It is difficult for dedicated organic gardeners not to sound inspirational, but the fact is, the world we live in is toxic. To be more specific, there are now manmade poisons in everything that grows—plant, animal and fish; there is poison in our air and in our water. The human animal itself now carries a sufficient concentration of DDT so that, in certain areas, its milk is actively dangerous to its young.

In the circumstances, if one has even a small plot, it makes the utmost sense to be doing organic gardening. You might be lucky enough to own several acres, but if not, even a pot of herbs on a windowsill is better than nothing.

The information is all here for you to use—for a tiny plot, a suburban garden, a small farm—with specific details about the value and the growing of specific vegetables and fruits.

And for those unfortunate enough not to be able to grow anything of their own, there is a complete list, by area, of sources for organic foods by mail.

Grow it! Do it!

The Basic Book of Organic Gardening

Edited by

ROBERT RODALE
Editor, *Organic Gardening Magazine*

Compiled by
GLENN F. JOHNS

BALLANTINE BOOKS • NEW YORK

The text was written especially for this edition and is based on material which appeared in *Organic Gardening Magazine*, Rodale Press, Inc.

ISBN 0-345-34522-3

Manufactured in the United States of America

First Printing: January 1971
Eighteenth Printing: July 1989

Contents

PART I

WHAT IS AN ORGANIC GARDENER?

An organic gardener knows that soil is a living, breathing organism, and because it is alive it should be fertilized and cultivated in a manner as close as possible to nature's own methods.

An organic gardener uses natural mineral and organic fertilizers to build his soil. Chemical fertilizers and poisonous insecticides are avoided by an organic gardener because he feels that these artificial stimulants and disinfectants compromise his desire for perfectly healthy soil and food and, indeed, can be actively dangerous. Water pollution from fertilizer and spray runoff reflect some of that danger.

An organic gardener wants healthy and better tasting food. He knows that a soil fertilized naturally produces richer food that will, in turn, give him and his family the vitamins and minerals they need in abundant supply.

Finally—and most important—the organic gardener knows that he is a living, contributing part of the cycle of life itself. He does not merely take. He is a giver, a sharer, a restorer.

How to Be an Organic Gardener

It's easy to be an organic gardener! In fact, it's so easy that we sometimes wonder why *all* gardeners aren't organic gardeners. Our prediction is that once everyone has a chance to see organic methods demonstrated, there will be few *artificial* gardeners left.

The main reason why organic gardening is easy and produces good results is because it forces people to pay attention to their soil and build its fertility. Organic gardening is basically organic soil building. We all know that probably 90 percent of all garden failures are caused by poor soil. By improving the fertility of the soil, the organic gardener prevents the major cause of poor gardening results.

The first step in becoming an organic gardener is to think about the step you are taking. Consider that you are embarking on a new adventure—a voyage of discovery into the world of nature's wonders. You are going to create in your own garden an environment for plant life that is supremely fertile and natural in conception. You are going to grow plants that are superior in size and in nutritional quality to the average produce available in the market—and immeasurably superior in taste.

Most important, think about the fact that your organic garden will be a demonstration of the *cleanliness* and spirituality of nature's design for life on this planet. Your organic garden will prove to you that our lives and the way we grow our food still are conducted best along the patterns set down by nature.

1. What Artificial Fertilizers Do to the Soil

Artificial chemical fertilizers have no part in the organic method. They symbolize the basic objections to unnatural gardening and farming. True, artificial fertilizers supply food elements that plants use, but their method of doing so is unnatural. Feeding a plant artificial fertilizers is basically the same as feeding a person intravenously. You can get needed food elements into the organism, but you are not doing it the natural way.

The food elements in artificial fertilizers are almost all soluble, while in nature plants are accustomed to getting nutrients from many insoluble sources. This solubility of artificial fertilizers leads to trouble in the soil. It unbalances the soil's supply of nutrients.

Another objection to artificial fertilizers is that they introduce into the soil various unnecessary and even poisonous elements that are added to them in order to make their nutrients soluble. Soluble food elements occur rarely in nature; so man in his factories adds various acids and other processing chemicals to insoluble minerals to make them into soluble fertilizers. After years of continued use, these processing chemicals, which weren't really needed in the first place, build up in the soil and can even change its structure and tilth.

The first practical step you can take in becoming an organic gardener is never to buy artificial fertilizers. If you are already a gardener, stop using artificial fertilizers! Throw them out, give them away, sell them—the important thing is to stop using them.

2. Replacements for Artificial Fertilizers

The organic method of gardening is just what its name implies—*organic*. As an organic gardener you will gain a new familiarity with compost, manure, garbage, spoiled hay, straw, sawdust, peat moss, weeds, and all the other sources of humus for the soil. Just as artificial fertilizers symbolize man's vanity in setting up a chemical method of gardening, humus symbolizes the spirit of cooperation with nature that is the core of the organic method. Humus and gradually pulverized rocks are the two elements that nature combined to form soil in the first place, and it is through these two elements that you as an organic gardener will work to maintain and improve soil naturally.

Pulverized rock powders assume a major role in organic gardening as a substitute for artificial chemicals. (In reality, artificial fertilizers were man's first substitute for the pulverized rocks that nature gave to the soil; so instead of substituting for artificial fertilizers we are just going back to the original product.) Major nutrients—calcium, phosphorous and potash—are supplied by those natural mineral fertilizers along with a flock of very necessary trace elements.

Phosphate rock is used widely as a natural rock fertilizer. It is mined in Florida and Tennessee and is an abundant source of phosphorus. Granite dust and greensand marl are two good natural sources of potash, an important major plant nutrient. Both these products also contain trace minerals, and phosphate rock carries with it quite a bit of calcium. Many of those organic products are available from local retail sources. You may find them sitting on the shelf alongside insecticides and artificial fertilizers, but they're probably there just the same. (We'll tell you more about where to get organic materials later.)

3. What About Insecticides?

Poison sprays are obviously the most unnatural element introduced by man into his farms and gardens. Because they disrupt the balance of nature and can be serious health hazards, practically all organic gardeners shun such poisons. Poison sprays are particularly dangerous when used in gardens because your garden is where you live and that's where the persistent poisons of an impure environment can hurt you most.

Organic growing and nonuse of pesticides go hand in hand. It has been shown time and again that plants and trees grown in fine organic soil do not suffer as much from insect and disease attack as plants growing on chemicalized soil. Scientific research has pointed out that many insects are the censors of nature—the destructive force whose purpose it is to kill off the weak so the strong can flourish.

Certainly, it is not logical to build a fine natural soil, rich in humus and free of the influence of chemical fertilizers, and then defile it with poison sprays.

One more thing to remember: When you decide to become an organic gardener, in your small way you have become part of a national energy—a real, honest to goodness, vigorous movement. Your decision to live compatibly with nature places you in the forefront of this serious effort to save the world. You have taken the first meaningful step away from the centric, superindustrial state toward a simpler, one-to-one relationship with the earth itself.

Organic Living—Why Is It So Vital?

The idea of conservation and natural living is on the verge of being a vital necessity—a life preserver within reach of people almost drowning in the effluence of their own mistakes. The virgin land is no more. The quiet places in the country are being built up. The air and water are dirty almost everywhere.

Under the conditions of today, it isn't hard to think like an organic gardener. On the contrary, you wonder why everyone isn't composting his garbage and tending a poison-free plot of land. What can be more valuable now than a small garden, free of synthetic fertilizers and pesticide poisons, yielding food that tastes as good as the vegetables and fruits we were able to buy in markets years ago? Valuable not only to the body but to the spirit.

Even before the technological world became so oppressive and obvious, the organic gardening idea was a full-grown philosophy. In fact, the unpleasant conditions of pollution and degradation which so many people are experiencing today were predicted almost 40 years ago by the founders of the organic method. They could see evidence then of trouble on a small scale, and knew that the isolated, eroded fields and polluted crops of that time would mushroom eventually into a pall of illness across all of society. The organic gardening idea goes back a long way. Even more significantly, organic gardening as an idea goes far into the future, projecting the possibility of a pleasant and rewarding way of life in an increasingly synthetic world.

7

Sir Albert Howard, an English agricultural advisor to the Indian state of Indore, first thought out the concept of growing plants and husbanding animals without using synthetic chemicals. Partly, his development of natural gardening and farming was a reaction to necessity. The area of India where he worked was so poor that local farmers couldn't afford to buy imported fertilizers. Sir Albert had to devise ways to recycle the natural nutrients available locally—the manure of animals and the waste plant materials that would otherwise be burned or overlooked. He saw that many potential sources of plant nutrients weren't being used because the native farmers didn't understand their value.

Sir Albert's practical solution to the Indian farm problem was the Indore method of composting. He taught farmers to combine rough weeds and crop wastes in layers with high-nitrogen manure and a little soil, making a pile that soon heated up to over 150 degrees as a result of the multiplication of bacteria and fungi. Lacking machinery and power, the native farmers had no mechanical means to deal with those wastes. By composting, however, they were able to break down stalks and leaves and to create a valuable soil conditioner and fertilizer that would replace the nutrients and humus removed from the soil by crops.

There was more to Sir Albert's thinking than just a solution to an immediate practical problem, however. He was disturbed by the trend of the scientific community toward advocating synthetic substitutes for many natural commodities, using the discoveries of the nineteenth-century German chemist, Justus von Leibig. Hailed as a pioneer of a new age of science, von Leibig had demonstrated the chemical simplicity of plant matter simply by burning it and then analyzing the ash for nitrogen, phosphorus, and potash, ignoring the organic portion of the plant. The chemical fertilizer industry was created out of the ash of von Leibig's experiment. Salesmen told farmers that N, P, and K were all that mattered in the soil, and that by replacing those chemicals in the form of a powder, they could assure fertility indefinitely. As we know, the chemical fertilizer message spread around the world quite effectively, and became the foundation upon which the current industrial type of agriculture is built.

Sir Albert perceived in von Leibig's doctrine something extremely dangerous—the rupture of the cycle of life. Under the "scientific" system of farming, soil became primarily something to hold up the plants so that they could be fed with artificial solutions. The age-old rhythms of nature that had built the soil were violated. Sir Albert began preaching that it was possible for thinking farmers to preserve the cycle of life by returning plant and animal wastes to the soil, countering insects by nonpoisonous means, and by avoiding the synthetic, soluble fertilizers with their burden of toxic residues. If the cycle of life wasn't preserved, said Sir Albert, future generations would be faced with declining fertility, hunger, and increases in disease and pollution.

My father, J. I. Rodale, first read about Sir Albert Howard's ideas in the late 1930s. Even then, the United States was so industrialized and technologically "advanced" that it was possible to see that what Sir Albert was predicting could easily come to pass. The American Dust Bowl experience of the Depression years was graphic evidence of the disruption of the cycle of life. But there were signs of trouble everywhere. Food quality was low. Pollution was intruding on our lives. Disease caused by physical degeneration—not just by microbes—was increasing. J. I. Rodale noted with dismay that the grim harvest predicted by Sir Albert and other philosophers of the conservation school was about to be reaped.

My father first used the word *organic* to describe the natural method of gardening and farming, mainly because compost, humus, and the organic fraction of the soil were emphasized so strongly. However, even in 1942, when ORGANIC GARDENING AND FARMING was born, J. I. Rodale saw that this method was more than just a way to husband the soil and grow plants and animals. He proclaimed that to be *organic* was to know and to understand the lessons of nature in all ways, and to use that knowledge to evaluate all of the "blessings" of science and technology. What good was it, he thought, to grow food without using chemical fertilizers or pesticides, and then to process that food so that its content of vitamins and minerals would be depleted seriously? In fact, not caring whether he was called an extremist or a crackpot, J. I. Rodale created what might now be called a *strict constructionist* interpretation of natural life under the banner of organiculture.

If it is synthetic, avoid it, he said. If it goes through a factory, examine it with special care. Follow the dictates of the cycle of life when growing things, he advised, and you will be blessed with foods of surpassing taste and quality that are less troubled by insects or disease.

Of course, there was originally much objection to the organic idea from the scientific community. Its members felt that anyone who said that all artificial fertilizers, pesticides, and foods were bad simply was not living in the twentieth century. Strangely, many "chemical" people who expressed violent disagreement with organic gardening and farming as a practical technique, admitted that it made sense theoretically. "Humus in the soil is important," they said, "but there isn't enough compost to go around." Almost everyone agreed that old-fashioned, natural ways of growing things produced tastier foods, but few would admit that it was possible to grow them now on a large scale.

Events of the past few years have changed a lot of minds. Many people can now see the direct result of the misuse of our environment, and of the failure of industry and agriculture to understand the importance of the cycle of life. You no longer have to be a prophet or a visionary to perceive that the way our world is being abused is leading to trouble. Of course, there is still much opposition to the organic method. Those whose reputations or livelihoods depend on continuing chemicalization of land, water, and air tend to refuse to believe that only a deep and sympathetic appreciation of natural ways can lead to a better and more pure world. There are still people who say that DDT is needed, and won't hurt anyone. And there are still strong voices raised in favor of burning garbage because to return it to the soil as compost might cost more this year.

I know, and I think you do too, that the organic way of living points down the right road, even though that road might have a few bumps and some hills to climb. Let's hope that everyone will soon start thinking as the organic gardeners and farmers have been thinking for 30 years.

—Robert Rodale

PART II

SECRETS OF THE BEST ORGANIC GARDENERS

Soil

1. What Is Soil?

Soil—What it is, how it is formed—with descriptions of the principal kinds of soil that exist, and their broad general distribution in the U.S.

The loose top layer of the earth's surface that supports the growth of plants, soil consists mainly of four parts—minerals, organic matter, water, and air.

An average topsoil of an active garden or farm might consist of about 25 percent air, 25 percent water, 49 percent minerals, and only one percent organic matter. In a virgin prairie soil, the organic matter could go to more than 10 percent. There are some soils that might contain up to 20 percent of organic matter. The amount of organic matter in the subsoil gradually goes down until, at a depth of about 30 feet, it may amount to only ⅛ of one percent.

Profile

In discussing soil, the word *profile* means a side view of a vertical section of the earth. If we could slice away a section of it, we could then regard the profile and see the various layers down to bedrock. A soil profile is often visible at a place where a road has been cut through a hill. An average profile might consist of five or six layers, beginning with the rock below and going through the various stages of subsoil to the uppermost layer, or topsoil. These layers, called horizons, are extremely significant in their effect on the processes of plant growth.

13

How soil is formed

Originally the entire earth was one mass of rock, and the only living things were microbes—single-celled organisms. Through their activities, these bacteria and fungi liberated carbon dioxide and certain organic and inorganic acids, which have a solvent action upon rocks, beginning the process of their breakdown into soil. The dead bodies of these organisms were the beginnings of the organic matter that was mixed with the tiny fragments of rocks to form soil. The action of heat, cold, wind, rain, glacier movement, and other influences and biological factors took a hand in the further gradual breakdown. The difference in temperature between day and night, and between summer and winter, caused expansion and contraction which produced open seams in the rock and detachment of fragments, permitting water to enter deeper into the rock.

Part of the process of soil formation consisted of the decaying remains of the low forms of plants such as lichens and mosses which soon began to cover the exposed rocks, digging their tiny tentacles into the rock. This slowly formed a film of soil over them. This bit of soil provided the foothold for the plants which are the next step up the evolutionary scale— the ferns—and gradually, as the soil thickened, other higher plants and trees began to grow, until there came into being overgrown jungles.

We must remember that without the soil organisms—the bacteria, fungi, actinomycetes, yeasts, etc.—no soil formation could take place. The making of soil is a biological process, meaning that living forces take a prominent part in it. We might say, therefore, that the process of soil formation consists of physical, chemical, and biological elements. The physical part is accomplished by the wind and the rain, the chemical by the excretions and respirations of the microbes, and the biological by the other activities of these organisms.

Soil has formed not only from the original bedrock, but also by rock that has been moved by glacial and other forces. And soil formation is still going on. Soil is constantly being created by the same forces which formed it originally—climate, decaying plant matter, etc. Deep down at bedrock, some of the rock is still gradually turning to subsoil. It takes these processes perhaps 500 years to make one inch of soil, but man with his destructive farming practices can destroy an inch in only a few years of soil mining, that is, farming that only takes out, putting nothing back that has staying power. It has been estimated that in about 200 years of farming in the United States, over 60 percent of the topsoil has been destroyed.

Soils are classified into groups, series, and types. The groups are based largely on climatic factors and associated vegetation, the series on parent material, and the soil types on the texture of the soil. The following information is based on government agricultural reports.

Texture

By texture is meant the relative amounts of the various sizes of particles making up the soil. These particles range in size from stones and gravel, through sand and silt to clay, the particles of which may be too small to be seen under the strongest microscope.

Structure

This refers to the grouping of individual particles into larger pieces, or granules. Good granulation or crumb structure of the heavier soils is essential to good results. Sandy soils show little if any granulation, due to the coarseness of their component particles. With soils containing a substantial percentage of clay, working them when wet results in destruction of the granular structure. Excessive tramping by livestock under the same conditions is likely to have a similar effect.

Alternate freezing and thawing, or wetting and drying, and penetration of the soil mass by plant roots are natural forces which favor the formation of soil granules, or aggregates. Such aggregation is developed most highly in soils near neutrality in their reaction; both strongly acid and strongly alkaline soils tend to *run together* and lose their structural character. Tillage also tends to break down the structure of many soils.

Porosity

Associated with both texture and structure is pore space, or porosity. These spaces may be large, as in the case of coarse, sandy soils or those with well developed granulation. In heavy soils, containing mostly finer clay particles, the pore spaces may be too small for plant roots or soil water to penetrate readily. Good soils have 40 to 60 percent of their bulk occupied with pore space, which may be filled with either water or air, neither of which can truly be said to be more important than the other.

Here, as in all other soil relationships, a satisfactory balance is important for productivity. Too much water slows the release of soil nitrogen, depletes mineral nutrients, and otherwise hinders proper plant growth. Too much air speeds nitrogen release beyond the capacity of plants to utilize it, and much of it is lost. In an overly aerated soil, the stored water evaporated the departure or difference from the overall soil description.

Soil groups

All soils are composed of particles varying greatly in size and shape. In order to classify them by texture as well as physical properties, four fundamental soil groups are recognized: gravels, sands, loams, and clays. (The last three make up most of the world's arable lands.)

The sand group includes all soils of which the silt and clay make up less than 20 percent by weight. Its mineral particles are visible to the naked eye and are irregular in shape. Because of this, their water-holding capacity is low, but they possess good drainage and aeration and are usually in a loose, friable condition.

In contrast, particles in a clay soil are very fine (invisible under ordinary microscope) and become sticky and cement-like.

Texture of the loam class cannot be as clearly defined, since its mechanical composition is about midway between sand and clay. Professors T. Lyon and Harry Buckman in their book, *The Nature and Properties of Soils*, (New York, Macmillan) describe loams

as such a mixture of sand, silt and clay particles as to exhibit light and heavy properties in about equal proportions. . . . Because of this intermixture of coarse, medium and fine particles, usually they possess the desirable qualities both of sand and clay without exhibiting those undesirable properties, as extreme looseness and low water capacity on the one hand and stickiness, compactness, and very slow air and water movement on the other.

Fortunately for the gardeners and farmers in the United States, most soils are in the loam classification. The majority of soils are mixtures; the most common class names appear below: (Combinations are given when one size of particles is evident enough to affect the texture of the loam. For example, a loam in which sand is dominant will be classified as a sandy loam of some kind.)

Sandy Soils
    gravelly sands
    coarse sands
    medium sands
    fine sands
    loamy sands
Loamy Soils
    coarse sandy loams
    medium sandy loams
    fine sandy loams
    silty loams and stony silt loams
    clay loams
Clayey Soils
    stony clays
    gravelly clays
    sandy clays
    silty clays
    clays

You can get a good idea of your soil's texture and class by rubbing it between the thumb and the fingers or in the palm of the hand. Sand particles are gritty; silt has a floury or talcum-powder feel when dry and is only moderately plastic when moist, while the clayey material is harsh when dry and very plastic and sticky when wet.

Observe Professors Lyon and Buckman: "This method is used in all field operations, especially in soil survey, land classification and the like. Accuracy . . . can be acquired by the careful study of known samples." If you're interested in developing an ability to classify soils, contact the local county agent for soil samples that are correctly classified.

The ideal structure is granular, where the rounded aggregates (or clusters) of soil lie loosely and readily shake apart. When the granules are especially porous, the term *crumb* is applied.

Water

Soil water occurs in three forms, designated as hygro-scopic, capillary, and gravitational. The hygroscopic soil water is chemically bound in the soil constituents and is un-available to plants. Gravitational water is that which normally drains out of the pore spaces of the soil after a rain. If drain-age is poor, it is this water which causes the soil to be soggy and unproductive. Excessive drainage hastens the time when capillary water runs short and plants suffer from drought.

It is the capillary water upon which plants depend very largely for their supply of moisture. Hence, the capacity of a soil to hold water against the pull of gravity is of great im-portance in ordinary agriculture. Organic matter and good structure add to this supply of water in soils.

But plants cannot extract the last drop of capillary water from a soil, since the attraction of soil materials for it is greater than the pull exerted by the plant roots. The point at which these two forces are just equal is called the *wilting co-efficient* of a soil. This term is used to express the percentage of water in a soil at the time the loss from transpiration ex-ceeds the renewal of the water by capillary means. Medium-textured loams and silt loams, because of their faster rate of movement of moisture from lower depths to the root zone, and the fact that they can bring up moisture from greater depths than either sands or clays, provide the best conditions of available but not excessive soil moisture for best plant growth.

Erosion

Generally erosion works this way: first, the main loss is by sheet erosion; each time it rains, the runoff water removes a thin layer of surface soil. Then, as the topsoil becomes thin-ner, miniature gullies appear. After most of the surface soil is gone, gullies become the main problem.

Usually there's a clear difference between the topsoil and subsoil. The subsoil is finer textured, more plastic, and lighter in color than the topsoil. Here's how erosion is classified:

No apparent erosion. All or nearly all the surface soil is present. Depth to subsoil is 14 inches or more. The sur-face may have received some recent deposits as the result of erosion from higher ground.

Slight. Depth to subsoil varies from 7 to 14 inches. Plowing at usual depths will not expose the subsoil.

Moderate. Depth to subsoil varies from 3 to 7 inches. Some subsoil is mixed with the surface soil in plowing.

Severe. Depth to subsoil is less than 3 inches. Surface soil is mixed with subsoil when the land is plowed. Gullies are beginning to be a problem.

Very severe. Subsoil is exposed. Gullies are frequent.

Very severe gullies. Deep gullies or blowouts have ruined the land for agricultural purposes.

There is a direct relationship between erosion and a soil's ability for intake of air and water. For example, when the soil surface becomes compacted, the danger of erosion increases, while the intake of water and air decreases.

Soil series

This refers to a subdivision of soil groups. A series is often given the name of a town, river, or other geographical feature near which the soil was first identified. Since many soils in this country are young, the original geological characteristics of the soil materials are still evident. Thus, members of the same soil series, or subdivisions, signify soils which have developed from the same kind of parent material and by the same processes.

A soil phase is a subdivision on the basis of some important deviation such as erosion, slope, or stoniness. It comes from the Finnish word *tunturi* which means a flat, barren plateau. The tundra lacks hills, and there is poor growth. There is much marsh and swamp. It consists of treeless plains and is closely related to the bog soils. The land is a mat of grass, moss, sedges, and lichen. Some berries, herbs, and dwarf shrubs grow. There is a tendency for the land to form peat. Cultivated crops are leafy vegetables, which thrive under cool growing conditions, and potatoes, which are grown from sprouts. There is a limited amount of dairying, and in some sheltered areas, there are hay and grain.

The soil is very shallow which is termed a lithosol type of soil. The topsoil is somewhat on the peaty side, under which is a thin layer of humus. Below that is about two or three inches of yellow-brown soil, beneath which is six inches of gray, sticky clay. Underneath the entire tundra region is a frozen layer that in some places extends downward for a thousand feet. This is called the permafrost. Only a few surface feet thaw out in the summer.

The tundra soils are in the Greenland, Siberia, Arctic Ocean, and Bering Sea regions. In some protected areas, alpine vegetation and forests will flourish. The activity of bacteria and fungi are at low ebb, and the soil is not necessarily acid.

Prairie soils

This is a semipodzolic type of soil, but differs from the latter in that no trees grew in this region in the formative period. The organic matter is high. There is only one prairie soil region in the world, and it is in the United States, covering an area of close to 300,000 square miles. This soil type includes most of Iowa, about three-fourths of Illinois, the southeast of Minnesota, the eastern half of Oklahoma and Missouri, a part of eastern Kansas, and some of central Texas. Soils somewhat similar to prairies are located in Oregon, Washington, California, and Idaho.

Prairie soils have a good granular structure and a high fertility. Some of the best farm land in the U.S. is of this type. It is a rich dark brown, but as it goes southward it becomes more reddish. There is a heavy accumulation of humus, from the native grass residues and due to the hot dry summers which deterred the activities of the decay-producing microorganisms. In the formative period, the grasses were more than six feet high. In some sections the humus layer is 20 inches deep.

The rainfall is from about 30 to 45 inches, spaced out nicely in the growing season, but there is usually a midsummer dry period. There is not the heavy rainfall of the podzol areas which cause a leaching of the minerals out of the top layer. The soil is not excessively acid.

Crops consist of the small grains, hay, corn, and soybeans. The farms are big and highly mechanized. Cattle raising and dairying are done on a big scale. This is the best soil in the country for growing the small grains and hay crops.

Planosoils

These are soils of the poorly drained prairie lands located in southern Illinois and Iowa and northern Missouri and in a few places in the humid forest regions. They are relatively flat lands where under natural conditions there is little erosion, but in cultivation, with poor management, they may suffer badly from the worst forms of soil destruction. There is always a hardpan or claypan in the subsoil. The surface soil is acid and leached.

These are not very productive soils, and the practices of the organic method would be a must. The soils in the spring are often too wet to work. Because of the hardpan, roots remain shallow. Crops suffer from extremes of climatic changes.

Locations of desert soils

Desert soils are in arid regions where grasses will not grow and are divided into three groups: (1) desert, (2) sierozem (gray desert), and (3) red desert. The sierozem and red desert soils are known as semidesert soils. The desert soils have the lowest rainfall, the sierozem having between 8 to 11 inches of precipitation. On desert soils, water is critically scarce, and there is usually a death struggle for it. Erosion is a serious factor. In some years, in desert areas there is no rainfall at all. In the red and sierozem soils, rainfall comes with more regularity.

Temperature

The sierozems have the lowest temperature of the three types of desert soils, the average being between 45° and 50° F. The red soils will go up to about 60°, but the desert soils, as the name indicates, have the highest temperatures. An unusual feature pertaining to the latter is that there is wide variation between day and night temperature, sometimes as much as 50°. This has been a factor in the process of soil formation in these areas in connection with the rock weathering, and due to the condensation of moisture, because of such fluctuating temperatures, there has developed more clay in the soils.

Color

Desert soils are usually gray in color, an indication of low organic matter which is the result of the sparse vegetation in this type of soil. The red soils have a variation in color from a light pink gray to red browns and red. The sierozems are a gray to a light gray brown. In Russian, the name sierozem means gray earth, in contrast to *chernozem* which means black earth.

The red color of the red soils was no doubt due to earlier conditions hundreds of thousands of years ago when the climate was more humidly tropical or subtropical and the weathering of rocks released iron into the soil.

Geography

The gray desert soils are located in Nevada, Utah, Oregon, Idaho, and Washington in the Great Basin intermountain desert plains and plateaus. The red soils are in the hot arid areas from Texas to southeastern California, which includes southern Nevada, western Arizona, and parts of New Mexico. The sierozems are in the drier parts of the Great Basin areas in western Colorado, eastern Utah, and smaller portions of Oregon and Idaho.

In the desert, there grow shrubs like the horsebrush, white sage, Indian ricegrass, rabbit brush, and cactus. On the red soils, there are the creosote bush, prickly pear, yuca, Mormon tea, wolfberry, and mesquite. On the sierozem there are black sagebrush, crested wheatgrass, juniper, blue grama, etc.

Unless there is irrigation, these lands are good only for cattle grazing, sheep raising being the main activity in some parts of these areas. When water is supplied in the form of irrigation, the land becomes extremely fertile, and a large variety of crops can be grown such as the grains, vegetables, fruits, beets, and pasture crops. There is evidence, however, that the nutritional value of irrigated crops is inferior to crops grown in the conventional manner.

The desert soils

In desert soils, the humus content is very low, and there is an accumulation of salts in the surface. Under conditions of irrigation, the soil suffers from alkali disease. These soils usually form a thin hard crust on the surface. Under the surface horizon, there is a layer of calcium carbonate (lime) which in many cases becomes a hardpan. Underneath that, the soil may be loose and crumbly.

In some places, the blowing of the wind clears off sufficient soil to leave an accumulation of pebbles and stones which are referred to as desert pavement, a hard, rocklike formation.

Sometimes this covers large areas. As a general rule, desert soils are sandy and gravelly. The content of organic matter is between ½ and 1½ percent, and conditions are usually on the alkaline side.

Adobe soils

These soils should not be confused with desert soils. The terms are not synonymous. Adobe can occur any place where the rainfall is less than 20 inches, and there must be clearly defined wet and dry seasons. The word *adobe* is of Spanish origin and has reference to sun-dried bricks. This kind of soil varies from fine sand to heavy loam, and clay. Usually, however, it refers to heavy clay soils only. These soils occur in Nevada, Colorado, Wyoming, Utah, California, Oregon, Idaho, New Mexico, Arizona, and Texas.

When dry, this type of soil cracks into irregular but roughly cubical blocks. Many gardeners and farmers obtain poor results in adobe soils unless they furnish it with an abundance of organic matter. The latter spectacularly destroys the adobe quality which makes it so difficult to cultivate. Sensational results are obtained on adobe soils when the organic method is practiced.

Chestnut and brown soils

These soils are closely related to the chernozems. They take in parts of Kansas, Texas, Oklahoma, Colorado, New Mexico, Idaho, Utah, Montana, Wyoming, Washington, Oregon, and Arizona. As with the chernozem, chestnut and brown soil has developed under grass, but due to lower rainfall, the grasses are shorter than the chernozem and the amount of organic matter less. The natural vegetation in these regions is shorter and more sparse than in the chernozem regions, the growth being of the steppe type.

Due to the small amount of rain and therefore a lack of leaching, a great deal of calcium carbonate (lime) accumulates in the subsoil. Where rainfall is very low, the calcium carbonate will be found nearer the surface. Usually gypsum will also be found in the subsoil (calcium sulphate). Under certain conditions, the soil becomes powdery because of lack of rain, giving rise to dust bowl blowing. There is a loss of crumb structure in the topsoil.

The chestnut soils are brown, reddish brown, and red in

color because they contain less organic matter than the chernozem, and sometimes because of oxidation of iron, due to higher temperatures. There are also grey and yellow chestnut soils.

These soils are referred to as the spring wheat belt. Cotton, corn, small grains, and sorghum are the principal crops. Cattle grazing is done on a larger scale than in the chernozems. Under irrigation, a much larger variety of crops is grown including orcharding and sugar beets. The pasturage consists mainly of dried buffalo and grama grasses.

The rainfall in these regions is only between 10 to 15 inches, and dry farming therefore has to be practiced on irrigated land in order to conserve the moisture. A grain is grown one year followed by fallowing the next, a type of fallow in which no crop is grown, the land merely being cultivated. This eventually leads to dust bowl conditions when an exceptionally dry period comes. The dust bowl region is in New Mexico, Texas, Kansas, Oklahoma, and Colorado.

Rendzina

Rendzinas represent dark soils on certain kinds of limestone formation, with a very high humus content, sometimes up to ten percent, and is found in humid regions. The color ranges from black to gray and sometimes brown. There are some rendzinas in Texas. The black belt of Alabama and Mississippi are rendzinas. The chalk cliffs of Dover, overlooking the English Channel are rendzinas. There is a wide range of fertility to these soils, being rich or poor depending on what kind of limestone they originated from.

Wiesenboden and bog soils

This type of soil is usually associated with the podzols. They are found in Illinois, Wisconsin, Ohio, Iowa, Indiana, and Florida, and especially in the area of prairie soils. They are very rich in organic matter. The bog soils are those that contain 18 inches or more of it. These are peat soils where well drained, exceptionally good crops may be obtained. The Everglades of Florida are an example of bog soil.

2. The Soil in Your Garden—How to Make It Right for Particular Plants

Why do azaleas flourish where iris will produce nary a flower? Why can you grow armfuls of huge carrots in the same patch that cannot raise one sweet potato? The answer to this rather puzzling problem is surprisingly simple. Plants, like all of nature's creatures, have their own special needs. Fundamentally, there are three soil conditions; acid, neutral, and alkaline. A plant that thrives in a light acid soil may go fruitless in a rich loam that is not acidic. Once you have determined the needs of your favorite plants, you are well on your way to peak garden yields.

Although some plants, especially herbs, will thrive in almost any type of soil, most of the more popular plant families are mighty choosy about their environment. Roses are a good proof of this. Fred S. Glaes, a director of the American Rose Society, stresses proper soil conditioning as one of the secrets of his show-winning roses. According to Mr. Glaes:

Prepare your soil carefully when starting new beds; dig them about 30 inches deep. Break up bottom of the hole, and remove about 4 inches of subsoil. Fill with a mixture of at least one-third compost, leaf mold or well-rotted manure to two-thirds good soil.

I mix one pound each of rock phosphate and greensand to every 4 feet of rose bed. When I finish preparing the bed, it's about two inches below the soil surface. I've found that new beds should be prepared 60 days before planting for best results.

Although the rich, organic loam produced by Mr. Glaes's formula gives him award winning roses, it would not be wise to use it for evergreens. Thriving on acid soil rich in humus, the evergreen could not take the heavy rose diet. Broad-leaved evergreens, members of the heath family, include heath, azalea, mountain laurel, rhododendron, trailing arbutus, cranberry, blueberry, and many other shrubs. When planting and caring for these plants, it is paramount to keep their acid-humus diet in mind. These plants are at their best when given an acid soil organically formed, a heavy mulch, constant moisture with good drainage, filtered sunlight, and absolutely no cultivation.

The acid soil required by these plants may be easily achieved by organic methods. Decayed pine needles have an extremely high acidity. Oak leaf mold and the decayed sawdust from oak, cypress, or hemlock are also acid, as is peat moss, which is excellent also for loosening heavy soils. If the soil where you are going to plant is alkaline, it should be dug out and replaced by acid soil. This may seem like a lot of trouble, but it will make plant care simpler in later years. You may obtain acid soil from pine or other coniferous forests or from the woods where acid-loving plants such as mountain laurel and blueberry are growing. Coarse sand and leaf mold mixed in makes a loose, crumbly soil that gives good drainage. Your plants will thrive in such soil, and after planting, the acidity can be maintained by proper mulching.

Even for the houseplant gardener, the proper planting medium usually means success or failure. Horticulturist Eva Wolf has a simple recipe for a potting mixture custom-made to ease houseplant cuttings through their usually traumatic starting period. Her mixture consists of equal parts of coarse builders sand, screened and well pulverized garden loam, and carefully prepared compost. A pint of bone meal is added to each bushel of mix.

The mixture is then turned and sprinkled with enough water to dampen. Variations can be made from this standard formula to meet your local conditions. If compost is not available, you can use shredded peat moss, well rotted manure, aged sawdust, and for acid loving plants, leaf mold. If your garden soil is sandy, merely increase the amount of organic matter and decrease the amount of sand.

If your flower gardens are lush with azaleas and rhododendron, but your efforts to get a vegetable patch going have met with failure, your soil may be overly acidic. This condition must be changed if you want to raise beets, broccoli, lettuce, and many other neutral to alkaline-loving plants. Crushed limestone or dolomite is the right prescription to get your garden to the correct pH (acidity-alkalinity scale). Dolomite has some magnesium present which is essential for plant nutrition and which is often deficient in many soils. Next to crushed limestone, wood ashes and marl are best. These may be added to limestone.

How is the need for lime determined? Most crops do best on soil within a 6.5 to 6.8 pH range—that is, just slightly acid. If it is lower than that—even only a little—the difference in yield can be tremendous. Corn, for example, that will yield 100 bushels to the acre at a pH of 6.8, will return but 83 bushels when this drops to 5.7. Food value in what is produced is affected, too. Crops supplied the right amount of calcium are richer in minerals and in protein.

The way to find out whether or not your soil needs lime, and how much, is by an accurate soil test. Adding it by guesswork is definitely a mistake. (Too much can be as detrimental as a deficiency.) Thorough soil tests are available through your county agent, from the nearest USDA state experimental station, from a number of reliable soil-testing laboratories, and through use of several available test kits and pH gauges. Since different sections of a farm or even a garden can easily vary, it's best to get an analysis of each before liming or planting. In general, wherever you find mosses, ferns, pine, laurel, blueberries or blackberries growing, you will find acid soil conditions. You will very quickly find that you can control soil conditions in quite specific areas by using a combination of compost and the proper mulch. (See the following sections.)

pH Preferences of Common Plants

QUITE ACID (pH of from 4.0 to 6.0)

azalea	heather	pecan
bayberry	huckleberry	pine
blackberry	lupine	potato, Irish
blueberry	lily	radish
chrysanthemum	lily of the valley	raspberry
cranberry	marigold	rhododendron
evergreens	mountain laurel	spruce
ferns	mosses	sweet potato
fescue	oak	watermelon
flax	peanut	yew
heath		

SLIGHTLY ACID (pH 6.0 to 6.5)

apple	gooseberry	rape
apricot	grape	rhubarb
barley	kale	rice
beans, lima	lespedeza	rye
bent grass	millet	salsify
bluegrass	mustard	snap bean
buckwheat	oats	soybean

cherry	pansy	squash
collards	parsley	strawberry
corn	parsnip	sudan grass
cotton	pea	timothy
cowpeas	peach	tomato
eggplant	pear	turnip
endive	pepper	vetch
gardenia	pumpkin	wheat
gloxinia		

NEUTRAL TO ALKALINE (pH 7.0 to 7.5)

alfalfa	cantaloupe	lettuce
alyssum	carrot	okra
asparagus	cauliflower	onion
beet	celery	quince
broccoli	clover	spinach
Brussels sprouts	cucumber	Swiss chard
cabbage	iris	zucchini
carnation	leeks	

3. Twenty Of the Best Organic Soil Builders

To make up your own fertilizer mixture, combine and apply a few of the materials listed below, which together are rich in the three major elements. You might combine cottonseed meal, bone meal, and granite dust; or manure, rock phosphate, and wood ashes. Any such combination will be effective and also will keep your soil supplied with trace minerals.

Always remember that the objective of the organic method is to feed the soil, not just supply the minimum amount of nutrients to produce a single crop in one season. Since most organic fertilizers are slow acting, that is, their nutrient content is released to plants gradually, there is a great residual power which improves soil for many years.

Following is a description of twenty organic soil builders. There are many more than twenty, but this list gives an indication of what they are, where they are available, and how to use them. Unless otherwise noted, these fertilizers can either be worked into the soil in spring or fall, topdressed around growing plants, added to the compost heap, or used as a mulch.

Basic slag

Basic slag is an industrial by-product, resulting when iron ore is smelted to form pig iron. Rich in calcium, slag also includes valuable trace elements as boron, sodium, molybdenum, copper, zinc, magnesium, manganese, and iron. Its efficiency varies with its fineness. Alkaline in action, slag is most effective on moist clays, loams, and on peaty soils deficient in lime. For light soils, tests show that it's better to mix with greensand or granite dust. Apply it in fall or winter; it is especially effective on such legumes as beans, peas, clovers, and alfalfa, available commercially.

Blood meal and dried blood

This is blood collected in slaughterhouses, later dried and ground. Blood meal analyzes 15 percent nitrogen, 1.3 percent phosphorus, 0.7 percent potash; dried blood contains 12 percent nitrogen, 3 percent phosphorus.

These materials can be used directly in the ground or composted. Because of its high nitrogen content, use very sparingly. A sprinkling is enough to stimulate bacterial growth; available in nurseries or wherever garden products are sold.

Bone meal

Years ago great amounts of buffalo bones were collected on western plains for use as fertilizer; nowadays the main source comes from the slaughterhouse. Consisting mostly of calcium phosphate, the phosphorus and nitrogen content depends mostly on the kind and age of the bone. Raw bone meal has between 2 and 4 percent nitrogen, 22 to 25 percent phosphoric acid. The fatty materials in raw bone meal somewhat delay its breakdown in the soil.

Steamed bone meal contains 1 to 2 percent nitrogen, up to 30 percent phosphorus, available in hardware stores, local nurseries or usually wherever garden products are sold.

Compost

Compost is so important that it has an entire section (below) devoted to it. It can include any or all of the other materials listed here. Like humus in the soil, compost is the storehouse for plant nutrients. Here are some general instructions about using compost: if notably fibrous, it can be applied in fall to soil, where it will decompose sufficiently by planting time; most recommended time for applying is about a month prior to planting. If storing in open, keep heap covered to retain nutrients. For best results, apply compost liberally, from one to three inches per year. The analysis of compost, of course, varies with the materials of which it is composed. For example, adding dried blood or cottonseed meal, tankage, activated sludge, or bone meal will increase nitrogen value. Rock phosphate, basic slag, bone meal, and sludge will add to phosphorus content, while potash will be increased through additions of greensand, granite dust, manure, and wood ashes. Generally the trace element content is good.

Certain materials and techniques act as compost activators and will speed up rate of decomposition. As previously mentioned, the high nitrogen and protein materials such as dried blood, bone meal, and manure do an effective job. It's also worthwhile to shred materials before adding to the heap, either using a rotary mower or a compost shredder.

Cottonseed meal

This is made from the cottonseed which has been freed from lints and hulls and then deprived of its oils. (Cottonseed cake is one of the richest protein foods for animal feeding.) Its low pH makes it especially valuable for acid-loving crops. Cottonseed meal analyzes 7 percent nitrogen, 2 to 3 percent phosphorus, and 1.5 percent potash. A truly excellent fertilizer, it is available commercially.

Grass clippings

Fairly rich in nitrogen, grass clippings are useful as a green manure to be worked into the soil, for adding to compost heaps, or for mulching. Clippings from most lawns contain over one pound of nitrogen and two pounds of potash for every hundred pounds of clippings in the dry state.

Greensand and granite dust

Both are highly recommended sources of potash. Materials can be applied as a topdressing or worked directly into the soil. General recommendation is 10 pounds to 100 square feet. Tests have shown that the granite dust or stone meal supply adequate amounts of potash to growing crops.

Glauconite greensand or greensand marl is an iron-potassium-silicate that gives a green color to the minerals in which it occurs. It contains about 6 or 7 percent potash.

Hulls and shells

Hulls and shells of cocoa beans, buckwheat, oats, rice, and cottonseed are commonly used as a fertilizer and mulch. They decay readily and may be spaded into the ground. The coarse shells are excellent as mulches, while the finer ones (sometimes almost in dust form) can be applied to lawns and elsewhere with a spreader. Hulls and shells make an exceptionally attractive mulch, and are most effective when about one inch thick, available commercially from nurseries, stores, or by mail.

Leaf mold

As fresh leaves are placed in a container (snow fencing or one of wood or stone), shred them, if possible, and keep them damp. Apply ground limestone to offset the acidity, unless you plan to use the leaf mold around acid-tolerant plants only. Leaf mold from deciduous trees has been found to be somewhat richer in potash and phosphorus than that made from conifers. Nitrogen content varies, sometimes as high as 5 percent.

Leaves

Leaves are an abundant source of humus and mineral material, including calcium, magnesium, as well as nitrogen, phosphorus and potassium. They are especially valuable for use around acid-loving plants such as azaleas, rhododendrons, and hollies. (Some leaves, as sugar maple, are alkaline.) They may be applied directly to the soil, as a mulch, for leaf mold, and for composting.

Manure, fresh

This has been a basic fertilizer used for centuries. Some manures, such as horse, hen, sheep, and rabbit, are considered *hot* manures because of their relatively high nitrogen content. Rabbit manure, for example, analyzes 2.4 N, 1.4 P, and 0.6 K. It's best to allow these manures to compost before applying directly to plants. Cow and hog manure, relatively wet and correspondingly low in nitrogen are called *cold* manures, and ferment slowly. All manures are excellent and should be included in an organic fertilizing program, when available.

Manure, dried

Commonly available at just about every fertilizer store, dried manure is always useful in the garden.

Peat moss

This is partially decomposed remains of plants accumulated over centuries under relatively airless conditions. Though it doesn't contain any nutrients, peat moss serves to aerate the soil, to improve drainage, ultimately to help plants absorb nutrients from other materials.

Phosphate rock and colloidal phosphate

An excellent source of phosphorus, phosphate rock also contains many valuable trace elements, including calcium, iron, sodium, magnesium, boron, and iodine.

Sawdust

A very useful mulch material, sawdust should be used more widely. When plants are about two inches high, a one-inch layer can be applied. Prior to spreading the sawdust, many gardeners side-dress with a nitrogen fertilizer as cottonseed meal, blood meal, tankage, etc. However, a recent OGF survey showed that many sawdust users do not apply a nitrogen supplement and were satisfied with results. It should be emphasized that this *must* be well rotted sawdust. Raw or pale colored sawdust will mat and cake and prevent proper penetration of rain.

Seaweed and kelp

Both are high in potash (about 5 percent) and trace elements. Many seaweed users apply it fresh from the sea; others prefer washing first to remove salt. It can be used as a mulch, worked directly into the soil, or placed in the compost heap. Dehydrated forms are available commercially.

Sludge

Activated sludge, produced when sewage is agitated by air rapidly bubbling through it, contains about 5 percent nitrogen, 3 to 6 percent phosphorus, that is similar to cottonseed meal. Digested sludge, formed when sewage is allowed to settle over filter beds, has about the same fertilizer value as barnyard manure—2 percent for both nitrogen and phosphorus. Sludge is usually on the acid side. It can be worked into the soil in fall or in early spring at time of initial cultivation.

Wood ashes

Containing 1.5 percent phosphorus, 7 percent or more potash, wood ashes should never be allowed to stand in the rain, as the potash would leach away. They can be mixed with other fertilizing materials, side-dressed around growing plants, or used as a mulch. Apply about 5 to 10 pounds per 100 square feet. Avoid contact between freshly spread ashes and germinating seeds or new plant roots by spreading ashes a few inches from plants. Wood ashes are alkaline.

Wood chips

Like sawdust and other wood wastes, wood chips are useful in the garden. They have a higher nutrient content than sawdust, and do a fine job of aerating the soil and increasing its moisture-holding ability.

—EVA WOLF

4. Seven Major Sources of Organic Fertilizers, Mulches and Conditioners

There are 7 major sources of organic fertilizers, mulches, and conditioners available in such profusion that the categories overlap—what you can't get in one, you can obtain in another. If animal manures are in short supply in your area, what about the blood meals, tankage, and fish scrap? If you can't get them, what about castor pomace, spent hops, cottonseed and soybean meal—all high in nitrogen? But the organic gardener is resourceful (he's got to be) and what he can't buy at the store or get from his local municipal composting plant or sawmill, he makes out of crop residues plus the contents of his garbage pail. Here are his almost never failing sources of supply:

1—*Animal manures;* cattle, livestock, poultry, rabbits.
2—*Animal tankage;* blood meal, dried blood, fish scrap.
3—*Vegetative manures;* the various bean and seed meals, spent hops, castor pomace.
4—*Minerals;* rock phosphate, colloidal phosphate, granite dust, greensand.
5—*Compost;* municipal, commercial, and homemade.
6—*Soil conditioners and mulches;* leaves, hay, straw, crop residues, most vegetable fibrous materials, including wood chips and sawdust.
7—*Large-scale, commercial organic fertilizers,* mulches and soil conditioners.

Below is a more detailed description of each.

The animal manures, chief source of nitrogen

The animal manures make things grow in the garden because they stimulate and release a lot of energy in the soil. They are the heart of the compost program, may be fed directly into the growing row without danger, can be used as topdressing for trees, bush fruits, flower beds, and borders. Whatever you have to fertilize, manure will help you do it better. So it's a good idea to keep rabbits on your place, poultry, goats, or livestock of any kind. If you can't, make every effort to contact a local dairyman, egg farmer, or riding stable. Chances are, the owner will be glad to supply you with this by-product just to get it out of his way.

But be ready to do your own trucking.

We get ours from a local dairyman, sometimes pay for it— $7 a ton—sometimes swap it for the loan of the shredder. One of the two heaps is used as an earthworm hill to which we add the family garbage after it is shredded or worked into a slurry. Bacterial and worm activity are so great in this hill that it never really freezes in winter, is readily opened to admit more garbage, and then closed over. Like a volcano, it's hot at top but cool down below where the worms stay at a safe distance from the heated part.

The commercial organic nitrogens

Tankage, blood meal, dried blood, and fish scrap may be had in all parts of the country whether or not you live near the ocean or have a slaughterhouse in your area. Meat tankage consists of waste processed into meal which contains 10 percent nitrogen and up to 3 percent phosphorus. Bone tankage has 10 percent phosphorus and 3 percent nitrogen.

Blood meal and dried blood contain 15 and 12 percent nitrogen respectively, and 1.3 and 3 percent phosphorus. Blood meal also assays at 0.7 percent potash. These materials may be used directly in or on the planting site, or they may be added to the compost pile. They should be used sparingly because of high nitrogen content—a sprinkling is enough to stimulate bacterial growth. Both are excellent in the compost pile, breaking down green fibrous matter and stimulating general bacterial action.

Vegetable residues are also high in nitrogen

If the budget is tight, or you just can't seem to secure animal manures or waste products, you still have the vegetable nitrogens. You can go down to your local brewery and get free dried hops—about 3½ percent nitrogen and 1 percent phosphoric acid. But go in August when the pile is fully dried—its easier handling. Castor pomace at 5½ percent nitrogen is another vegetable by-product that is excellent both in the compost heap and the planting row. Castor pomace is the residue that is left after the oil is extracted from the castor bean. It is handled by fertilizer dealers in various parts of the country.

We use cottonseed meal and soybean meal whenever we turn wood chips or old hay under in the garden. It gives the soil bacteria extra nitrogen to work with. Cottonseed meal offers the extra advantage of a low pH, which makes it fine for acid-loving crops, and is rated at 7 percent nitrogen, 3 percent phosphorus, and 1½ percent potash. It's easily obtained at any grain or feed mill.

Mineral fertilizers high in phosphorus and potash

But nitrogen-rich manures and meals don't tell the whole story. No plant can grow successfully, attain a ripe maturity, or reproduce its own kind without the phosphorus and potash found in the rock minerals. And you can get all you need in local stores at very moderate prices, although the stuff is admittedly heavy and hard to handle.

There are 4 important natural rock fertilizers. Rock phosphate and colloidal phosphate respectively contain 30 to 50 percent and 18 to 30 percent phosphoric acid. Granite dust yields 3 to 5 percent potassium, while greensand, originally an ocean deposit, contains 6 to 7 percent. Since phosphorus has been called the "master key to agriculture," its lack can cause low crop production. These mineral fertilizers are essential for top results in the garden patch.

Ground to a fine powder to speed and ease release of its nutrients, rock phosphate does particularly well on acid soils and, combined with raw animal or green vegetable manures, is a most effective fertilizer. This is due to a reciprocal action which makes the nitrogen in the manure more available to the plant while the acids work on the rock, making its phosphorus more assimilable by as much as 200 percent.

The potassium in granite dust—a slow working and long lasting fertilizer—helps carry carbohydrates throughout the plant's system to form strong stems and fight disease. It improves the keeping qualities of fruit, is essential to cell division, while it reduces the plant's water needs and helps it to utilize nitrogen. Some granite dusts contain 11 percent potash.

Commercially processed "fortified" granite dusts are now available, sold as complete natural soil conditioners. Produced on a large scale in the region where they are abundant and packaged, they are then distributed on a nationwide basis. Just such a product comes from Georgia where the raw granite juts up out of the ground, and 10,000 chicken egg farms are common. The product is a combination of the chicken droppings and pulverized granite, colloidal phosphate, ground meat scraps, and humus composted and heated to 160 degrees, then allowed to cool off gradually. A Pennsylvania-made product combines such organic materials as blood meal, castor pomace, fish meal, cocoa bean shells, phosphate rock, greensand, and seaweeds. It is packaged and marketed in 4 different blends, for maximum effectiveness with different soils and growing problems. These commercial fertilizers or additives may be combined with the gardener's own home-made compost or applied separately.

Greensand, containing about 7 percent potash, is an excellent soil builder with the ability to *thin* dense, clayey textures, and also to *fatten* loose, sandy aggregates. It absorbs and retains large amounts of water, contains plenty of trace elements, may be left on the surface as a mulch, used in the compost pile, or tilled under with other nutrients. An undersea deposit, greensand has up to 50 percent silica, 23 percent iron oxide, and 7½ percent magnesium.

Once in short supply, greensand is now mined and processed in New York, New Jersey, Maryland and Ohio, where-ever the deposits exist, then packaged and distributed over a great part of the country. To these marine sources of soil fertility and texture must be added the new material called humate, which is abundant along the Florida coast and the Gulf of Mexico.

What about composting?

Composting is almost, but not quite, perpetual motion put to work on the homestead, because what you take from the land is later returned. But there's more to the problem—composting is the only safe way to dispose of municipal wastes.

Municipal sludge, packaged and sold by many communities, is even given away for the hauling in some. But make sure that the sludge you use has been subjected to microbial decomposition. Such material has a pH of 5 to 6 and assays at about 3 percent nitrogen. It is especially recommended for use on new and old lawns, trees, shrubs, and considered an economical way to replenish the soil. Find out if your community makes it available, it's a good way to build soil fertility.

Gardeners report improvements in home composting methods

But the organic gardener is a self-reliant individualist who does his own composting. Recent reports from our readers stress experimentation which results in improvements in quality, quantities, and time consumed. Microbial action is more complete, achieved in less time, and with less work. In last year's April issue, F. W. Bassett reported how he obtained "Continuous Compost Without Turning" by getting his pile up off the ground — one full foot in the air. Improved circulation of air completely matured the pile.

Then in the December issue, Frederick J. Barnett reported from "Down-Under" Australia that he had made a revolving composter-digester which continuously aerates the churning mass by forcing air through a hollow shaft pierced with 32 holes. A reversed vacuum cleaner, geared to the turning mechanism, drives the air to very center of the pile, while bacterial action brings the inside temperature up to 160 degrees. Total cost of the homemade apparatus, he reports, was $8.50.

PERCENT OF N–P–K IN ORGANIC MATERIALS

Material	N	P	K
Brewer's grains (wet)	.90	.50	.05
Ground bone, burned		34.70	
Cocoa shell dust	1.04	1.49	2.71
Coffee grounds (dried)	1.99	.36	.67
Cottonseed	3.15	1.25	1.15
Cottonseed meal	7.00	2.5	1.5
Fish scrap (red snapper)	7.76	13.00	3.8
Hoof meal and horn dust	10.00	1.50	
King crab (dried and ground)	10.00	.26	.06
Lobster shells	4.60	3.52	
Molasses (residue)	.70		5.32
Seaweed (Atlantic City)	1.68	.75	4.93
Wood ashes		1.00	4.00
Blood meal	15.00	1.30	.70
Bone meal	4.00	21.00	.20
Tankage	6.00	8.00	
Rabbit manure	2.4	1.4	0.6
Hen manure	1.1	0.8	0.5

Sheep manure	0.7	0.3	0.9
Horse manure	0.7	0.3	0.6
Duck manure	0.6	1.4	0.5
Cow manure	0.6	0.2	0.5
Pig manure	0.5	0.3	0.5
Oak leaves	.8	.35	.15
Pear leaves	.7	.12	.4
Apple leaves	1.00	.15	.35
Raspberry leaves	1.35	.27	.63
Vetch hay	2.8	.75	2.3
Alfalfa hay	2.45	.5	2.10
Immature grass	1.00	.5	1.2

Applying compost and organic fertilizers

This brief discussion of the availability and varieties of organic fertilizers would be incomplete without some mention of the best ways to put them to work. Here are some practical ways recommended by experienced gardeners:

1. Spreading the fertilizers in the seedbed *before planting*
2. Sowing them along the seed row *during planting*
3. Setting fertilizers in or around the hill *before or at planting time*
4. Applying fertilizer along the plant row *during the growing season.*

Rate Per Acre, in Pounds

	250	500	750	1000	1500	2000
12"	9 oz.	1 lb.	1½ lb.	2¼ lb.	3½ lb.	4½ lb.
15"	12 oz.	1¼ lb.	2 lb.	2½ lb.	4 lb.	5 lb.
18"	14 oz.	1½ lb.	2½ lb.	3 lb.	5 lb.	6½ lb.
24"	1 lb.	2 lb.	3 lb.	4½ lb.	6½ lb.	9 lb.
30"	1¼ lb.	2½ lb.	3¾ lb.	5¾ lb.	8½ lb.	11 lb.
36"	1½ lb.	3½ lb.	4½ lb.	7 lb.	10½ lb.	13½ lb.

Amount of Fertilizer Per Row for Various Rates of Application
Approximate amounts per 100 feet, for rows different distances apart

Spreading fertilizer in the seedbed before planting raises the general fertility level of the soil. Done annually, it may also be supplemented with subsequent top-dressing or side-dressings. It's good practice to mix it into the soil by raking, disking, or rotary tilling.

Sowing fertilizer in a narrow furrow at planting time puts the nutriments close to roots, making them readily accessible.

Fertilizer should be placed deeper then the seed, but we put matured compost all around the seed, sometimes literally planting the seeds in it. Placing fertilizers around hills at planting time is good for widely spaced plants. The fertilizer should be kept 2 to 3 inches away from the seed and 1 inch deeper. When we've got enough, we use compost as a mulch around the hills, or work it into the soil at seed level.

Fertilizers applied after growth has been made should be set in furrows 3 inches deep— 2 inches if the plants are small. The furrow is then filled with soil and moistened by sprinkling. When we use compost, we merely distribute along the row, leaving it as topdressing and mulch. If you plan to use fertilizers and are not sure about amounts, the accompanying chart should be consulted.

Materials for mulching and composting are practically interchangeable. You can get all the leaves you want or need for making leaf mold, for composting, and for mulching. If you've got the room, keep two piles of everything—wood chips, sawdust, corncobs, hay, and crop residues of all kinds. All of these materials are free for the hauling and asking, as are the contents of the family garbage pail which should always — but always! — go into the compost pile or worm pit. And finally, there are the commercial, mass-processed organic fertilizers, mulches, and soil conditioners.

—MAURICE FRANZ

5. Where to Buy Organic Fertilizers and Mulches

We went shopping for organic fertilizers and mulches one wintry day so we could tell you what's available right in your own backyard even on one of the most unlikely days of the year.

We wanted to find out what you can buy, how far you may have to go to get it, and just how hard it might be to get some pretty scarce items—seakelp and bagasse, for example. This is what we found out.

Nowadays everybody stocks organic materials

We covered about 100 miles, fanning out in a 25-mile radius from our Emmaus, Pennsylvania editorial offices, stopping at two feed mills, three garden supply shops, a flower shop with an attached greenhouse, and two dealers who specialize in organic supplies. But we found that nowadays everybody stocks organic mulches, fertilizers and soil conditioners right along with the chemical stuff. All you've got to do is ask and, not only do they know what you're talking about, they've got it, and at a price that's competitively right.

The moral of the story is that you can get all the organic supplies you need for the garden and homestead.

These are some of the places we deliberately passed up although we knew we could get all the free materials we could use:

1. The feed mill that gives you all the free ground corncobs you can haul away
2. The city dump that lets you take all the leaves you want
3. The brewery that keeps spent hops in the yard—free for the taking
4. The lumberyard with a sawdust shed that's handy for backing into
5. The city sewage treatment plant that fills your truck with sludge for $1 a load

We passed these places on the road—didn't have to detour —but didn't stop because we were on an "organic shopping spree." Regarding that argument, "It's hard to get organic materials," we can only stress that we could have made 13 calls within our self-imposed 25-mile radius instead of a mere 8.

Plenty of organics at garden supply center

Our first call at a real "old country" garden supply store revealed a good variety of meals—blood, bone, and cottonseed—plus cocoa bean shells, shredded pine bark, and a soil amendment and mulch called TURFACE which was new to us. Technically described as a "montmorillonite clay," it seems to be Mississippi River mud which has been heat treated at high temperatures to resist decomposition. List price for a 50-pound package is $3.38.

Second call, 3 miles away, was at a high-pressure farm co-op and feed mill with a quickly spotted display of chemical fertilizers and sprays, and a really impressive display of farm power tools of every kind and size.

But when we said, "Organic fertilizers, bone meal, blood meal, cottonseed meal," the man behind the counter asked briskly, "How much do you want?" He also had cow manure, sheep manure, raw limestone, and soybean meal. When asked about mulches, he offered to sell us Canadian peat moss, cocoa bean shells, sphagnum moss, and shredded pine bark.

Next call, at the garden supply center of one of our largest national retail distributors, was something of a disappointment, because this is a seasonal-minded chain store operation. But they had 5 pounds of cow manure for 69 cents.

On the way to the following call, the flower shop and greenhouse, we passed the city dump, the sewage plant, the brewery, and the lumberyard without stopping. The woman at the flower shop apologized "for our poor supply" but had sphagnum moss, peat moss, and cocoa bean shells available. Like the man at the big chain store, she urged us to "come back in the season; we'll have everything you can use."

Lots of mulches at country feed mill

The next visit, a good-sized country feed mill, was perhaps the most rewarding call of the day, because the inventory of mulching materials was unexpectedly wide ranging. The manager and his young assistants knew exactly what we were talking about and frequently anticipated our next questions. They stocked and willingly displayed huge bales of bagasse, minced sugar cane residues, from Louisiana, and pine planing mill shavings from Maine. This was well packaged organic merchandise, designed from the eye-appeal point of view to compete with other mass distributed products.

More than anything else, the freshness of the packages and the obvious care taken in their presentation showed that there is an organic market, and that the suppliers are both conscious of it and mean to reach it.

The same feed mill also stocked ground corncobs, crushed granite, Canadian peat moss in 6-foot bales, crushed limestone, cow manure, and cottonseed and soybean meal. Bone meal was in short supply, available only in 10-pound bags.

Nearby, in a small garden-supply shop, the dealer reported he would carry a fuller inventory of organic materials "as soon as I know what they want." Meantime, in January, he stocked Canadian peat moss, cocoa bean shells, and two organic fertilizers which are distributed nationally.

A few miles away we stopped—just for the record—at a

local organic researcher who composts coffee grounds, selling the product in 50-pound bags, for $2. Its name is CINAGRO, Which is ORGANIC spelled backward.

Last stop, 27 miles away, at organic supplier

The last stop of the day was a bit distant, 27 miles away. But we wanted to see Paul Degler who makes a specialty of dealing in organic fertilizers and mulches. (See Appendix for address.) He has been supplying us for years, keeps a very complete inventory at all times, and we wanted to check on what we had possibly missed elsewhere. While Degler had just about everything you would need to run an organic garden and homestead, it should be stressed that visits to perhaps three other dealers nearer home would give you all the materials you need.

We also noted complete organic fertilizers which, although processed regionally in Georgia and Pennsylvania, are distributed nationally. There was also Sea Born, a Norwegian seaweed meal product, packaged in 100-pound sacks.

It may be helpful to list here some of the products he stocks in eastern Pennsylvania.

> *blood meal*
> *feather meal*
> *bone meal*
> *cottonseed meal*
> *ground granite*
> *colloidal phosphate*
> *rock phosphate*
> *dolomitic limestone*

The organic gardener has opened up a new market, and that market is being supplied, catered to, and courted increasingly.

Don't worry about a shortage of organic supplies, there's more than enough to go around.

—MAURICE FRANZ

6. Getting Humus into the Soil

There are two ways to get humus into the soil, you can put it there, or you can grow it in. Which is best for you?

The method depends on the kind of place you have, where it is, how big, and the kind of soil you have to work with. To maintain soil fertility, texture, and structure, you can spread compost, animal and vegetable manures, and then work them under. But if your soil is extremely poor, too much sand or clay, you should consider green manuring or cover cropping seriously.

Sheet composting is an efficient, quick way to add organic material to the garden patch. Instead of being composted in heaps, materials are spread directly over the planting area and turned under with a rotary tiller. It provides a highly concentrated organic mixture of animal manures, crop residues, rock minerals, and soil which creates a balanced condition for healthy, vigorous plant growth.

Down in Florida, "where spring is fall and the end of the growing season is June," Jeanne Wellenkamp follows a program of "sheet composting combined with organic minerals and green manuring."

First, year-old chicken manure is combined with granite dust, phosphate rock, and bone meal "in amounts determined by the crop that will follow." These are worked into the soil at the same time, weather permitting. Otherwise they are worked in singly.

About July 1, a nitrogen-fixing legume, sesbania, is planted as a cover crop, 30 pounds of seed to the acre. Six weeks later, about August 15, "when this green manure has shot up to 8 to 10 feet and is beginning to bloom, it is cut down, chopped and plowed in." In 3 weeks the fields are ready for cultivation and planting.

In the meantime, Mrs. Wellenkamp notes, "the earthworms have been having a field day for themselves and millions of them are propagating in the sweet sesbania compost."

Up in Needham, Massachusetts, Jerome Sisson likes sheet composting for another reason, "it's a one-time operation that doesn't call for the periodic all-summer attention required in maintaining a compost heap," he writes. "Besides saving time and effort, the spread-and-turn-under system allows the gardener to make direct, soil-enriching use of many materials—

probably more than he would process into compost," he stresses.

Two different systems of sheet composting are used by Mr. Sisson. First, he spreads weeds, manure, and other organic materials over the garden and field where they are worked into the soil to decompose. Second, he spreads "about 8 cubic yards of ground leaves over my 30-by-30 garden where they lie 1 to 2 inches deep." After spreading a generous application of ground limestone, he works them in "thoroughly with a rotary tiller, and then I leave the rest to Mother Nature."

What about garbage—and the compost pile?

But the now classic compost pile cannot be either ignored or neglected. Maybe it does take longer to make finished compost this way, 14 days with considerable turning, and then maybe you do have to haul it away and spread it. But in the summer's greatest heat, we have made good, usable compost in 6 days with our open-hearth composting technique. The trick is to raise the pile off the ground, with about 12 inches of space under it. Convection does the rest. As the heap heats in the blazing sun, cool air is sucked in at the bottom and pulled up through the pile, aerating it completely.

This rapid conversion of compostable material permits us not only to make good and full use of our kitchen garbage, it also allows us to maintain a schedule of successive midsummer and late summer plantings. Into the new planting rows or into the second plantings, go spadefuls of compost with the seeds or seedlings to give them a good start. We like this system which gives us late tomatoes and corn, and also side-dressings and booster feedings right through the summer.

As for the garbage, since it is necessary to any organic gardening program, don't treat it as though it were a nuisance. Mix it with straw, hay, wood chips, sawdust; get it into your compost pile, and put it to work out in the garden rows!

It's an old trick, using garbage on "hard spots"

Kitchen wastes are a good supply for our compost, but out in Michigan, Marilyn Pearce also buries garbage directly in the paths of her garden. "Lifting up the spoiled hay mulch which covers all the pathways, I dig a hole and bury some of the kitchen wastes," she writes. The mulch is then replaced and she leaves her "small shovel right in place to know where to dig next time."

Come spring, compost is placed "all over the garden which we work into the soil with a rotary tiller. By now the former sand we began with has turned into rich-looking soil," she notes, "a pleasure to dig into with your hands."

"Organic cores" beat harsh Texas conditions

Another organic gardener, Fred L. Christen writes from Texas that "hardpan is what the building contractor leaves after he is finished with his heavy equipment." Confronted with such a situation, Mr. Christen bought a 6-inch posthole auger and started to plant in 2-foot-deep holes filled with "organic cores."

Each hole was filled with "a mixture of compost and uncomposted organic materials," watered down to drive out the air, and then a plant was set down right on top. Only organic material was used to fill the hole, and the removed soil was "thrown on the compost pile for the worms to aerate."

The results, he reports, were "spectacular." Although it was one of the hottest Texas summers on record, "38 days reached 100 degrees or higher," the peppers and tomatoes thrived, and insects were "only a slight problem." When he checked out the root systems at the end of the season, he found them "healthy and husky, ample testimony to how well the method works!"

The "hole method" was also used to save peach trees, writes an Oklahoma hardpan gardener, Mrs. Marjorie Bingham. Although they were badly stunted, the trees responded to holes dug around them and filled with fresh cow manure. "The results have been wonderful," she notes, adding that the "hardpan presents such a barrier to roots that very little growth occurs unless it is broken."

Cover cropping saves manure

The Binghams also report that the "first cover crop planted was so scant that it was scarcely worth turning under, although one of our first purchases was a rotary tiller which has since proved invaluable." However, by continuing to plant cover crops, and practice green manuring and sheet composting, "the soil gradually improved." The Binghams estimate they have spread about 40 tons of manure and litter on the orchard and garden. Manure, which at first "seemed almost a must in order to start production," is no longer relied on to maintain soil fertility. "We always have a winter cover crop such as rye and vetch," Mrs. Bingham reports.

The advantages of green manuring your garden plots are many and they add up to better crops because it encourages a normally functioning soil microbial life. Here they are:

1. ADDING NITROGEN to the soil for use by productive crops
2. INCREASING FERTILITY by mobilizing minerals and building up organic matter
3. REDUCING LOSSES caused by erosion
4. IMPROVING PHYSICAL CONDITION of the soil, thus permitting a more efficient use of plant nutrients
5. CONSERVING NUTRIENTS by cutting down losses caused by leaching.

Hairy vetch is the "most dependable" green manure crop, writes T. Hayden Rogers and Joel E. Giddens in their joint USDA article, "Green Manure and Cover Crops," In a 6-year planting experiment conducted in Alabama, vetch was superior to commercial nitrogen fertilizer. Other studies revealed that the "residual effect of vetch preceding corn in a cotton-corn rotation was equivalent to 214 pounds of seed cotton."

Green manure crops may be used with considerable success in rotating vegetables, the authors report. Green manure "increased the yield of potatoes an average of 53 bushels an acre" in experiments conducted over a period of 16 years in Maine. When the green manure crop was removed, "the yield of potatoes was reduced 38 bushels." Green manuring is quite profitable from the commercial aspect. "The average value of the organic treatment on all vegetables studied was $135 an acre above costs."

Your choice

By now it should be fairly obvious that what you do to maintain soil fertility and structure in your garden is up to you and depends on what you've got to work with in terms of soil and the weather conditions that prevail in your area. In any case, use what is abundant and cheap locally. Grow a cover or green manure crop, sheet compost, bury garbage or compost to break up hardpan. Do them all, but *do what conditions demand* and then check results *honestly and carefully!*

And, if you really want to add humus, don't forget to mulch. It also puts humus in the soil, which is dragged down by the worms and broken up into layers, just like on the forest floor, below the mulch. Also, plant some deep-rooted annuals for show and soil improvement. Their roots aerate the soil and, after they die, turn into humus down in the deeper top-soil and subsoil.

7. Fertilize Organically and Forget the "Numbers" Complex

Fertilizing garden soil with organic materials is a simple job, except perhaps for the person doing it for the first time. For example, take the case of Mr. J. D., an organic gardener from Louisiana. He's just had his soil tested by the State University and was advised to use 800 pounds of 8-8-8 per acre. He writes: "Since I'm gardening the organic way, and don't want to use commercial fertilizers, I thought of the following substitutes that I can easily get: cottonseed meal (7 percent N, 2-3 percent P, 1.5 percent potash), phosphate rock (30 percent P), and wood ashes (1.5 percent P, 7 percent K). How many pounds of each should I apply to equal the fertilizer amount in 8-8-8?"

Like so many other organic growers, Mr. D. has a good, clear idea of what materials to use and where to get them. His main trouble, as we see it through, is that he's suffering from a "number" complex. Because some expert told him to use 8-8-8, he's going to struggle to match it—only with organic fertilizers instead of chemical. Aside from the needless mental activity (perhaps even anguish) caused by this complex, there are other disadvantages.

First, it's often difficult to equate the organic ratio with the chemical one. The results may be that the "new" organic gardener may say that the organic method is difficult or confusing.

Secondly, and perhaps the most common trouble, a lot of gardeners and farmers make the big mistake of not using organic fertilizers heavy enough on their first applications. We found this to be true time and again. Advertisements of chemical companies who have just come out with an expensive fancy mix or super blend may advise applying at the rate of 200 pounds per acre, or a pound or two for the whole vegetable garden. Then when the organic grower wants to convert, he still thinks of such applications.

Fertilizer program for you

That's what harm the "number" complex can do in terms of worry, confusion, and inefficiency. Our advice to Mr. D. of Louisiana (and every organic gardener and farmer worrying about chemical ratios) is to forget about the numbers, and concentrate on a long-range fertilizing program. Once you do this, you'll find yourself growing better plants, and sleeping better too.

Soil tests are a valuable guide to all gardeners and farmers, as they will indicate when and how to increase fertilizer applications. At first, these tests will show what elements are needed most; future tests will tell how well your fertilizing program is working out. But when these results are accomplished by suggestions for chemical fertilizers, don't feel you *must* come up with the *exact* mixture in organic *fertilizers*.

Now here are some general recommendations for making the best use of organic fertilizers.

Nitrogen Sources. For vegetable gardens, pastures, etc., we believe cottonseed meal is one excellent source of nitrogen. The price is somewhere between $4.50 to $5.50 per 100 pounds. When you consider what you are getting in the meals compared to nitrate of soda which costs only a little less, you are definitely better off using the meal. General early spring application rates are 200-300 pounds per acre or heavier depending upon conditions, 5 pounds per 100 square feet for flower and vegetable gardens, and the same rate for lawns.

Blood meal, costing about the same as cottonseed meal, is quicker acting, as its nitrogen is readily available. (It's also useful for keeping rabbits from eating young plants in the garden.) Fish meal is another good N source, especially for corn (about two pounds per 60-foot row). Generally speaking, with all organic fertilizers, use those which are easily obtainable in your area.

Phosphate Application. One thing a farmer or gardener must remember: to get best results, you must have your phosphate level built up along with your organic matter. The normal supply of phosphate in our virgin soils averaged about 1,200 pounds per acre. In many areas, this level is now down to 125 pounds per acre.

The trouble of "too light applications" often pops up with rock phosphate. After a soil test shows a phosphorus deficiency, the new organic grower may continue to apply less than 500 pounds per acre, only substituting rock phosphate for superphosphate. It is impossible to build up the phosphate level with this application.

When we recommend phosphate to a farmer, we want him to use 1,500 to 2,000 pounds per acre on his first application. Say the phosphate cost him $34 per ton. If he is on a four-year rotation, that figures out at $8.50 per year for phosphate. Then follow this up on each rotation with 1,000 pounds plus crop residue and you're increasing the mineral content as well as the fertility of your soil. Many farmers go by the rule: "Feed your phosphate to your clover, feed your clover to your corn, and you won't go wrong."

Tests with different crop rotations at the University of Illinois showed that corn, beans, and clover did just as well on applications of rock phosphate as superphosphate. The work also revealed that a four-year rotation of corn, soybeans, wheat, and legume hay uses fertilizers more efficiently than a two-year rotation of corn and soybeans.

Adding Potash. Potash is another element deficient in many soils. Green manuring with deep-rooted crops like sweet clover and alfalfa, helps to restore potash to depleted land. Greensand and granite dust applied at from 1,000 to 2,000 pounds per acre will definitely help correct the problem. Many farmers feed phosphate to small grains and greensand to their corn. Many we know use 500 to 1,000 pounds per acre through the corn drill when they plant and are harvesting 100 bushels per acre.

The suggested amounts for applying the rock powders—colloidal or rock phosphate, greensand and granite dust—in the garden are the same: spread about 10 to 15 pounds per 100 square feet. In fall or winter, you can spread it right on top of the ground. In spring, dust a mixture of phosphate and potash (equal amounts) in the row; mix a good handful in around plants such as tomatoes, cabbage, etc. The following year, use in the row only. In this way, you're returning more than what you drew out the previous year.

Other recent experiments at Illinois showed that a single application of potash per acre—applied ahead of either corn or wheat in a four-year rotation of corn, soybeans, wheat and mixed hay—is just as effective as split applications on both corn and wheat. Therefore, growers can save time and money by applying the full amount of rock potash once instead of two or three times in a rotation.

One caution about liming: never assume that your soil needs tons of limestone. Always test first to see what is needed. Sample both the topsoil and subsoil to get a correct answer. If you do need lime, use dolomite limestone for the high magnesium content of this rock.

Disregard the numbers

When you want to add nitrogen to your soil, take your pick of tankage, manure (fresh or dried), homemade or commercial compost, sludge, any of the vegetable meals as cottonseed, linseed, soybean, or peanut. Because of the high nitrogen content of blood meal and dried blood (12 to 15 percent), use these materials more sparingly.

For phosphate, you have your choice of rock or colloidal phosphate, bone meal, and some materials named above as dried blood, the meals, and manure. Natural potash sources include granite dust, greensand marl, wood ashes, cocoa shells, kelp, and many plant residues.

All these materials can be worked into the soil in spring or fall, topdressed around growing plants, used as a mulch, or added to the compost heap. Keeping a high humus content in your soil means that many of these fertilizers will be more readily available as well as stay available over several years.

A variety of organic fertilizers are available at local garden supply stores, feed mills, farm cooperatives, etc. Most often, a few phone calls will tell you where to obtain all you need. If you have any difficulty locating sources of natural rock powders or anything else, write to organic fertilizer advertisers for the names of dealers nearest you.

Whether you're just beginning as an organic grower or are a veteran of many years you needn't fret about formulas or converting chemical mixtures to organic ones. Our advice is follow the general recommendations for amounts to apply and be assured that your soil (and plants) will make the best use of them.

8. Natural Mineral Fertilizers Get Results

Although they are considered mainstays of organic gardening and farming, natural rock fertilizers have been more or less neglected by the average gardener. This oversight should be remedied because natural rock fertilizers furnish ample supplies of phosphorus and potash without which *no plant can grow successfully, attain a ripe maturity, or reproduce its own kind.*

Of equal organic significance is the fact that natural mineral fertilizers put these essential nutrients into the soil gradually, literally over the years, so they are absorbed as the plants need them. And because there is no "feast or famine," the soil and plants are in sound balance and the soil structure improves as the nutrients are released.

There are four important natural fertilizers. Two of them, rock phosphate and colloidal phosphate, respectively contain 30 to 50 and 18 to 30 percent phosphoric acid. Granite dust and greensand, which originally was an ocean deposit, yield 3 to 5 and from 6 to 7 percent potassium respectively.

The basic importance of these elements cannot be overstressed. Their available presence in the soil is absolutely necessary to successful gardening and farming. Phosphorus has been called the "master key to agriculture" because low crop production is due more often to a lack of this element than any other plant nutrient.

Potassium is almost as vital to the well being of the plant. Root and tuber crops require enormous quantities of potassium, while its sufficient availability insures plump kernels in grains and good straw structure.

What do these facts mean to the average gardener? Just this, he isn't going to grow the kind of organic foods he wants and needs unless he pays strict attention to a sound rock fertilizer program. For real results in the garden and field, we must fertilize the soil with both phosphorus and potassium. Let's start with the phosphates.

Rock phosphate

Rock phosphate is a natural mineral, ground to a meal or dust. In recent years, it has been reduced to a fine powder to facilitate release of its nutrients in the soil. It does particularly well on acid soils, and we will see that, combined with raw animal or green vegetable manures, it is a most effective fertilizer.

It has been determined that, due to the reciprocal action of the manures and phosphate powder, the fertilizing availability of each agent is increased when they are mixed together. The manures ripen more quickly and the nitrogen in the manure is absorbed more readily by the plant. The manure acids correspondingly work on the phosphate rock, making it more assimilable.

A series of experiments conducted in the Soviet Union reveal that soil fertilized with phosphate rock mixed with fresh manure yields 60 percent more potatoes; 158 bushels per acre, compared to 97. When the manure and phosphate rock were not mixed, but applied separately, 145 bushels were raised. It has been estimated that combining the phosphate and manure increases the availability of the phosphorus to the plant by 150 to 200 percent.

The next step is to mix phosphate rock and manure. Reports on the value of this extra procedure are lacking, but it is almost self-evident that the same benefits which derive from mixing phosphate and manure may be obtained. In any case, the experiment of mixing the two rock powders, phosphate and granite, with animal or vegetable manures should be made. The successful outcome means the creation of a complete organic fertilizer of augmented nutrient availability.

Colloidal phosphate

This is also a natural mineral product, found chiefly in Florida in sedimentary deposits of soft phosphate with colloidal clay. It is also obtained from ponds which occur where phosphate rock is mined hydraulically. It contains 18 to 25 percent phosphoric acid, and you should apply 50 percent more than you would with rock phosphate.

Rock Fertilizers—Application Rate Pounds Per Acre	
Rock phosphate	1,000 lbs.
	2,000
Colloidal phosphate	1,300 lbs.
	2,300
Granite dust	4–8,000 lbs.
Greensand	4,000 lbs.
Basalt	5,000 lbs.
Diabase	10,000 lbs.

Potassium from granite dust

The value of potassium is indicated by its position in the scale of nutritional values; it is the third major plant food. It helps carry carbohydrates throughout the plant system, forms strong stems, and fights disease. It improves the keeping quality of fruits; aids in the production of sugar, starches, and oils; reduces the plant's water requirements; is essential to cell division and growth; and helps the plant utilize nitrogen.

Granite dust is an excellent source of organic, slow working potash. Its potash content varies from 3 to 5 percent, but granite dust has been obtained from a Massachusetts quarry with a potash content of 11 percent.

The potash-bearing minerals in granite dust are the potash feldspars and micas, the latter containing the most readily released potash. Small amounts of trace elements are also present. Two tons of granite dust should be applied to the acre. However, as noted under the rock phosphate section, we believe granite dust should previously be mixed with the manure-phosphate combination, spread, and then turned under. This should be done in the spring, before planting, when you would normally start working the land. Smaller applications call for 20 pounds to 100 square feet and 200 pounds to 1,000 square feet of this complete fertilizer.

Greensand—product of the sea

Greensand or greensand marl contains more potash than granite dust; 6 to 7 percent compared with 3 to 5. Being an undersea deposit, it contains most if not all of the elements which are found in the ocean. It is an excellent soil builder.

Superior deposits of greensand contain 50 percent silica, 18 to 23 percent iron oxide, 3 to 7½ percent magnesia, and small amounts of lime and phosphoric acid.

Greensand has the ability to absorb large amounts of water and provides an abundant source of plant-available potash. Its minerals or trace elements are also essential to plant growth. Because it is versatile, it may be applied directly to the plant roots, left on the surface as a combined mulch-compost, or used in compost heaps to stimulate bacterial action and to enrich the heap. Once again, combining it with the manure-phosphate rock mixture should be seriously considered, if not put into actual practice.

Summing up—in general

Don't be afraid to use relatively large amounts of natural minerals. They are slow working and cannot burn young plants. If the soil is alkaline, increase the amount of manure either in the mixture or put it directly into the ground before applying the mixture.

Rotating crops and growing legumes, will also reduce an alkaline condition. But if you apply rock phosphate, remember to turn it under thoroughly so the nitrogen-fixing bacteria growing on the legume roots can go to work on it.

Remember that plant symptoms of nutritional deficiency are helpful indicators, but not the whole story. When you observe them, it is too late to correct the situation that year. You can only plan steps for the next to prevent its recurrence.

Mixing fresh animal manures with natural mineral fertilizers may well be a real advance in organic fertilizing. Based on past experience, the various elements work reciprocally, their interactions increasing the potency of each nutrient. Getting this complete fertilizer into the ground promptly reduces nutrient-loss sharply and increases its plant availability.

In all, the use of natural minerals in combination with animal and plant manures is recommended soberly as the cornerstone of a gardening and farming program that will extend over the years. You are putting vital nutrients back into the soil where they will work gradually and naturally to improve soil structure and produce ripened, wholesome, nutritious crops year in and year out.

9. What's an Earthworm Worth?

Call him a wiggler, an angleworm, fish bait, or anything else you may choose, the earthworm is a valuable adjunct in the soil's expression of fertility. He digests the soil, eats it and conditions it. Our topsoils have practically been made by earthworms. That is why Aristotle called them the intestines of the soil. Their castings are far richer minerally than the soil which they ingest. It is said that an average earthworm will produce its weight in castings every 24 hours. They burrow into the ground, as far as 6 feet down, aerating the soil, making holes for rain to penetrate. They break up hardpans, which have been created by chemical fertilizers and other artificial horticultural practices. Each year their dead bodies furnish a considerable amount of valuable nitrogenous fertilizer, which may amount to more than a thousand pounds per acre in a highly "organic soil."

An earthworm-worked soil will absorb a 2-inch rainfall in 15 seconds due to its porous consistency and spongelike structure, whereas its neighboring clay soil takes sometimes as long as 2 hours for the same amount to sink in. Every earthworm burrow hole is a watering tube.

These subterranean workers aerate the soil, allowing the much-needed air to penetrate to the roots. In turn, this oxidizes and nitrifies the earth. It dissolves the soil and makes it soluble in the water that carries the food to the plant roots. I have seen an earthworm take a fairly good-sized globule or tiny clod of earth and watched its passage through its body. It draws leaves and other green matter below the surface, much of which decays and enriches the soil. Many roots use the long tunnels as a means to get to lower levels. As these tunnels are lined by the worms with a fertile liquid casting, the roots benefit accordingly.

As the life of the earthworm is a bare year or two, their dying and decaying bodies furnish a substantial amount of fertilizer each year. The worms have a very high nitrogen content as well as a potent oil which immeasurably enriches the soil. Some earthworm breeders, incidentally, claim that persons with eczema of the hands have cured it by running their hands in the soil of the earthworm boxes which seem to be impregnated with this oil.

Worm castings are richest humus

Earthworm castings are the finest form of humus known. At the Connecticut Experimental Station, it was found that the nitrogen in these castings is almost 5 times greater than in the ordinary topsoil, the phosphate 7 times greater, potash 11 times, and magnesium 3 times. California florists pay a high price for earthworm castings. They report this material as the best they have ever been able to secure for raising flowers. Experts from Great Britain have estimated that in the intensive 6-month cotton-growing season, following the overflowing of the Nile, earthworm castings amounted to almost 120 tons per acre. This is more than 8 times the figure given by Darwin, and would seem to indicate an earthworm population of about 1,500,000 an acre. Such a gargantuan quantity of worms is made possible by the organic material (their food), which the overflowing Nile deposits on the land.

Darwin's figures of the number of earthworms per acre were very conservative. In Ohio, government investigators found 1,000,000 worms per acre on bluegrass pasture. Here the topsoil was over 18 inches thick, whereas in England Darwin found the upper layer of rich soil where he conducted his researches only 5 or 6 inches deep. Government investigators in Oregon found earthworm populations from 500,000 to 1,500,000 per acre.

More than a thousand types of earthworms

There are over 1,100 species of earthworms, but for our purposes we need consider only two. This group doesn't include cutworms, which are really caterpillars, nor grubworms, which are larvae of insects such as beetles. Neither do they include the parasitic nematodes—threadworms or roundworms so small that they are barely seen by the naked eye. Eelworms are in the same class.

We are concerned mainly with two types of earthworms: the bluish, long thin type, which works in the soil, and the smaller, thicker reddish type, which lives on fresh manure and in compost heaps. The blue, soil type earthworm will not thrive in a compost heap, and vice versa. When a heap is first made, no earthworms will be seen. They soon begin to propagate (the red type), and when the heap turns to humus they die and decay. Where incomplete compost is spread on the land, any of the red earthworms in it will die. The blue earthworm works on organic matter in the soil and turns it into humus. Sometimes when a compost heap is in the final stages, the blue earthworms may migrate into it.

Chemicals and Earthworms don't mix

Organic matter and mineral rock fragments are the earthworm's natural food. The gardener should use no other fertilizers, for if he does, he will be destroying a very valuable ally. Where strong chemical fertilizers are used, conditions distasteful to earthworms arise and their numbers decrease to the vanishing point. Ammonium sulphate, a fertilizer extensively used by farmers, is particularly harmful to these soil workers. The U.S. government itself acknowledges this fact by recommending ammonium sulphate as a specific where earthworms are to be killed off, such as on putting greens of golf courses!

Many other chemical fertilizers are slowly but definitely killing off the earthworm population. This was proven at the research laboratory at Dornach in Switzerland, where experiments showed that earthworms did not like soil saturated with artificial fertilizer, and if given an opportunity chose earth fertilized with biodynamic compost, in preference even to soil that was not fertilized at all.

Strong insect sprays containing lead, arsenic, copper, lime sulphurs, and tar oil, etc., are even more destructive to earthworms. In tracts of potato-growing land where much of these sprays are doused periodically on the land, nary an earthworm can be found. What is equally as bad is the fact that much of the bacteria population is adversely affected. The result is that the soil becomes almost sterile, and the farmer is working in a dead medium. Therefore, each succeeding year requires the use of progressively more spray and more chemical fertilizer to get the necessary yield.

Likewise in vineyards or orchards which have been intensively treated with sprays for many years, no earthworms are to be found. In such places, the earth becomes hard packed and extremely difficult for cultivation. Bird life will move away because of the lack of its usual food, the earthworm, and the land will suffer further because birds destroy fabulous amounts of noxious insects and their larvae.

"Bacteria test" shows worm's value

The boring into the soil of earthworms increases the porosity and aeration of the soil. This is of great aid to other kinds of soil life, such as bacteria, for example. In well worked soil, there is to be found about 600 pounds of bacteria to the acre. Where earthworms are absent, the bacteria population greatly decreases, to the serious detriment of the soil's fertility.

Bacteria is a potent factor in the formation of humus. It gives the soil the power to quickly digest organic matter. Place a piece of burlap on top of the soil that is saturated with bacteria. It will be eaten up by the soil and completely disappear from the surface in a few months. Do the same thing on land strongly chemicalized and sprayed. It will remain for years. That type of soil has lost its natural powers of digestion. It is sterile. It is dead.

Where any one item in nature's cycle is disturbed, it will be found that others are automatically affected. Nature consists of a chain of conditions, interrelated and interlocked. Remove any one factor and you will find that she cannot do her work efficiently and becomes less friendly to man. It never fails.

—J. I. RODALE

Compost

1. Garbage Is Gold; Compost Is Beautiful

At the very base of the organic method lies compost. In its many forms and variations, compost is the beautiful substance which gives fertility to soil, productivity to plants, and health to man. It is the combination soil conditioner-fertilizer of the organic gardener, and the hub of all his gardening activities. If you are a successful compost maker, chances are 100 to 1 that you are a successful organic gardener.

In the past two decades, there has been a great amount of research in composting methods, resulting in the 14-day method, sheet composting, anaerobic methods, and many more variations of these. Behind them all, however, lies the original Indore method, invented by the father of organic gardening, Sir Albert Howard. The Indore method is still the most widely used, and is still practical and productive.

Sir Albert Howard found that by layering different organic materials, decomposition took place more quickly and more completely. He first placed down a 5 or 6-inch layer of green matter, then a 2-inch layer of manure (blood meal, bone meal, sewage sludge, or other high protein material may be substituted), and a layer of rich earth, ground limestone and phosphate rock. This simple formula produced a crumbly compost, rich in nutrient value and valuable as a soil structure builder. In further research, Howard found that a heap 5 to 10 feet wide, and 5 feet high was ideal (the length is optional). He also found that decomposition was facilitated by aeration, and so he placed pipes or thick stakes through the pile as it was being built, then pulled them out when the heap was 5 feet high. He then lightly pressed the entire outside surface to prevent blowing, formed a shallow basin on top to catch rainwater, covered the entire surface with a thin layer of earth, and left it to decay.

Organic gardeners have taken Howard's core of compost research and produced beautiful compost and beautiful gardens. Take the example of O. A. Severance of Watertown, New York, who transformed a completely unproductive piece of land into a lush garden spot, all through the use of compost. Mr. Severance makes compost in a pit, surrounded by a wall of loose field stone 7 feet square on the inside and 2 feet high. The wall is laid on top of the ground, and the soil inside is dug out a foot deep.

Into this pit go hen and stable manure, leaves, weeds, garbage, lawn clippings, sunflower stalks, some sod, and ground limestone. This pit, layered according to Howard's Indore process, is level with the top of the stones when it is completed. Severance turns the pile in 3 weeks when he estimates the temperature has reached 150 degrees. Four weeks later he turns the pile again, in order to be sure all material has a chance to get into the center of the heap where decomposition is proceeding most rapidly. In a total of 3 months, he takes out well over 2 tons of finished compost. In this way he can make 2 piles each season.

From experimenting, gardeners often find ways to improve the Indore method, at least in their own gardens. Lois Hebble of Decatur, Indiana, uses a strip composting method. In the middle of the growing season, she lays heaps of organic materials on top of vegetable rows from which she has just harvested early crops. The material is partially composted by the next spring, but is not broken down enough for small seeds. Into these rows she plants melons, squash, or cucumbers.

"For each hill," says Mrs. Hebble, "I scoop out a small hole and fill this with a shovelful or two of garden soil, then plant the seeds in this. Later in the summer, just before the vines start spreading out too much, I cover the strip with a good weed-smothering layer of old hay. By the following spring, the soil under this strip has become mellow and homogenized enough to plant the smaller seeds. This method also keeps the garden crops in constant rotation."

Other gardeners use variations of the earthworm bed, sheet composting, mulching, pits, bins, plastic, shredding, and numerous devices in trying to find the best method for them. You, too, can experiment with different methods to find *your* way of composting. But remember that the key to success is the Indore method. Learn it well and anything is possible.

2. Helpful Hints on Compost Making

When to make compost

In temperate climate zones, autumn is generally the most suitable time to make compost. Among the reasons for this are:

1. Garden production is completed for the season; time and attention can more readily be given to preparing humus.
2. Plant wastes, leaves, and various other organic materials are plentiful and easily available.
3. Either finished or partially decomposed compost can be readied and applied to all sections of the garden with minimum effort or interference and with ample time to replenish the soil well before spring planting.

October and November are excellent for making compost heaps or pits because at no other time of the year are plant materials more abundant for this purpose. Garden wastes, autumnal leaves, roadside weeds, wastes from food-processing plants, and other materials are easy to obtain at this time of year. Also by making the compost heap then, the compost will be ready for use at spring garden making time.

Compost, however, can and should be made during any part of the year. In subtropical climes, any time is best for compost making. In the North, however, you often have extremely dry summers, when the decaying process is held up. We recently made a pit of compost of very resistant ingredients—shredded corncobs and leaves—in the middle of the winter, and by July it had been turned into wonderful compost, with earthworms doing the mixing. During the winter warm spells, compost can be made in a pit. The pit sides keep it warm and accelerate the decay processes in the winter. It wouldn't pay to assemble a compost heap in the open.

For winter composting, pile up the manure with a covering of soil and burlap bags or canvas. Also have available, in a

protected place, topsoil and green matter that are not frozen.
Leaves that have been gathered in the fall are excellent.

If you do have to make a compost in the open during winter, choose a protected place, as on the south side of a building or wall. You could also make a protective barrier of corn
stalks tied together. An extra heavy layer of soil on top would
help, or a very heavy hay or straw mulch a few feet thick to
keep the heap warm.

What grinding does

Grinding is the key to quick composting. What grinding
materials actually does is greatly increase the total surface
area of the material. The conversion of raw organic matter
into colloidal humus is accomplished by a series of fermentations. These fermentations consume the plant and animal residues like a living fire. The finer the particles, the faster they
will be consumed. In breaking up a large particle into smaller
particles, the volume decreases so much faster than the surface that in finely ground matter the ratio of surface to volume is very great. It is the large surface and relatively small
volume of the fine particles that makes it possible to make
finished compost in so short a time as from 3 to 5 days. The
same principle applies to the burning of such a substance as
charcoal. A large piece of charcoal may burn for hours or
even days. If the piece of charcoal is reduced to a fine dust,
complete combustion will be accomplished in a fraction of a
second with explosive force. The compost made in less time
than one week will be even better than that made over a
period of months, because there is less time for the dissipation
of valuable gases and the leaching out of essential elements.

Ventilating the heap

It is absolutely essential that the compost heap be well
ventilated so that there is a sufficient flow of gases between
the atmosphere and the interior of the compost heap. The
soil organisms which break down the plant and animal residues and convert them into compost are aerobes, i.e., they
must have the oxygen from the atmosphere to carry on their
life activities. Here is a suggestion for a simple but effective
way of ventilating the heap. As soon as the pits have been
dug or the soil has otherwise been prepared for the compost
heaps, a number of ordinary fence posts are set up and held

in position by driving 3 small stakes around the base of each post. The posts are placed where the ventilators are desired. By using chalk or heavy pencil, marks can be made on the posts 8 inches apart to serve as a guide in building the various layers of the heap; 6 inches for plant material, 2 inches for the fresh manure, a sprinkling of raw ground limestone, and a ¾ inch or less of good earth. When the heap has been built to its usual height of 5 feet, the posts are pulled out to form the ventilating chimneys. To facilitate the removal of the posts, a board can be laid on the heap to serve as a walk, and a cross piece nailed near the top of the post to serve as a handle to pull out the post. The size of the ventilator is determined by the size of the post used.

Where to make compost

There are no set rules on the best place to make compost. We know of gardeners with imagination who have set up a composting area on their front lawns in such a way that it added to the overall attractiveness. For the most part, though, gardeners prefer to do their compost making in back of their lots, where the heap can be easily "disguised" in some way.

For example, on one suburban place, the home owner chose an area behind the fireplace alongside the rail fence at the rear of the property. It's just a few yards from the vegetable patch, so it's a simple procedure to carry weeds, plant wastes, etc., to the pile, as well as take the finished compost to the garden.

Just as important, whenever large quantities of waste organic materials are available, it's a simple job to drive up the alley at the end of the yard and dump the materials directly onto the heap. So in that case the composting area has these three advantages:

1. It fits into the landscaping plan without being an eyesore.
2. It's close to the source of organic waste materials and to where most of the compost is used.
3. It's little work to bring in outside materials, since they can be dumped directly from a car or truck.

There are a great many ways to improve the appearance of composting areas on your own home grounds. There are wooden bins specially designed for this purpose, where the slats are removable for easy withdrawal of the finished compost. Many gardeners we know use cement blocks, often without mortaring them together, around 2 or 3 sides of the heap. (Hay bales make an excellent "door" on the fourth side). Still others make use of hedges to "fence off" their home fertilizer factories.

What you decide to do depends a great deal on the size of your grounds. If you have several acres, there's probably little need to think about disguising the heap; your main objective is to choose an idea that's accessible and large enough to make all the compost you need.

On the other hand, if you live in a highly developed suburban area with fussy neighbors, you'll want to be extra careful. Besides the camouflage techniques mentioned previously, you might want to think about making compost in pits.

Here's an idea which John Adamson of East Lansing, Michigan, recently sent in. one that might suggest a solution for your own composting problems.

> I've been trying to come up with a systematic arrangement for making regular use of kitchen and garden refuse. What I have in mind are sunken dual compost heaps, that is, two pits side by side. These are to be dug in the rear of my garden, surrounded by shrubbery for screening and protection. The rectangular depressions are to be about 2 feet deep, 2 feet wide, and 4 feet long, with wooden covers to go over them to keep the neighborhood dogs from scattering the contents, and to keep these receptacles from filling up with snow in the winter season.

> In a surburban area as I live in, it would not be acceptable to try to maintain my compost on top of the ground, even with 3 framed sides. The dimensions mentioned would provide relatively small compost heaps, to be sure, but half a loaf is better than none, and I can get away with this size and also get a more rapid turnover than if they were larger.

The main thing to remember is that in just about every yard, there *is* space for composting.

Collecting and assembling materials

When it comes to getting materials for your compost heap, the big point is to use imagination and initiative. You'll have a certain amount of waste materials available without moving off your home grounds, such as grass clippings, garden residues, leaves, weeds, kitchen wastes, and so on. If these supply you with enough of the vegetable matter for your composting, that's fine. But don't feel that you are limited to just those sources. If you need more, there are scores of places within a short drive of your home where valuable wastes are available—for the most part *free*.

Using power equipment

When done correctly, compost can be made according to the Indore method in about 3 months. The pile is turned after 6 weeks and again at 12 weeks, to allow air to penetrate all parts of the heap.

However, in recent years, various power garden equipment has been developed which cuts down the composting time to as little as 10 days. Foremost among these machines are the grinders and shredders which cut up the green matter and manure going into the compost heap. Shredding materials can also be done with a rotary mower by running it back and forth over a pile of green matter.

Without power equipment

While a great many gardeners have access to power equipment of some sort, there are still many who don't. If you're one of the latter group, perhaps you're wondering if you have to give up on the idea of making "speed" compost. This is not the case. We definitely believe that compost can be made quickly without the use of special equipment or chemical activators. Here's how:

When making the compost heap, be sure to mix material such as grass clippings, vegetable tops, weeds, etc., with materials high in nitrogen (manure, cottonseed meal, dried blood, and tankage). All material should be moist to start with, and the heap should be kept wet. A brief watering for the first 3 days should be sufficient.

Turn the heap often. The fastest working bacteria thrive in the presence of air, and turning the heap is the best way to aerate it. Initially, every 3 or 4 days is not too often. It's best not to make the speed compost heaps too large. Remember, a ton of compost occupies a space only 4 feet square and 4 feet high, and will last the average gardener for quite a while.

Adding earthworms to the compost heap has also been found an effective way of hastening decomposition.

Improving value of compost

Many homemade composts have relatively little plant foods, that is, a low nitrogen, phosphorus, and potash content. Yet they accomplish a conditioning effect in the soil which is beyond the power of the most expensive high analysis fertilizers. Besides increasing the soil's water-holding capacity, improving its tilth and aeration, compost also makes plant nutrients already in the soil more available to plants.

However, there are many ways in which you can make compost even more valuable. If testing shows that your soil is acid, mix in ground limestone when assembling the materials. Regardless of what kind of soil you have, it will always help to add some rock phosphate and potash, as well as other natural mineral fertilizers. Manure and other nitrogen-rich materials speed up the compost material, while increasing the N content of the finished compost.

Watering and turning

When the materials are shredded in the 10–14 day composting technique, it's relatively easy to turn the heap with a pitchfork, so you can do it as often as time permits. However, the heap should be turned at least twice during the first 14 days.

If the materials are not shredded and you want finished compost as fast as possible, it's best to keep the heaps relatively small so they can be turned often without too much effort.

Regarding watering, it's especially important to have the heap quite moist during the initial days. It's well to have the top of the heap sloping toward the center, so that rainwater and water from a hose will seep down through the heap. A good practice is to check the heap at regular intervals to make sure the heap is always moist.

Mistakes to avoid

Most people get in trouble with their compost heaps by making them of one ingredient. They make a pile of only leaves, or weeds, or grass clippings and are disappointed when nothing happens. Last year we made a test heap consisting only of shredded hay. Although we kept this heap moist and turned it frequently. little decomposition took place. It's essential to add some nitrogen-rich material such as fresh or dried manure, dried blood. or compost previously made. or even a small amount of rich soil, because the nitrogen in these materials is needed food for the decomposing bacteria.

Just as important as not letting the heap dry up, is not keeping it in a perpetually soggy condition.

Difficulties can arise also if the compost heap is too large. Five feet is about the right height. as it allows air to get into every spot, provided that the heap is not too wide either (no more than 10 to 12 feet wide at the bottom, generally not less than 5 feet).

During the winter months, little decomposition usually takes place in the heap because of the cold. Many gardeners get around this by covering the heap with burlap bags or canvas, or by even using soil.

How to tell when finished

Some people think the finished product of their composting process should be crumbly like old leaf mold, but generally we're satisfied with a compost in which the straw, grass clippings, and more refractory substances such as cornstalks are broken up and have a rich, dark color.

When we apply compost, the mass is crumbly, not soggy; very often, on close inspection, you can determine its origin. Of course, if you're in no rush to use the compost, there's no harm in letting the compost break down into finer material. For ordinary gardening purposes. this is not necessary though, since the final decay can take place right in the ground. For flower growing, especially potted plants and for starting seedlings, it's good to screen the rougher material or to use the finer material which develops later.

When and how to use compost

Many gardeners schedule their compost applications about a month before planting, when the materials are decomposed and rather fine. Others "double up" on their composting production by applying it half finished, or notably fibrous, in the fall, and allowing it to break down right in the soil. In this way, they can make a second compost heap in the same space as the first and have twice as much finished compost by the time spring comes.

For general application, the soil should be turned thoroughly; then the compost is added to the top 4 inches of soil. When adding compost to growing crops, it can be mixed with topsoil and together applied as a mulch, so the roots of established plants will not be disturbed. This procedure is called a topdressing of compost.

Compost should be applied annually—anywhere from 1 to 3 inches in thickness. You can get by with less, but in gardening with small plots put it on heavily. As a guide, an average figure of weight for one cubic yard of compost is 1,000 pounds.

When composting trees, start about 2 to 3 feet away from the trunk and go to a foot beyond the drip line at the end of the branches. First cultivate the soil under the tree; then work about an inch or more of compost into the upper 2 inches annually.

When adding compost to your lawn, make sure that it is finely ground, so there's no chance of smothering the grass. An excellent way to improve your lawn is to first use an aerator to slice up the sod; then apply a thick covering of fine compost. As an optional final step, you could use a rotary mower to distribute the surface compost into the crevices. In this way, the compost provides the roots with moisture and nutrients and prevents soil from compacting.

3. A Steady Compost Supply for the Small-space Residential Gardener

Want the richest flower beds in town? Want an ever ready supply of rich humus, and built-in humus beds? Want to stop giving away kitchen garbage to the city truck? If so (and who doesn't), then you should try this simple, but wonderfully efficient, composting method devised by J. J. Bartlett. He combines kitchen garbage, manure, green matter, and earthworms into a neat, workable system, especially suited to the small-space residential gardener.

The first step is to build or find a box (no bottom or top). It can be of any size, but Mr. Bartlett has found that a long narrow one is more suited to inconspicuous placement along fences, in front of hedges, in borders, and other small spaces. His boxes are 4 feet long, 1 foot high, and 1–2 feet wide.

Next, pick a spot and dig a rectangular hole about 18 inches deep and just slightly smaller in dimensions than the box, so that the box will rest firmly on the ground above the hole. After this is done, you are ready to begin composting. The hole is filled in layer style—kitchen garbage, manure, and green matter, in that order. Mr. Bartlett has found kitchen garbage to compost faster when run though a meat grinder, but this is not essential. He keeps a bag of pulverized manure and a pile of shredded green matter at the side of the box, and each time garbage is introduced he follows immediately with the other two layers. After each addition, he covers the pit with a burlap bag and wets it down, then places a board on top of the box. In this way there is absolutely no odor, nor any pest problem.

In about three weeks when the bottom layers have decomposed to a great extent, introduce about 500 earthworms. You may have to buy these, but they will be the only ones you'll ever have to buy; you'll soon have thousands, to use all around the garden. These little composters will work through successive layers, which you add to the pit, mixing and breaking down the heap for you. Be careful, though, not to introduce the earthworms during the terrific heat of the initial breakdown. Heat of successive layers won't bother them, because they'll remain below until the above layer cools.

Continue this layering process until the pit is filled all the way to the top of the box. Then allow it to decompose for 5 or 6 more weeks, keeping it moist. In the meantime you can start another box.

After the first pit is fully composted, remove the compost down to soil level, place it in several cone-shaped piles on a large board or tarpaulin, and leave it exposed to the sun for 1 or 2 hours. The worms will have balled up at the bottom of each pile, and can be easily removed and introduced to the second pit. The finished compost piles may be sifted and bagged for future use. Meanwhile, you have just created the richest 18-inch-deep flower bed in town, which you can use as is, or tempered down with soil—any way you like.

Now you may begin pit number three, using the box you have just emptied. Using this system, you'll have a new load of compost each sixth week, you'll be able to make flower beds rich in humus from the worst clay or sand; you'll be raising thousands of earthworms for general garden use; and you'll have done it with little trouble or expense in a small space, with no odor or pest problem.

4. Eighteen Tons of Compost with the Fourteen-day Method

You can make 18 *tons* of crumbly compost in six months, in a space *8 x 4 feet!* This is enough compost to put a two-inch layer—an ample annual dosage—over 6,000 square feet of garden area, or a space 75 by 80 feet!

How is it done? Easily—using a shredder or rotary mower with the 14-day composting method, you begin in early spring, making a 4-foot high heap in a space 8 x 4 feet. After 3 weeks (we have allowed an extra week for possible slow heating), remove the finished compost—110 cubic feet, weighing about 2 tons—and begin the next pile. By midfall— 6 months later—your ninth heap should be finished, giving you a 6-month total of 18 tons.

The 14-day method has passed many trials with flying colors. Initially devised by an agricultural team at the University of California, the method was tried first at the Organic Experimental Farm in 1954, and since that time many readers have reported success with it. Here is the basic formula and procedure. This is not absolute, of course, and it may be altered to suit your individual needs and supply of materials:

Day-to-day to two-week compost

First day. Your basic material can be one of a number: leaves, spoiled hay, weeds, or grass clippings. To this should be added one of the nitrogenous materials (manure is best) and any other material available. In the editorial experiments, equal parts of leaves, grass clippings, and manure, with a liberal sprinkling of natural rock powders, were found to work very well. Remember, too, that leaves tend to mat down, slowing the composting process; they should be mixed with other material. Shred everything, including the manure, with a compost shredder or a rotary mower; mix materials together and place in a mounded heap. If your materials are low in nitrogen, be sure to add a sprinkling of dried blood, cottonseed meal, or other nitrogen supplement on each series of layers.

Second and third days. By now, the heap should have begun to heat up. If not, add more nitrogen. Bury a thermometer in the heap to check temperature. Keep the heap moist, but not soggy.

Fourth day. Turn the heap, check temperature, and keep moist.

Seventh day. Turn it again, check temperature, and keep moist.

Tenth day. Turn it once more. The heap should now begin to cool off, indicating that it is nearly finished.

Fourteenth day. The compost is ready for use. It will not look like fine humus, but the straw, clippings, and other materials will have been broken down into a rich, dark, crumbly substance. You may want to allow the heap to decay further, but at this stage it is perfectly good for garden use.

How to make compost in winter

While winter winds and snow may be blowing, your compost heap can still be alive and hot. Many gardeners successfully make compost during the wintertime; following are some ideas they've used:

Pits and earthworms. If compost is made in a pit in winter, the pit sides keep it warm and accelerate the decaying process. Even such resistant materials as ground corncobs and leaves will be ready for soil-building use by late spring with the pit method, especially if earthworms are used to do the mixing. Depth of pit can be 3 feet, length and width about 4 feet. After placing the materials in the pit, cover them with soil, burlap bags, canvas, straw, or similar materials to retain heat and moisture for faster decomposition.

Insulating heaps. If you do make the heap above ground, choose a protected place, as the south side of a building or wall. You could also make a productive barrier of cornstalks tied together or use snowfencing as a windbreak. Here again, an extra layer of soil on top, or a very heavy hay or straw mulch would help keep the heap warm.

It's even possible to insulate a compost heap outdoors for faster decomposition. You can do this by enclosing the heap with a larger enclosure and filling the space between the two enclosures with leaves, hay, straw, sawdust, or other insulating material.

Greenhouses and cold frames. When compost can be made in a greenhouse, barn, or outbuilding, winter compost making is naturally less of a problem. Some gardeners have had fine results using a cold frame as a winter bin. One Pennsylvania organic gardener reports that the temperature inside the cold frame was as much as 50 degrees warmer than that outside.

In any winter compost project, it's important to use as much manure, tankage, blood bone meal, sludge, or other high nitrogen material as possible. These will aid the heating-up process in spite of the weather.

Compost for starting seedlings

Make a mixture of 2 parts good garden loam, 1 part fine, sharp sand, and 1 part compost. (It's a good idea to let this mixture age for several months before seeding, so January is about the right time to prepare it.) You may want to sift the mixture through a ¼ inch mesh screen, placing the coarser particles in the bottom of the flat to improve drainage.

There is enough plant food in this mixture without adding manure or other organic fertilizers high in nitrogen. Used too soon, these can cause young plants to grow too rapidly, unbalancing their natural growth.

Starter solution

Plant starter solutions made from compost can be a big help in growing plants. According to Ralph Clark, extension horticulturist from Oregon, greenhouse operators have long made use of this method to bring their crops to a rapid and profitable production.

The main benefit received from these solutions is that the plant is provided with immediately available plant food. This stimulates leaf and root growth, giving the plant a thick pickup after transplanting. These solutions are used especially on young lettuce, tomatoes, celery, peppers, melons, eggplants, cabbages, cauliflower, and all kinds of transplants.

Here is a recommended starter: Fill barrel or other container ¼ full of compost. Continue to fill container with water, stirring several times during next 24 to 48 hours. In using, dilute to a light amber color with water. Pour 1 pint around each plant when setting out, or later as necessary to encourage growth. Liquid compost can be used at 10-day to 2-week intervals, especially when soils are not high in fertility.

Tests have shown that seeds sprout more than twice as well when soaked in a solution of this kind. In the wild, practically all seeds depend upon the moisture which seeps to them through a layer of nature's compost. In soaking the seed flat, place it in a large container holding 1 or 2 inches of starter solution. Allow the flat to soak until its sandy surface shows signs of dampness.

Seed flats containing mature compost and handled in this way seldom suffer loss from "damping-off" of seedlings.

5. Building the Best Compost Bin

The best compost bin is the one that turns your homestead's organic wastes into soil fertility quickly, cheaply, and easily.

The materials don't matter, but the results do. For years, organic gardeners have been making compost bins with bits of old wire, scrap wood, discarded lumber, old cement blocks, and battered, secondhand steel drums. They've been using whatever they could lay their hands on (free donations are always appreciated!) to make compost bins that fitted in with their gardening programs. Here's how they've been doing it for the last ten or more years.

Three-by-three wire bin cost $4 in 1961

Back in 1961, Lyman Wood built a wire and wood bin using scrap 2-inch-square lumber, which he covered with ½-inch chicken-wire mesh for a total cost of $4. Made of 2 L-shaped sections held together with screen-door hooks, the cage provided him with 18 to 24 cubic feet of finished compost in 14 days, which was par for the composting course then.

Composter Wood reported that the pile heated up to 140 to 160 degrees in 2 days, and could be turned in 4. He damped down each layer—leaves, grass, garbage, and manure— as he added it, and counted on the well ventilated cage to encourage complete bacterial action.

Turning was extremely easy. He unhooked the sides, separated each of the L-shaped sections, and then reassembled them next to the square sided heap. "You will be pleasantly surprised at how neatly and firmly the heap stands," he wrote, adding: "It is now a simple and satisfying task, using a fork, to peel the layers off the pile and toss them in the now-empty cage." During the turning operation, he kept a hose handy to wet down the heap as the material was transferred.

"I have used this cage many times," he concludes, "for 14-day rapid composting, and each time it is a satisfying successful venture to harvest the cube of dark, moist crumbly humus."

The same idea—a portable compost bin that can be lifted, leaving a pile ready for turning—was used about six years ago by the Peter Seymour Company of Hopkins, Minnesota. The "Cake-Maker" was made of wood and metal framing, and was light enough to be lifted off the pile, leaving a "cake" of compost, and ready to be filled again.

Bales of hay make a winter compost bin

Alden Stahr once made an all-winter compost bin out of old bales of hay stacked around secondhand storm doors and windows which he put up in the garden. Composter Stahr mixed in garbage and manure to help heat up the pile, while the glass lid—slanted to the south to pick up the long, low, midwinter rays of the sun—also kept out scavenging cats and dogs.

Although he recorded a 50-degree difference in temperatures between the inside of the bin and the outdoors one cold January morning, he achieved an extra supply of compost, which he had ready for early-spring use, "thanks to the billions of happy bacteria hard at work."

The New Zealand bin—air from all sides

The classic among compost bins is the wooden New Zealand box which was originally designed by the Auckland Humic Club to admit as much air as possible from all sides. Many variations exist, so don't hesitate to change your design to fit your material and budget.

The important factor is air circulation and ventilation from all sides, so be sure to leave 1-inch spaces between your slats or boards. It's a good idea to start with a rugged frame work —two-by-fours are excellent—and then nail a lattice of boards over it. The top and bottom are left open, although some composters prefer to cover the top of the pile in rainy weather to prevent leaching. One or two good coats of linseed oil should be allowed to soak into the wood to make it weather and rot resistant.

Steel drum composters for the suburbanite

West Coast gardener John Meeker reported several years ago how he solved the twin problems of running a compost pile in a congested suburban area without offending his neighbors, while getting enough compost to run his garden. He circulated air into the heap, using a steel drum which cost him $1, and had it raised 6 inches off the ground by setting it up on a circular metal frame with legs. Meeker's frame, worth $15 if done in a commercial shop, cost him nothing. But other readers have set their steel drums on 8-inch cement blocks, which get them up into the air for practically nothing.

Meeker reported that the construction has several advantages over the piles and pits that I used before. *The air can circulate up from the bottom of the barrel.* The six-inch space allows easy removal of the compost. The moisture content of the compost can be carefully regulated by covering the barrel with a lid . . . leaching of the compost is perfectly controlled. *By simply covering and uncovering the top, one can regulate the amount of air introduced into the mass.*

There is always a bushel or two of compost ready, Meeker noted, even with so small a composter "once the cycle has begun." This includes such seasonal bonuses as summer grass clippings, autumn leaves, and crop residues which are "ready to enrich the garden by the time one gets ready for spring planting."

As for the neighbors "who have gladly shared" his bumper harvests while "turning up their noses at my deposits of leaves, cuttings, manure and—worse—garbage," Meeker reported the solution to the odor problem.

"When I have a large amount of lettuce leaves, beet tops, grass cuttings, or kitchen refuse, *I whiten the top of the dampened pile with a sprinkling of ground limestone,* and over that I add a thick layer of dried steer manure.

The limestone helps to decrease the smell and lessen the acidity of the green refuse and garbage."

A more complicated application of the steel-drum composter calls for nesting one drum on the bottom third of a slightly larger container, and installing a metal lattice grate between them to hold the pile up so air can get at it. Built by Ralph Poe of Canton, Illinois, the drum composter also featured a hollow, vertical, 3-inch-wide pipe with ¼-inch perforations that was thrust down into the heap's center and left there for additional ventilation.

Revolving drum composters mix materials with air

An even more effective way of getting air into the compost pile *by using the drum as a mixing chamber as well as a ventilating device* was reported by Julian Fletcher of California and Frederick J. Barnett, an Australian retired engineer. It is good to be able to report that, while these composters are somewhat complicated, *their cost was very low*.

Although the Australian machine was run by a quarter-h.p. electric motor, it cost $8.50 because it was made almost completely of discards. The California hand-turned drum cost more—$12.15, of which $7 went for the drum and extra welding. The moral of both composting stories seems plain; you can do almost anything you want to for your homestead, if you're willing to plan carefully and work hard.

Fletcher spent the extra money for a very tight welding job that secured his 50-gallon drum diagonally to a 1½-inch pipe set 42 inches above the ground, which made "it easy to get a two-wheel garden cart under it for quick loading." The supporting pipe was 50 inches long, and measured 47 inches between the two-by-four, 58-inch-long posts that were set 18 inches deep into the ground.

Retired engineer Barnett, who was in his 80's when he perfected his revolving drum, reported that "as the years went on, it got harder to turn compost in the bins." So he decided to make "practically effortless" compost using "a rotating square container that was easier to make" and producing it economically from materials "that had been lying about for years." Cost of materials came to $8.50, including the motor, the pipe on which the box revolves, the wheels from a baby carriage and bicycle, and the pulleys. Although inventor Barnett "likes" the motor, he concedes that "a crank handle may be easily attached to the shaft and do as well."

Vacuum-cleaner motor blows air into pile

Complete air ventilation of the entire mass has been achieved by the Barnett revolving drum. The fan section of a vacuum cleaner, sealed to one end of a hollow rotating shaft, blew air through it and out into the compost through a series of 32 opposing holes.

It is almost impossible to overemphasize the importance of this ideal mixing of air with the layers of grass cuttings, kitchen refuse, sawdust, and fowl manure. Also, each layer is dampened as it is applied, and the box is rotated for 30 minutes. It is then rested for 24 to 48 hours with the lid on top, and covered with three layers of sacking.

The resulting bacterial action caused inside temperatures to reach 160 degrees. After five days, the box is again rotated for 30 minutes, with *the blower again forcing air through the shaft into the center of the mass.* This time the box rests with its bottom on top to permit air to circulate through 12 quarter-inch holes drilled along the bottom. Intermittent turning, the inventer reported, "seems to produce better heating results."

Raising pile off ground eases circulation of air

But you don't have to build a revolving drum to get air into the center of your compost heap. Just raise it off the ground—10 inches is fine—by building a substantial open lattice support right into your bin.

You can also make a wooden base for your compost pile, reinforcing it with ½-inch netting to get it the recommended 10 inches off the ground.

Researchers at Phoenix, Arizona found that a ton of rapidly decomposing compost uses up 18,000 to 20,000 cubic feet of air daily, and that turning of the pile doesn't always get the job done. But "forced air" composting—raising the pile off the ground—stimulates uniform decomposition of the entire pile, not just the top 12 inches.

The "open-hearth-bottom" bin is made of wood with a sturdy grid of 1-inch piping holding the compostable mass 1 foot above the ground. It's 4 feet square, made of sturdy secondhand lumber. A user reports never having to turn the pile, and advises that you don't have to worry about "mass and bulk as long as you have the open-hearth-bottom, and you'll always have plenty of good compost."

The compost bin will pay its way

A compost bin will soon pay for itself in reduced garbage disposal expenses. But there is more to composting than that. A compost bin pays for itself in a more productive and beautiful garden, and tastier, more healthful food for the entire family.

The bin shouldn't cost more than $10, and it shouldn't take more than three hours to make. Use whatever materials are cheap and abundant in your area, and don't be afraid to accept handouts. Put the bin where it will get both sun and air, and is handy both to the garden, where the compost will go, and the driveway, where so much of its material will come in.

Finally, every homestead—the little ones as well as those in crowded towns—should have its own compost-making bin in this time of widespread and mass pollution of the environment. Remember, composting is the only safe way to handle the family's organic wastes and leftovers.

Better start building that bin—now.

—MAURICE FRANZ

6. Materials for Composting and Soil Conditioning

Leaves

Leaves are valuable fertilizer material since they are rich in minerals. For fast composting, never use leaves as the exclusive green material. They should be mixed with weeds, lawn clippings, plant residues, etc., so not to pack and impede aeration.

If you have a power mower, the best practice is to make shallow piles of the leaves and go over them with the mower, shredding them fairly fine before adding to the heap.

Hay

In its early stages, all green matter, including hay, contains more nitrogen than when grown to maturity. Therefore, if you can get hay such as alfalfa or clover during its first year's growth, it will break down faster in the compost heap. However, it's worthwhile using all the hay you can get—young or old; shredding with a mower or shredder will hasten decomposition of the hay.

Sawdust and wood wastes

Sawdust has excellent properties for building soil, and can be added to the compost heap. You probably can obtain as much sawdust as you want free by checking with a local lumber mill.

Since sawdust does not break down completely unless used in fine sprinklings, it should not be packed too heavily lest it prevent aeration of the heap. Incidentally, sawdust also makes an excellent mulch material around shrubs, flowers, and vegetables.

Garden residues

Tomato and squash vines, cornstalks, flower stems, and all plant remains make a rich harvest for the compost heap. These are among the most available of green matter for your compost.

Weeds

Weeds are a very valuable addition to the compost heap because they belong to different plant families and therefore extract different elements from the soil. All these valuable elements are incorporated and made serviceable to the gardener when properly composted. It is essential to use weeds in green form, so that the nitrogen in them is fully utilized; if the compost is made properly, the bacterial action and heat will destroy live seeds. The more seeds on the weeds, the more manure or other organic nitrogen should be used to insure proper heating. Although it is best to use weeds fresh for compost making, a special weed pile may be started in order to let the seeds drop out. This weed material can then be used as the basis of a compost heap.

Grass clippings

Cut grass is most always sufficiently wilted by the time it is added to the compost heap so that it will soon start heating.

The nutrient value depends on the fertility of the soil and the maturity of its growth. A fertile soil produces a grass rich in nitrogen, and grass cut before blooming is richer in nutrients.

Sewage sludge

As a rule, sludge is classified as a source of nitrogen and will act as a bacteria stimulator in the compost heap, even though the nitrogen content may not be above 1 percent.

Garbage

In using garbage, it is best used as a part of the green matter of the compost heap. Its relatively high nitrogen content produces quicker decay. All kitchen wastes can be used with the exception of soapy water and fat. Soapy water contains dangerous chemicals, especially soda, which is not good for most plants. Only beets like it well. Fat, besides being an attraction to ants, does not break down very well and had best be used elsewhere. That leaves us with garbage of all kinds, scraps, bones, etc.

Brewery wastes

Spent hops is the residue after hops have been extracted with water in the brewery. In their wet state, they have about 75 percent water, 0.6 percent nitrogen, 0.2 percent P205. Moisture content varies considerably, and the analysis expressed on the dry matter is the most satisfactory figure. On this basis, the nitrogen ranges from 2.5 to 3.5 percent and the phosphoric acid about 1 percent. Spent hops in their natural condition are to be regarded mainly as a source of nitrogen. In many areas, gardeners and farmers have been successfully using the hops in their natural condition, spreading it in the same way as farmyard manure. Many other growers have been composting the hops before applying to the soil.

Another brewery waste available is the material left over from the mashing process, composed of grain parts.

Leather dust

Leather dust makes an excellent fertilizer material high in nitrogen. The nitrogen content varies from 5.5 to 12 percent, and it also contains considerable amounts of phosphorus. Available from leather tanneries.

Nut shells

The composition of nut shells varies according to the nuts. Almond shells and pecans decay readily; black walnut shells, which contain greater amounts of lignin, take longer; filberts and English walnuts decompose without trouble; Brazil nuts and coconuts could be used only in ground-up form, in the same manner in which cocoa shell meal is utilized. The only analyses available refer to the latter product, which is given as 2.5 percent nitrogen, 1 percent phosphoric acid, and 2.5 percent potash.

Peanut hulls

Peanut hulls are rich in nitrogen. Here is an analysis:

	Nitrogen	Phosphoric Acid	Potash
Peanut shells	3.6	.70	.45
Peanut shell ashes	.8	.15	.50

Tobacco stems

The nutrients contained in 100 pounds of tobacco stems are 2.5 to 3.7 pounds of nitrogen, almost a pound of phosphoric acid, and from 4.5 to 7.0 pounds of potassium. Thus tobacco stems make a good potash fertilizer in organic form.

Coffee wastes

Coffee chaff seems to be an excellent material for use in home gardens as well as farms. Over 2 percent in both nitrogen and potash, chaff also appears very suitable for use as a mulch material.

Dried blood

Dried blood is the blood collected in the slaughter houses and afterward dried and ground. The nitrogen content of dried blood is 12 percent or over, while the phosphorus content ranges from 1 to 5 percent. It can be used on the ground but in sound gardening practice is composted. Its high nitrogen content makes a sprinkling of it sufficient to stimulate bacterial growth. Before applying such a sprinkling, it is advisable to soak the plant matter thoroughly or to apply the dried blood in moist form. A relatively fast-working compost can be secured with the use of dried blood.

Manure

The most common domestic animals which are a source of manure are horses. cattle. goats, sheep. pigs, rabbits, and poultry. The dung consists of the undigested portions of the foods which have been ground into fine bits and saturated with digestive juices in the alimentary tract. It also contains a large population of bacteria which may make up as much as 30 percent of its mass. Dung contains, as a rule, 1/3 of the total nitrogen, 1/5 of the total potash, and nearly all of the phosphoric acid voided by the animals.

Percentages of Nitrogen, Phosphate, and Potash
in Different Manures

KIND OF ANIMAL MANURE	% NITROGEN	% PHOSPHATE	% POTASH
rabbit	2.4	1.4	0.6
hen	1.1	0.8	0.5
sheep	0.7	0.3	0.9
steer	0.7	0.3	0.4
horse	0.7	0.3	0.6
duck	0.6	1.4	0.5
cow	0.6	0.2	0.5
pig	0.5	0.3	0.5

Manure, dried

Commonly available at just about every fertilizer store, dried manure is always useful in the garden. Pulverized sheep, goat, and cattle manure have about 1 to 2 N, 1 to 2 P, 2 to 3 K, while poultry manure analyzes 5 N, 2 to 3 P, 1 to 2 K.

Cottonseed meal

This meal is made from the cottonseed which has been freed from lints and hulls, then deprived of its oils. (Cottonseed cake is one of the richest protein foods for animal feeding.) Its low pH makes it especially valuable for acid-loving crops. Cottonseed meal analyzes 7 percent nitrogen, 2 to 3 percent phosphorus, 1.5 percent potash. A truly excellent fertilizer it is available commercially.

7. How to Use Compost

Your compost is finished. After carefully following the recommended steps for turning the year's bounty of organic material into rich, mellow humus, you want to be certain that it's used right—that it benefits your soil most and helps to insure a natural abundance and health in your coming crops.

Let's examine some of the better methods of garden compost application. By doing so, perhaps many people who have recently begun gardening the organic way will find a number of very practical and worthwhile suggestions on making the optimum use of nature's valuable fertilizer. Even those who are "old hands" at tilling the land and following the recommendations of the organic method may discover some downright helpful ideas and hints.

When to apply

The principal factor in determining when to apply compost is its condition. If it is half finished, or noticeably fibrous, it could well be applied in October or November. By spring it will have completed its decomposition in the soil itself and be ready to supply growth nutrients to the earliest plantings made. Otherwise, for general soil enrichment, the ideal time of application is a month or so before planting. The closer to planting time it is incorporated, the more it should be ground up or worked over thoroughly with a hoe to shred it fine. A number of garden cultivating tools and machine equipment offer an excellent time-and-labor-saving hand in accomplishing this. Several will help spread it evenly and mix it thoroughly with the soil.

If your compost is ready in the fall and is not intended to be used until the spring, it should be kept covered and stored in a protected place. If it is kept for a long period during the summer, the finished compost should be watered from time to time.

How to apply

For general application, the soil should be stirred or turned thoroughly. Then the compost is added to the top 4 inches of soil. For flower and vegetable gardening, it is best to pan the compost through a ½-inch sieve. Coarse material remaining may then be put into another compost heap.

Orchard composting

To save time, the compost, instead of being made in a separate place and then hauled to each tree, can be made right under the tree. Thus it acts as a mulch also. The reason it is called the *ring method* is that since you start about 3 feet away from the trunk, the material looks like a ring. Apply the raw materials under the tree as if you were making compost, but instead of making the heap 5 feet high, make it only about 2 feet high. To hasten the formation of compost, a large quantity of earthworms can be placed in the material.

For flowers

All flowers, like any other growing plants, respond well to the organic method and of course to applications of compost. Compost may be safely applied even to acid-loving flowers such as the rhododendron. If a gardener has a considerable number of acid-soil plantings, which include several of the berries as well as many flowers, it would be advisable that he prepare an acid compost. This is done by making the compost without lime or wood ashes, just as it is for those soils that are quite alkaline.

For potted flowers, compost should not be used alone, but should be mixed with soil. Try screening and applying friction to it before using in a flower pot. Then mix about ⅓ compost and ⅔ rich soil.

Lawns

Want a lawn that stays green all summer, has no crabgrass, and rarely needs watering?

Then use compost liberally when making and maintaining it. You want a thick sod with roots that go down 6 inches, not a thin, weed-infested mat laying on a layer of infertile subsoil.

In building a new lawn, work in copious amounts of compost to a depth of at least 6 inches. If your soil is either sandy or clayey (rather than good loam), you'll need at least a 2-inch depth of compost, mixed in thoroughly, to build it up. The best time to make a new lawn is in the fall. But if you want to get started in the spring, dig in your compost and plant Italian ryegrass, vetch, or soybeans, which will look quite neat all summer. Then dig this green manure in at the end of the summer and make your permanent lawn when cool weather comes.

To renovate an old, patchy lawn, dig up the bare spots about 2 inches deep, work in plenty of finished compost, tamp and rake well, and sow your seed after soaking the patches well.

Feed your lawn regularly every spring. An excellent practice is to use a spike tooth aerator, then spread a mixture of fine finished compost and bone meal. Rake this into the holes made by the aerator. You can use a fairly thick covering of compost—just not so thick it covers the grass. This will feed your lawn efficiently and keep it sending down a dense mass of roots that laugh at drought.

Where compost is desired to aid a growing crop, there are cautions necessary to avoid injuring plant roots growing near the surface. In order not to disturb these roots of established plants, the compost may be mixed with topsoil and together applied as a mulch. This is the best means of adding what is often termed a topdressing. It serves a double purpose in that at the same time it is providing plant food, which will gradually work itself down to the growing crop, it also affords an effective mulch to the soil, giving protection from extremes of temperature, hard rains, and so forth.

How much to apply

In gardening for best results, compost should be applied liberally, let us say from 1 to 3 inches in thickness per year. Within a few years, your garden will become the wonder and envy of your neighborhood. Of course, you can get by with as little as ½ inch of compost, but in gardening with small plots, put it on heavy. There is no danger of burning due to overuse, such as is always the case with the chemically concocted fertilizers. You can apply compost either once or twice a year. The amount would depend, of course, on the fertility of your soil originally and on what and how much has been grown in it. Incidentally, an average figure of weight for 1 cubic yard of compost (27 cubic feet) is 1,000 pounds. There would be variations depending on the materials used and the length of time composted.

For orcharding and trees

Compost should be applied under each tree. Start about 2 to 3 feet away from the trunk, and go to about a foot beyond the drip line at the end of the branches. How thick shall it be applied? If you are going to apply it every year, a ½ inch to an inch will do. First cultivate under the tree to work the grass mat into the soil, then work in the compost, keeping it in the upper 2 inches. It is a good practice then to apply a mulch of old hay or other green matter. A layer of compost about 3 or 4 inches thick would be sufficient for 3 or 4 years.

Where there are poisons in the soil from many years of spraying, a 3- or 4-inch layer of compost worked into the soil will tend to counteract somewhat their harmful effects.

Mulch

1. There's More to Mulch Than Meets the Eye!

A gardener who hasn't mulched is like a restaurant gourmet who hasn't tasted organic foods. He just doesn't know what he's missing! But when he finds out, his garden will give forth a bonanza of tasty treats.

Mulch, technically speaking, is a layer of material, preferably organic material, that is placed on the soil surface to conserve moisture, hold down weeds, and ultimately improve soil structure and fertility.

But there's more to mulch than meets the eye. Be it a fluffy blanket of hay, a rich brown carpet of cocoa bean shells, or a smooth sheet of paper disguised with grass clippings, that topping for the vegetable patch and flower bed serves as much more than frosting on the garden cake.

Mulch acts. It performs in several wondrous ways. It fills a role as protector of the topsoil, conserver of moisture, guardian against weather extremes, and comfortable, bruise-saving cushioner under ripening produce.

As with composting, mulching is a basic practice in the organic method; it is a practice which nature employs constantly, that of always covering a bare soil. In addition, mulching also protects plants during winter, reducing the dangers of freezing and heaving.

Advantages of mulching

1. We know that a mulched plant is not subjected to the extremes of temperatures of an exposed plant. Unmulched roots are damaged by the heaving of soil brought on by sudden thaws and sudden frosts. The

mulch acts as an insulating blanket, keeping the soil warmer in winter and cooler in summer.

2. Certain materials used for a mulch contain rich minerals, and gradually, through the action of rain and time, these work into the soil to feed the roots of the plants. Some of the minerals soak into the ground during the first heavy rain. Therefore, mulch fertilizes the soil while it is on the soil surface as well as after it decays.

3. For the busy gardener, mulching is a boon indeed. Many backbreaking hours of weeding and hoeing are practically eliminated. Weeds do not have a chance to get a foothold, and the few that might manage to come up through the mulch can be hoed out in a jiffy. And since the mulch keeps the soil loose, there is no need to cultivate.

4. The mulch prevents the hot, drying sun and wind from penetrating to the soil, so its moisture does not evaporate quickly. A few good soakings during the growing season will tide plants over a long dry spell. It also prevents erosion from wind and hard rains. Soil underneath a mulch is damp and cool to the touch. Often mulched plants endure a long, dry season with practically no watering at all.

5. At harvest time, vegetables which sprawl on the ground, such as cucumbers, squash, strawberries, unstaked tomatoes, etc., often become mildewed, moldy, or even develop rot. A mulch prevents this damage by keeping the vegetables clean and dry. This is the season when most gardens begin to look unkempt. But the mulched garden always looks neat and trim, no matter what the season. In addition, mud is less of a problem when walking on mulched rows, and low-growing flowers are not splashed with mud.

Disadvantages of mulching

1. Seedlings planted in very moist soil should not be mulched immediately. The addition of any organic matter which keeps the soil at a high humidity encourages damping-off of young plants. Damping-off is a disease caused by a fungus inhabiting moist, poorly ventilated soil, and can be 90 percent fatal. Allow seedlings to become established then, before mulching.

2. It is wise, too, to consider the danger of crown rot in perennials. This disease is also caused by a fungus. If there has been especially heavy rains, postpone mulching until the soil is no longer waterlogged. Do not allow mulches composed of peat moss, manure, compost, or ground corncobs to touch the base of these plants. Leave a circle several inches in diameter. The idea here is to permit the soil to remain dry and open to the air around the immediate area of the plant.

3. Do not mulch a wet, low-lying soil, or at most, use only a dry, light type of material, such as salt hay or buckwheat hulls. Leaves are definitely to be avoided as they may mat down and add to the sogginess.

The heavy mulching method, described by Ruth Stout and others, stands a better chance of success if the soil contains some humus (well decayed organic matter) and is fairly high in nitrogen content.

Where the soil is poor and mostly clay in composition, it is well to test the soil and apply the needed elements, as nitrogen, phosphate, and potash, according to test results. Then spread the mulch in thin layers without packing, so as to permit air and moisture to start breaking down the raw material. When the first layer of mulch shows signs of decay, sprinkle some cottonseed meal, blood meal, or other nitrogen-rich material and apply another thin layer of mulch. By this method, any danger of the heavy mulch taking too much nitrogen from the soil is avoided.

With the instructions given above, it is simple enough to know when and where not to mulch. Except for these instances, the gardener really can't do without mulching as a wonderful labor-saving helpmate.

—Virginia Brundage

2. What Mulches to Use

When you set out to mulch a home garden of any considerable size, there are three factors to be considered: (1) how the material will affect the plants most intimately concerned, (2) how the completed mulch will look, and (3) how easily and inexpensively the mulch may be obtained. Following is a list of commonly used mulch materials that have been found beneficial by many organic gardeners.

Grass clippings

Fairly rich in nitrogen, grass clippings are useful as a green manure to be worked into the soil, for adding to compost heaps, or for mulching. Clippings from most lawns contain over 1 pound of nitrogen and 2 pounds of potash for every 100 pounds of clippings in the dry state.

Leaves

Leaves are an abundant source of humus and mineral material, including calcium, magnesium, as well as nitrogen, phosphorus, and potassium. They are especially valuable for use around acid-loving plants such as azaleas, rhododendrons, and hollies. (Some leaves, as sugar maple, are alkaline.) They may be applied directly in the soil as a mulch, for leaf mold, and for composting. Leaves mat and seal in moisture, keeping thaws from heaving fall-planted stock. They also decay rapidly, giving their benefits more quickly than slower decomposing mulches.

Leaf mold

As fresh leaves are placed in a container (snowfencing or one of wood or stone), shred them, if possible, and keep them damp. Apply ground limestone to offset the acidity, unless you plan to use the leaf mold around acid-tolerant plants only. Leaf mold from deciduous trees has been found to be somewhat richer in potash and phosphorus than that made from conifers. Nitrogen content varies and is sometimes as high as 5 percent.

Hulls and shells

Hulls and shells of cocoa beans, buckwheat, oats, rice, and cottonseed are commonly used as a fertilizer and mulch. They decay readily and may be spaded into the ground. The coarse shells are excellent as mulches, while the fine ones (sometimes almost in dust form) can be applied to lawns and elsewhere with a spreader. Cocoa shell dust analyzes 1 N, 1.5 P, 2.5 K. In general, the hulls are richest in potash, although peanut shells analyze 3.6 N, 0.7 P, 0.45 K. Hulls and shells make an exceptionally attractive mulch, are most effective when about 1 inch thick, and are available commercially from nurseries, stores, or by mail.

Paper

Newspapers and magazines have excellent moisture-retaining qualities and can be set out in the vegetable garden and nursery. A layer of hay, straw, corncobs, or wood chips over the paper will improve the appearance and keep the wind from blowing them away. Paper has a deadly efficiency in preventing weed growth. Because it is dense enough to keep rain from readily passing through to the soil underneath, it is best applied after a heavy rain. Use 4 to 6 thicknesses. Paper eventually, though not quickly, decays and adds humus to the soil.

Stones

Stones are one of nature's natural mulches and have all the standard advantages of most mulches plus a few additional ones. Rains and snows leach minerals from the rocks and return them to the soil, creating a valuable fertilizer. Rocks give an added boost of adding warmth to the soil, particularly in the spring and fall when certain plants have a big need for it. Conditions under stones are ideal for bacteria, earthworms, and other beneficial organisms. Rocks are permanent and rustically attractive to the eye.

Sawdust (well rotted)

Here is a very useful mulch material that should be used more widely. When plants are about 2 inches high, a 1-inch layer can be applied. Prior to spreading the sawdust, many gardeners side-dress with a nitrogen fertilizer as cottonseed meal, blood meal, tankage, etc. A recent survey showed that many sawdust users do not apply a nitrogen supplement and are satisfied with results. The sawdust must be well rotted, or it can be lightly mixed with a few shredded leaves or bits of straw to aerate.

Seaweed and kelp

Both are high in potash (about 5 percent) and trace elements. Many seaweed users apply it fresh from the sea; others prefer washing first to remove salt. It can be used as a mulch, worked directly into the soil, or placed in the compost heap. Dehydrated forms are available commercially.

Wood chips

Like sawdust and other wood wastes, wood chips are useful in the garden. Some people are afraid that the continued application of wood chips will sour their soil, that is, make it too acid. A very comprehensive study of sawdust and wood chips made from 1949 to 1954 by the Connecticut Experiment Station, reported no instance of making the soil more acid. It is possible, though, that sawdust and wood chips used on the highly alkaline soils of the western United States would help to make the soil *neutral*. That would be a very welcome effect.

Plentiful quantities of wood chips are becoming available in many sections of the country and are being widely used by gardeners and farmers. In some ways, wood chips are superior to sawdust. They contain a much greater percentage of bark, and have a higher nutrient content. Bark chips, available commercially, are a fine addition to your list of mulching materials.

The general verdict on sawdust and wood chips is that both materials are safe and effective soil improvers. They do a fine job of aerating the soil and increasing its moisture-holding capacity.

Corn stalks

To the depth of 3 or 4 inches, they provide a well aerated winter mulch, but do not use stalks from a field which was heavily infested with borers. Lay the stalks crisscross with tops and butts alternating. Shredded, the stalks make a fine garden mulch.

Straw

This is clean, contains no weed seeds, is inexpensive, quick, and easy to lay down, and it looks presentable. Once it has been applied, it remains in place an entire season. In fall, dig it in, and by spring it will have become an indistinguishable part of the soil. It is estimated that 1 ton will give a 1-inch mulch on an acre of land.

Corncobs

Ground into 1-inch pieces, they have many uses. The sugar content will help to increase the microorganisms in the soil, and these will give a better soil granulation.

Finely ground corncobs are highly recommended for seed flats. Use lightly here as a protection against too much nitrogen which forces premature growth in seedlings. It is interesting to note that florists using this material claim 100 percent more production and 30 percent saving on operating costs as germination takes place more rapidly, and there is not the need for frequent watering.

In the opinion of L. C. Chadwick, Professor of Horticulture, Ohio State University, a ground corncob mulch helps to prevent black spot on roses.

Contact the mills in your community that shell corn. They'll probably give you mountains of corncobs merely for the hauling.

Pine needles

These are good for strawberries the year around. Keep in mind that they can be a fire hazard when dry. Use a 2-to-4-inch mulch and renew every year. Particularly good for acid-loving plants, or to change neutral soil to acid. Pine needles alone are not good on alkaline-loving plants.

Alfalfa hay

Coarse and ragged in appearance, it is most easily handled when green and freshly cut. It has a high nitrogen percentage and will supply the requirements of fruit trees. Rain-spoiled hay can always be used as a mulch material, so there need be no waste here.

Oak tow

Oak tow is like sawdust, but contains coarser wood strings. It is made by tearing the wood lengthwise in sawing stave bolts. If you can get the material from a saw mill, you'll find it does not compact or blow as readily as sawdust.

Rotted pine wood

Like pine needles, these materials are excellent for mulching such acid-loving plants as azaleas, camellias, and rhododendrons. Before being used for plants that require a neutral or slightly alkaline soil, these materials should be composted.

Packing materials

Trees and plants ordered from nurseries usually come packed in sphagnum moss or redwood shavings. Breakables shipped from out of town arrive packed in excelsior or shredded paper. Save these materials and use them as mulches, alone, or mixed with other materials.

Weeds and native grasses

These make an excellent mulch around trees, where it is important to build a deeper covering than we use in the gardens and where this sort of mulch does not look out of place. They should be exposed to the air before applying to prevent rooting. They may be shredded to make a neat appearance, and can be mixed with grass clippings.

Peat moss

This is partially decomposed remains of plants accumulated over centuries under relatively airless conditions. Though it doesn't contain any nutrients, peat moss serves to aerate the soil, to improve drainage, ultimately to help plants absorb nutrients from other materials. Established lawns can be topdressed with a ½-inch layer of peat moss twice a year, and an inch or more can be spread and worked into vegetable gardens and flower beds. Extremely useful as a mulch.

3. How Much Mulch Is Enough?

When it comes to getting top garden or farm results, mulch makes a difference. Agreement on that score is just about unanimous, particularly among followers of the organic method. The value of a layer of material placed on the soil surface is pretty well recognized today by gardeners of all shapes, sizes, and sections of the country.

The catch, if really there is one, lies in deciding on the *amount* of mulch to use. Should a good mulch always be the same depth? Must it be measured to slide-rule accuracy to function right? Do any other considerations influence the proper quantity? In other words, *how much mulch is enough?*

Generally, gardeners mulch crops that are in the garden for most of the summer. How much? During the growing season, the thickness of the mulch should be sufficient to prevent the growth of weeds. A thin layer of finely shredded plant materials is more effective than unshredded loose material. For example, a 4- to 6-inch layer of sawdust will hold down weeds as well as 8 or more inches of hay, straw, or a similar loose, "open" material. So will 1 or 2 inches of buckwheat or cocoa bean hulls, or a 2- to 4-inch depth of pine needles. Leaves and corn stalks should be shredded or mixed with a light material like straw to prevent packing into a soggy mass. In a mixture, unshredded leaves can be spread 8 to 12 inches deep for the winter. To offset the nitrogen shortage in sawdust and other low-nitrogen materials, add some compost, soybean, or cottonseed meal.

Other good mulches not already mentioned include cotton-gin wastes, shredded cotton burs, oats, rice, and cottonseed shells, sphagnum moss, a variety of weeds, crop residues, grasses, and different types of hay.

Stout method heaps hay

Speaking of hay leads us to Ruth Stout, the nation's foremost advocate of year-round mulching. She relies almost exclusively on spoiled hay, which is peeled off in convenient layers, or "books," from bales standing ready for use, or tossed on by the armful to smother a solitary weed or two that may poke through the existing cover. After years of experience working out the permanent-mulch technique, Ruth has emphatic notions on its proper application.

How much mulch do you need? For her system, Miss Stout replies: "The answer to that is: more than you would think. You should start with a good 8 inches of it. Then I'm asked: 'How can tiny plants survive between 8-inch walls?' And the answer to that is: the mulch is trampled on, rained on, and packed down by the time you are ready to plant. It doesn't stay 8 inches high."

What about specific crops? Such acid-loving plants as strawberries, blueberries, cranberries, raspberries, peanuts, radishes, sweet potatoes, watermelons, azaleas, camellias, mums, rhododendrons, etc., do well with an acid-material mulch—most leaves, pine needles, sawdust, wood shavings, salt hay. According to the Wisconsin Experimental Station, a 1½- to 2-inch layer of salt hay makes the best mulch for strawberries. Pine needles are another excellent topping for this plant, and have been found effective at a 2- to 4-inch depth. Tests at the Ohio Agricultural Experiment Station showed that mulched blueberries yielded more fruit than cultivated plantings, and that sawdust at a rate of 6 to 8 inches gave the most consistent results.

Actually, a mulch program maintained for several years will let you practically forget about acid or alkaline soil problems. Ample organic matter acts as an effective buffer and helps to neutralize extremes of pH in any soil.

Mulch timing is often important

Some vegetables, like tomatoes and corn, need a thoroughly warmed soil to encourage ideal growth. A mulch applied too early in the spring, before ground temperatures have had a chance to climb a little in frost-zone areas, may slow up such crops. Once plants are well started, though, and the weather levels off, mulch is definitely in order to conserve needed water, stimulate topsoil microorganisms, and generally condition the soil.

Author-gardener John Krill pinpointed the importance of logical mulch timing for tomatoes. His experiments, and the experiences of others, show that early ripe tomatoes cannot be expected if the spring-thawing ground is cloaked too soon. In summing up his findings, Krill writes:

I have learned this lesson: That if mulch is applied before the earth is thoroughly warmed, it will delay the ripening of tomatoes. I apply mulch now only when the flowers are profuse, or may even wait until the fruit sets before mulching the plants. Then the mulch seals the heat in instead of sealing it out . . . . For late-ripening tomatoes I mulch my plants heavily when I set them out. For the earliest possible fruit I set out enough to get ripe tomatoes in unmulched soil until the juicier and better-flavored tomatoes are ripened in the mulched rows. By the wise use of mulch you can prevent tomatoes ripening all at one time.

Much the same is true of corn, despite a long-continuing difference of opinion about whether it should be mulched at all. Organic gardeners throughout the northern planting zones consistently get improved crops and growth response by mulching when plants are up about a foot high. Other vegetables which do best in well warmed soils include the melon and cucurbit families.

Potatoes started in mulch

Still another way mulch makes home gardening more rewarding with less work is in growing potatoes. Richard V. Clemence outlines the system:

> Large crops of the highest-quality potatoes can be grown by laying the seed (preferably small whole potatoes) on top of the remains of last year's mulch. I make double rows, 14 inches apart, with the seed the same distance apart in the rows. The idea of this is not only to get a heavy yield, but to make it easy to inspect the vines from both sides occasionally, and take care of a rare potato bug or a bunch of eggs that the lady-bugs have missed. Having laid the seed in straight rows with the aid of a string, I cover the rows with 6 or 8 inches of hay, and do nothing more until several weeks later. After the blossoms fall, I begin moving the hay carefully to see how things are progressing. Small potatoes an inch or two in diameter can be separated from their stems without disturbing the parent plants, and the hay then replaced.

As for the soil-type factor, along with curbing weeds, a carpet of mulch performs yeoman service in a number of less frequently realized directions. USDA horticulturist E. P. Christopher explains that cultivating a hard-packed soil will favor moisture percolation and air penetration, but the dry, bare surface may be completely eroded in a flash storm. Furthermore, he adds, "continued cultivation may speed up organic matter loss and thus destroy favorable soil structure."

Mulches, Christopher points out, influence moisture penetration in several ways:

Bulky materials such as wood chips, sawdust and straw temporarily hold a considerable volume of water, and thus prevent loss by runoff when the rate of application —natural or artificial—is too rapid for soil penetration. This may be more important with a heavy silt than with a porous sand soil. However, maintaining the soil structure loose and open may be the most important factor involved. Rain beating on an exposed soil compacts it and subsequent baking in the sun almost completely eliminates its capacity to absorb water rapidly. The open soil structure found under a mulch is also favorable to rapid air exchange. Roots require oxygen for the respiration process through which energy for growth is released.

Harvest and winter protection

At harvest time, vegetables which sprawl on the ground, such as cucumbers, squash, strawberries, unstaked tomatoes, etc., often become moldy or even develop rot. Others may be damaged by falling onto uncovered soil. A mulch prevents such injury by keeping the vegetables clean and dry, and by providing a cushioned layer on which they can rest or drop.

Besides this aid, a late-summer mulch helps to prolong the growing season. By buffering the effects of early frosts, it allows more time for second plantings or late crops to mature. At both ends of the summer, mulched soil and plants derive a noticeable benefit in this guard against weather extremes.

As Indian summer wanes and fall makes its mercury-dropping entrance, the usefulness of a mulch follows the season. There's a somewhat different prime purpose in the fall and winter mulch, though, and it's important to keep this in mind. Protection—especially of bulbs, perennial roots, shrubs, etc—is the objective now; protection, that is, from sudden temperature changes, from up-and-down thermometer readings which can harm overwintering plants.

The mulch now should be applied *after* the first hard frost to prevent alternate thaws and freezes from heaving soil, roots, or bulbs. Its purpose once winter sets in is to hold the lower temperature *in* the soil, avoid a rise and subsequent refreezing which shifts the earth and plants, often exposing enough to cause winter-killing. To protect young shrubs, and particularly roses, mound several inches of earth around them early in autumn, then mulch after the first freeze with several more inches of leaves, straw, yard trimmings, etc. Young trees can be protected from rabbit or field mouse damage by wrapping hardware mesh loosely around their base before the circle of mulch is applied.

Of course, the winter carpet of organic matter also helps condition the whole garden area for the next spring.

How much mulch?—the amount that does the best job for you, your soil, and your plants. Working out an ideal mulch program takes some experimenting, some trials with various materials and depths. It's only common sense to check on the most plentiful free and reasonable sources, to test the effects of different mulches in your climate locale, your own soil type and timing. But the program more than pays—in handsome dividends of better home-grown foods, a finer soil, and happier gardeners. Get going on your blanket of benefit, no matter where you garden—from Weed, California, right across the continent to Mulch, Virginia.

—M. C. GOLDMAN

4. A Report on Four Mulches

One summer we had the opportunity to test 4 different organic mulches—grass clippings, rotted sawdust, ground cork, and shredded pine bark. These materials were spread on the richly fertile beds and borders in our garden, and we checked each one for its desirability as a mulch.

Grass clippings

Our lawn, green, healthy, and practically devoid of weeds, has always provided a more than abundant supply of clippings to cover, thin layer by thin layer, every bed and border in our garden. The pale gray green color of the drying grass deepens to brown and is not unpleasant. It readily permits raindrops to penetrate to the soil beneath, while its decomposition enriches the soil, and its shady protection keeps the earth beneath it both cooler and damper than cultivated soil exposed to the elements. On a day in July when the air temperature was 98° F. and the temperature, in direct sun-

light, at the surface of the mulch registered 120, the surface
of the soil beneath the dried grass mulch was 94°.

These grass clippings, however, require almost weekly re-
plenishment in order to keep the mulching depth a preferred
3 inches. This rapid decomposition necessitates the constant
addition of organic fertilizers, rich in nitrogen, to the soil;
and the protected plants, even in a season of fairly normal
rainfall, are very often in need of additional moisture.
Furthermore, by freeze-up time very little dried grass is ever
left for use as a winter mulch.

Rotted sawdust

Another material available to us at the expenditure only
of time and physical effort was some *very well rotted* hardwood sawdust which had been lying in a shady woods for
some 20 years, host to centipedes, worms, and beetles, and
overgrown with Virginia creeper, honeysuckle, and green-
brier.

This sawdust was, of course, moist and very heavy to
handle, but its dark color was most pleasing to the eye. Even
the lightest of rains seemed to go directly through to the garden soil and very little additional water was needed throughout the summer by the herbaceous annuals and perennials
protected by it, nor did they show any overt need for additional fertilizers during the growing season. The vegetable
garden grew lushly, and strawberries, raspberries, and rhubarb all produced prodigiously, surrounded and protected by
this sawdust mulch.

No replenishing of the mulch was necessary from spring
to fall. Not one garden weed penetrated the 3 inches of sawdust, and only an amazing few of the broken roots of the
creeping woods plants gave rise to new growth that had to
be pulled from the loose, unresisting medium.

On the same July day when the soil beneath the dried
grass registered 94° F., that beneath the rotted sawdust registered only 82°. These temperature readings were taken in
the same test bed, in the same direct rays of the sun, and
within 4 feet of each other.

In early November, checking the decomposition and/or
loss of the sawdust, I found approximately 2 inches of loose
mulching material, while the first inch or so of soil immediately beneath was so mixed with the sawdust as to be in-
separable one from the other. It was, in effect, a rich, black,

moist soil, brought about, probably, by the action of rain water, soil bacteria, and little earth animals. Approximately ⅔ of the original material, by bulk, was still available for use as winter mulch or to be raked and stored according to the desires of the gardener.

This particular material, though, as far as this gardener is concerned, is exhausted at the source, and fresh sawdust, while satisfactory in its way, is not to be compared with the well rotted substance.

Shredded pine bark

When the commercially marketed bags of shredded pine bark are opened and their dark, brown red contents spread 2 to 3 inches deep around the needled and broad-leaved evergreens of the foundation planting, the woodsy fragrance that rises is so heavenly that the gardener is apt to feel that even if its mulching capabilities are nil, it is worth its price in nostril-tingling value alone. But, fortunately for the garden, it is an excellent mulch. Its pine-woods aroma vanishes after a few weeks' exposure to the elements, but its dark color remains pleasing to the eye for at least the 2 years I have used it.

It does not rob the soil of moisture and, instead, appears to allow every falling drop to penetrate to the earth. Its fine, dusty particles are, of course, quickly absorbed by the soil, but this is such an extremely small percentage of the mulch that its disappearance is scarcely noted, either in the depth of the mulch on the ground or in the bulk recovered if it is raked up for storage during the winter months. The dust absorbed presumably increases, to a slight degree, the acidity of the soil, but does not noticeably increase the demand for nitrogen.

Possibly because the larger pieces and consequent greater unevenness of the shredded pine bark mulch allow some moisture to escape, but more likely because the foundation planting suffers from being in the rain shadow of the house, a considerable amount of additional moisture was required by these large evergreens. So, too, the smaller-rooted cuttings in the test bed required a great deal of additional water, but this need not necessarily be laid at the door of the pine bark mulch.

When the surface temperature of this mulch was 120° F., the temperature of the soil directly beneath it was 86°, while a temperature of 90° was registered in medium shade with the soil beneath it registering 82° F.

Ground cork

The fourth mulching material tested was ground cork—not yet, to my knowledge, on the open market.

This material was so light and so easy to handle that a 90-pound woman could spread it with ease. It was also so light that I feared the first Howard County breeze would blow it across the countryside and that even the moderate force of an ordinary raindrop would dislodge it from place. But I was wrong.

Scarcely had we spread this mulch when an early-summer thunderstorm raced across the land. Preceded by violent winds, it let loose a volley of pounding, outsize raindrops, and then sluiced down veritable waterfalls upon the earth. The storm passed, the sun shone, and we went out to view the end of a mulch test that had not yet fairly begun; and there lay the ground cork, smoothly and evenly spread upon the ground, completely unruffled by either wind or water. The cork itself was damp, the ground beneath it soaked, and from that moment through the entire growing season that section of the test garden relied on nature for its watering.

This ground cork is reported, authoritatively, to test 1 percent nitrogen, a fairly negligible amount; but its deterioration is so unbelievably slow that it appears almost to be an inert material, and its effect for good or ill on the nitrogen content of the soil is not observable except probably by highly scientific testing methods. Measured by bulk, there appears to be exactly as much cork in November as there was in May.

Well known for its insulating qualities, there should be no surprise that where its surface registered the same 120° F. mentioned before, the temperature of the surface of the soil directly beneath was 82°; and in light shade where the mulch surface showed 94°, the soil beneath showed 78° F.

Dry or wet, it is completely odorless. Its only drawback—and it is no doubt quibbling to mention it in view of its other excellences—is its pale tan color which does not enhance the beauty of a planting as a darker color would do.

—MARY LEISTER

5. Mulch Your Way through the Summer

Put mulch to work for you during the hot, parched stretches of summer. Let it stop weeds in their tracks and hold on to needed moisture. Let it keep soil temperature down and garden production up.

Ruth Stout, for example, has roared for years about how a good mulch helps close the "work gap" between spring planting and autumn harvests. A champion of the year-round hay mulch, Ruth emphasizes in her books and articles that there's less labor, less struggling with watering, wilting, weed competition, insects, or soil conditioning when a constant layer of thick hay blankets the garden. "The whole thing," she exclaims, "can actually almost be said in one sentence: Keep your ground (vegetable patch and flower beds) covered with mulch, and from then on just use your brains."

Lots of things besides hay make effective mulches. The list of usable materials seems to be growing nearly as fast as the plants in a well mulched plot. Basically, there are two main divisions of mulch: organic and inorganic.

Experiment pace quickens

Serious interest in mulching has climbed sharply in the last few years and the tempo of mulch experimenting has spurted. At the New Mexico Agricultural Experiment Station, for instance, orchard-management studies showed that apple trees given an alfalfa hay mulch produced larger fruit than trees kept either in permanent sod or under chemical-spray weed control. Grapevines mulched with a layer of straw outyielded cultivated vines by 25 percent at the Ohio Station, where raspberries mulched with wheat straw also showed a 10 percent increase over cultivated plants, as well as a boost in berry size. And at the same station, peat moss or sawdust mulches on blueberries brought as much as 80 to 152 percent higher yields than cultivated berries. Raspberries mulched with grass clippings, wood chips, sawdust, newspaper and maple leaves grew faster and had remarkable flavor improvement for Vermont nurseryman Lewis Hill.

Soil scientists at the Texas Station have worked out a "mulch recipe" for reclaiming land in the Rio Grande Delta that has been ruined by salt accumulation. The barren clay-loam plots, so saline they produce almost no crops at all, are covered in March with a 5-inch layer of cotton-gin trash (dried bolls, stems, and leaves). The plots are left idle at least 6 months, then plowed and planted to crops. Within 5 months of applying 30 tons of mulch per acre, researchers found 84 percent of the salts had been leached from the top 30 inches of soil.

Noted garden-author Cynthia Westcott relates that she's found blackspot of roses "a disease that can often be reduced in extent by the use of a proper mulch." She usually mulches her New Jersey rose garden with buckwheat hulls applied 1 inch deep. A 50-pound bag will cover about 60 square feet or more at that depth, she notes. Cocoa bean shells, adds Miss Westcott, seem to be equally effective and attractive, although 50 pounds won't spread quite so far. Ground corncobs, also a recognized preventive of blackspot, she found more conspicuous.

Best mulches for the home garden

For the home gardener, the most practical and popular mulches are those easily available and cleanly handled. Baled hay, usually "spoiled" for livestock feed, is readily moved and spread by peeling convenient layers or "books" from the bale. Leaves and leaf mold, grass clippings, pine needles and coffee grounds (both acid) are helpful, common mulching choices. So too are a variety of waste or by-products of food processing: cocoa and buckwheat hulls, shredded cotton burs and gin trash, ground tree bark, shredded sugar cane (bagasse), and the shells from peanuts, oats, rice, cottonseed, etc. Shoreline dwellers have seaweed and often salt hay available, both rich in minerals and free of weed seeds; sawdust is offered at planing mills and wood chips frequently by power-line pruning crews. Spent hops, the waste product of breweries, are quite moist, light colored, more resistant to fire hazard than straw, etc., with an odor that persists a few weeks; chopped tobacco stems are coarse, may help discourage some insect pests.

Ground corncobs are a highly recommended mulch. Light and bulky, they help to "fluff up" the soil, thus preventing crust formation. Peat moss, although it doesn't contain any nutrients, improves soil tilth, aeration, and drainage, ultimately helping plants absorb nutrients from other materials. An old standby, it can be spread an inch or more in vegetable gardens and flower beds, and used as a ½-inch top-dressing twice a year on established lawns.

Sawdust no puzzle

To offset the nitrogen shortage in sawdust and other low-nitrogen materials, add some compost, manure, blood meal, tankage, soybean or cottonseed meal to the soil before mulching. Actually, there is no basis in fact for many of the old accusations tossed at sawdust. Used properly, it's not a "devil" that sours soil or robs plant food. Weathered or un-weathered, from hardwood or softwood, sawdust is not acid, nor is it toxic in any way. It is organic matter, beneficial as both a mulch and soil conditioner. Used about 3 inches thick, it serves efficiently around fruit trees, shrubs, perennials, evergreens, and in border plantings. Like other carbon-rich materials, sawdust will sometimes turn plants yellow if used alone. The reason is that soil bacteria and fungi temporarily use so much nitrogen to decompose sawdust that little is left for the plants. The yellowing is a hunger sign—and the diffi-culty can be prevented by adding any of the nitrogen-rich organic fertilizers.

Just how effectively a good mulch performs might be seen in the results that L. Winston Hamm gets in S. Wolfeboro, New Hampshire. His half acre of Kennebec potatoes, ferti-lized in the fall with 500 pounds each of compost and cotton-seed meal, has a mixed mulch 6 to 8 inches deep of hay topped with 6-year-old pine sawdust. Another planting gets cottonseed meal and sawdust in a 4- to 6-inch combination. Fifty- to 60-bushel yields to the half acre of top quality potatoes are what Mr. Hamm harvests. He has no insect troubles, no potato scab, and plenty of customers. His moun-tainside soil, originally hard packed, is now so friable he can poke 8 to 10 inches into it with his finger. As a test, Hamm compared mulched and unmulched potato hills, found he picked 2 to 3 times as much from the mulched ones.

—M. C. GOLDMAN

6. Getting Along Without Plastic

Ironically, organic gardeners, dedicated to preserving a healthful and attractive environment, are nevertheless unwittingly contributing their share to the nation's reputation as a plastic society. Without giving it a thought, most of us end up with at least half a dozen disposable plastic packages every time we go to the supermarket. But more than that, *we actually use plastics deliberately in our gardening.*

A freshly dug unpotted plant will keep for days in a sealed plastic bag. A vacationer can swathe his house plants in a plastic bag and find them flourishing when he returns from a two-week vacation, without any interim watering. Greenhouses made of plastic are supposed to be almost as good as glass ones, and much less expensive. Plastic mulch has been used for keeping down leaves and retaining moisture. Cuttings can be rooted in damp vermiculite, even in a dry wintry house, if you enclose the whole business in plastic.

It's true—plastics are convenient, quick, durable. (Boy, are they durable!) But these characteristics, desirable though they may be, are not the be-all and end-all of organic gardening.

Commercial fertilizers are also quick and convenient. But the organic gardener doesn't use them. He prefers to spend the extra time and put up with the extra inconvenience in order to protect his environment and his health from the pesticides which the big-time operators use, and from the commercial fertilizers which not only produce inferior food but contribute to the destruction of our waterways in the form of nitrate pollution. Plastics are nonorganic substances which add nothing to the soil except trouble if you try to grow crops where they have been buried. There is, in fact, some reason to believe that the formaldehyde given off in small amounts by some plastics can actually kill soil bacteria and thus interfere with plant growth. At any rate, the organic gardener can do very well without plastics. And when you stop to think of it, what could be more unnatural than a product like plastic mulch? It keeps the soil untouched by air, sunshine, dew, or rainfall. It does nothing to enrich the soil, while an organic mulch breaks down into compost, humus, and minerals. It also lets the air, dew, rainfall, and sunshine seep through it to the plants beneath.

Of course there is more work with an organic mulch. You must provide a new mulch at least every year, for the old one has a way of disappearing into the soil so completely that you wonder where it went. The answer is it went to nourish the soil—a "problem" you will never have to worry about with plastic.

Hay, straw, and leaves make good organic mulches. Old newspapers and magazines are excellent materials for making organic mulch—and waste paper is one of the most plentiful discarded materials in the world.

Lay it in very thick layers to mulch almost anything. The most expensive evergreen border, a box hedge, a row of rhododendrons, a perennial bed—these are all garden spots that lend themselves well to a paper mulch. If you use a permanent mulch on your vegetable garden, you will be amazed at the absence of weeds. The paper can then be covered with something attractive, and organic like compost, hay, straw, leaves, wood chips, peat moss, cocoa beans, ground corncobs, sawdust, or almost anything else.

Cover the papers with something or the wind may scatter them over the neighborhood. They are not hard to spread into a mulch if you work on a fairly windless day and keep the layers thick, preferably with a helper coming along after you and spreading the topping.

What can you use instead of plastic bags? For big jobs there are burlap bags, inexpensive and durable. You get them free with lots of things like ground corncobs or peat moss. Clean and dry, they can be used again and again. And when they are too worn out to use any more, tear them in strips and use them for mulch along with the paper. For rooting cuttings, old-timers used to save pickle jars and jelly glasses. Fifty years ago any self-respecting rose garden had rows of upside-down mason jars on the ground. Inside these miniature greenhouses, precious cuttings were rooting, safe from bugs, worms, and stray animals, and kept at exactly the right degree of moisture. Instead of throwing out the old peanut butter and mayonnaise jars, why not switch over to using them instead of plastic for your cutting chores and for raising seedlings? When you dig up a plant to take to a neighbor, put it in a jar and screw the lid on. Your neighbor can check on the moisture inside until he can find time to plant it.

The plastic industry has been with us for about 25 years now, and during that time manufacturers have made it the great thrust of their research to develop more and more indestructible materials. Their great success is the sanitation department's—and the public's—great headache.

You can garden as well or better without plastics, but even if that were not true, it is time that organic gardeners truly concerned with the exploding volume of environmental contaminants made up their minds to avoid using as much as possible one of the fastest-growing pollutants of all, plastics. A biodegradable plastic is probably not an impossibility, but development of it will require industry to spend a sizable portion of its income in serious research. Until that research is done and a plastic developed which will decompose within a reasonable time, the fewer plastics used the better.

In the past, when pollution control had not assumed its present "now-or-never" aspect, we favored the use of black plastic in the garden. But the reports reaching us have been extremely disturbing; plastic is practically indestructible, unless you burn it. It cannot be composted or digested, and it is estimated that discarded plastic will litter the land—a memento that will endure, an eternal synthetic, a memorial to our times, non-biodegradable, and incapable of assimilation into the organic cycle.

How much nicer it would be if that archaeologist 10,000 years from now would stomp his shovel into clean rich soil, breathe our fresh air, drink our pure water, and then name us for those characteristics, instead of the plastic which is fast overburdening our society.

PART III

WHAT TO GROW—AND HOW!

The Best Laid Plans

1. "Stretch the Harvest" by Planning

The successful organic vegetable garden will give you and your family a ready and inexpensive supply of fresh, nutritious vegetables throughout the year. With careful planning, you can get a continuous supply of vegetables from early spring to late fall. Robert Stevens, extension horticulturist at the University of Delaware, calls this "stretching the harvest season."

You'll also be able to double the harvest by interplanting and succession planting. Careful planning will decrease the need for canning, freezing, and storing great quantities of food. Vegetables picked fresh for 7 or 8 months of the year not only decrease the amount needed to be preserved, but also provide a fresh source of vegetables for the family table.

Another advantage of having a definite plan for the garden is that the kind and amount of seed can be determined fairly accurately in advance, and proper amounts purchased. If you have no plan, you are likely to get too much of some seeds and not enough of others. These 10 points should be considered while drawing the plan, according to Stevens:

1. Perennial crops such as asparagus, strawberries, and rhubarb should be located at one side of the garden.
2. Tall-growing crops, such as corn, must be kept away from small crops like beets and carrots to avoid shading.
3. Provide for succession crops—a fall garden, small fruits, and overwintered crops to mature early in the spring. In this way, space for spring crops which will be harvested early, may be used again for later crops. Examples: tomatoes after radishes; cucumbers after spinach.
4. Early planted, fast-growing, quick-maturing crops

111

should be grouped together. Examples: radishes, lettuce, early cabbage, scallions, etc.

5. Provide plenty of vegetables for canning, freezing, and storing.
6. Do not overplant new varieties, vegetables which the family does not like, or too much of any one vegetable at one time.
7. Rows should follow across the slope (on the contour) in hilly areas.
8. Make sure the plan provides the best spacing between rows for the method of cultivation that you intend to use (hand, tractor, horse).
9. Run rows north and south if possible to prevent plants from shading one another.
10. Long rows save time in care and cultivation. Several crops may be planted in the same row if the distance between rows is the same.

Getting the most out of your garden

Actually, the entire purpose of careful planning is to get the most out of your garden. Managed correctly, a small garden will yield more and certainly satisfy you much more than a poorly run, large plot. Consider the average suburban home with the yard obviously not large enough to produce everything wished for. Is here anything that can be done about it? Definitely yes! Here's how one Pennsylvania organic gardener, Dr. Lewis Theiss, suggests solving the problem:

Production in a restricted garden area can be very largely increased by making a two-story garden. In a way, such a garden is like an old-fashioned house with two stories. That type contains twice as many rooms on one plot. Similarly, a two-story garden greatly increases the productive area.

Some years ago, I had to limit my plantings to an enclosed garden that was just about 50 feet wide. The two-story garden enabled me to produce a very generous supply of vegetables in this restricted area.

To begin with, I narrowed the space between plant rows. Instead of cultivating, I mulched. That not only did away with a lot of work, but it kept the ground moist in a way that had never happened before. And this generous supply of moisture certainly helped the vegetables to secure more plant food.

But spacing my rows closer did not entirely meet my needs. So I resorted to the two-story garden. Suppose your garden is 50 by 50 feet. You have 200 feet of fence that ordinarily goes to waste. Yet that fence will hold plants as well as bean poles, trellises, or other supports. Those 200 feet, of course, are the equivalent of 4 50-foot rows of vegetables. So the thing to do is to make use of the space along your fence.

What do gardeners usually grow that needs support? There are climbing beans—several varieties of them. There are cucumbers, melons, squashes, and so on. All have tendrils for climbing. So all the gardener has to do is to plant his seeds, or set out young plants, in a long row at the bottom of his fence wire, mulch the ground well, and see that the young plants get hold of the fence wire. The plants will do the climbing.

You needn't be skeptical when it is suggested that squashes can be grown on a fence. If you have ever seen a farmer's cornfield, you must have seen some of his pumpkin vines climbing the cornstalks. And if your farmer is of the thrifty sort, and planted some beans along the corn rows, you will see lots of bean vines going up the cornstalks—and out in a great field at that, where there is ample room for all sorts of plantings. The farmer is simply trying to save himself some work.

I have suggested climbing beans as an illustration. Some crops that are ordinarily grown on the level will do better if grown vertically. Take cucumbers, for instance. If you get a wet spell, and especially if your ground is heavy, your cucumbers will in all likelihood begin to rot. If you raise China cucumbers—and every gardener who desires a very superior product *should* raise them—you will be surprised how much can be grown on a fence.

If you want something more attractive in your garden, try scarlet runner beans on the fence. You will not only get some good beans, but the showy sprays of brilliant flowers will make your fence a thing of real beauty. Even beans with inconspicuous flowers add living charm to a fence. The long and sightly pods, hanging in heavy clusters, are also a thing of beauty.

And, when it comes to picking the beans, you never had it so good as you will have it if you put your beans on a fence. There will be no more backbreaking stooping to gather the beans. Harvesting them will be as easy as taking a can off a shelf. I know. I have done it.

You can also tie your tomatoes to the fence. Staked tomato vines always have to be trimmed some. You can trim off the shoots that want to grow through the fence. Fruits on the opposite side of the fence are of little use to you. If you grow some of the little red-fruited tomatoes, you will be amazed at the beautiful picture they will make on your fence. The small red cherry or red pear tomatoes, or the yellow pear or plum tomatoes, are indeed colorful and decorative—as well as tasty. The fruits grow in brilliant clusters. But they need to be hung up to be seen well.

Climbing peas, such as telephone peas, were really made for fences. They absolutely *have* to have high support. They will cover the woven wire with their beautiful foliage, and the hanging pods are like striking figures worked into a lovely green fabric.

But you don't need to limit your fence-row growths to climbing vines. A row of corn can be grown hard against the fence—with beans to climb the stalks, at that. And so can any other tall, upright growths successfully occupy the little swath of ground along the foot of your fence. All such growths can be looped back flat against the wire.

In earlier days, folks grew many products on the sides of their houses, espalier fashion. They thus grew apples, pears, apricots, and other tree growths. Grapes have long been a favorite for the sides of houses. They can be for you, or you can grow them on your garden fence.

This is not intended to be a complete list of things you can grow in your two-story garden. It is meant merely to suggest that, if your garden space is limited, you try two-story gardening—an excellent plan for you to get the most from any garden.

2. Motto for March: "Be Ready!"

Here's some advice from Connecticut gardener-mulcher Ruth Stout, author of *How to Have a Green Thumb Without an Aching Back,* on planning your garden:

By about March, your seeds should all be arranged in 3 boxes, marked Early, Middle, Late. They should be in alphabetical order, so it will be easier when planting time comes to pick out the ones you are ready to put into the ground.

But whether you have bought your seeds or not, you can get out the catalogue from which you intend to order them and make out your list so that you will know exactly what space you can allow for each and what you are going to put where. This done, find a big white sheet of good thick paper, a ruler and soft black lead pencil. Unless you are one of those skillful people who never makes a mistake, you will be better off with an eraser at the end of the pencil.

After outlining the measurements of your vegetable garden, you can settle down to putting your crops on paper. It's a little unbelievable how much time and space a person can save if he has a complete plan to follow when he is ready to plant.

I rotate my vegetables because the experts tell us to, and hardly anything makes me feel so virtuous as following the advice of the experts on those rare occasions when I feel it isn't hazardous to do so. Every other year I put corn and tomatoes in the upper half of the garden, the following year in the lower half. Why not?

Maybe you know how many feet of corn you want to plant this year. If you don't, figure how many ears you can use, how many you can get from a foot of corn, and that's it. With my year-round mulch, no plowing, no weeds, I average almost two ears to a stalk and I can also plant very closely because my 14 years of rotting mulch has given me such superb soil.

Let's say you're going to plant three varieties, two early and one main crop, so that you can eat corn for at least two months. Draw lines on the paper for the rows, and put planting dates and name of the varieties on each line. It's wonderful when planting time comes just to glance at the diagram and waste no time in figuring where you want to put what.

Next, choose a spot for tomatoes and mark that. Do you plant too many? I do.

I put peas, including bush edible pod, between the rows of corn. This saves a lot of space and peas being an early crop, corn a late one, the two don't interfere with each other. I find Lincoln peas infinitely more satisfactory than any kind I've ever tried and so do many other people to whom I have recommended them. Keep them well propped up with hay so they won't steal sunshine from the young corn.

I plant about the same amount of spinach, onions and peppers each year, I always plant these in two rows, the length of the garden, next to the row of strawberries, rotating by putting the onions next to the berries one year, and the spinach there the following year. I put pepper plants in the same row with spinach, since one is so early and the other so late. Spinach is eaten or in the freezer by the time the peppers are old enough to feel the need of a little space and privacy.

If you are like me you are always dashing out for a handful of parsley, so you may want to do as I do: put it at the near end of the garden. Have you ever tried making a border of it around a flower bed?

Most of the other vegetables are a matter of ruling your paper, 1, 2, 3 feet apart as each vegetable requires, and writing the names on the lines. When you choose the rows for cabbage, broccoli and cauliflower you can, if you need the space, put kohlrabi seeds between the plants. I drop a few seeds of the larger plants every 18 inches and put the kohlrabi along the rest of the row. You can also crowd the lettuce and bush beans with any of the later crops; they will mature and be out of the way fairly early. I put lettuce and beets extremely close to each other; neither seems to mind.

Dill seeds itself copiously but if you mulch, it is more practical to plant it each year. We're so fond of it when it's young and fresh that I plant it several times a season. But ignore this when you plant your garden because you can sow the seeds in the same rows with cabbage and so on, unless you have kohlrabi there. Radishes take no space; you can drop their seeds right on top of carrot, parsley, parsnip seeds.

I've come across very few people who grow edible soy beans, but it seems a shame not to. This year when the frost took all our limas on June 19th, the soy beans, which we think are as delicious as limas, came through bravely. But you have to give them plenty of space. They get huge and sometimes flop around, showing no consideration whatever for any less demanding crop which may be unfortunate enough to be trying to live close to them. If you can plan your garden so that the soy beans are next to the early corn it may be that the corn will get such an early start that it won't mind the soy beans. I somehow have not found it convenient to do that, but I see no reason why it wouldn't work.

I put poles for beans along one end of the garden and they take up practically no space.

Cucumbers, pumpkins, squash and gourds are the worst space-grabbers. You might think they were human the way they invade other people's territory. Cocozelle squash (zuccini) can go right in a corn row because it doesn't spread. Besides, very few hills go a long way. But if you grow things in the corn which creep between the rows they become a great nuisance. Perhaps you can put these things along one end or one side, or both. I put them all along the asparagus one year; last year I crowded the pole beans with them. They ran outside the garden over the grass and were most prolific.

This is no good for Hubbard squash, however, if you want to root it in several places along the vine, as I have learned to do, to outwit the borers. It works beautifully. So I scrabble around to find a special spot for it. One successful Hubbard squash vine provides enough squash for the winter for a small family, which is a very good thing, considering that a healthy Hubbard squash vine has less restraint than anything I have seen, with the possible exception of a Russian sunflower.

In planning the garden, you will want to consider the size of the area available, the needs of the family, and their likes and dislikes. Keep these points in mind when you take pencil and paper and start to draw the plan. A rough sketch will do, but it must be fairly accurate to be useful. Make the plan to scale if possible. You can use a scale of ⅛ inch to 1 foot. Outline the shape of your garden, put down the length and width, space between rows, names of vegetables to be planted in each row, and the names of late vegetables that will follow the early ones.

Suggested Vegetables for a Garden 50' x 100' or Larger
Planned for Power Cultivation—Northeastern Area

DISTANCE BETWEEN
ROWS IN FEET   ◄————— 50 feet —————►

3	early potatoes
3	late potatoes
3	late potatoes
3	peas, early as possible ⎫ Follow with plantings of any
	⎬ of the following: beets, car-
3	peas, 10 days after 1st ⎬ rots, snap beans, endive, fall
	⎬ lettuce, turnips, whatever the
3	peas, 20 days after 1st ⎭ family likes
3	spinach (late cabbage plants) parsley
3	lettuce (follow by late cauliflower) radish
	radish (10 days later)
3	early cabbage (rutabagas for fall storage)
3	broccoli (late beets) early cauliflower (late carrots)
3	onion sets (fall spinach)
3	onion sets (fall lettuce)
3	early carrots (snap beans) early beets (snap beans)
3	early snap beans (lettuce) kale or swiss chard*
3	shell beans
3	shell beans
3	lima beans (bush)
3	parsnips
3	peppers eggplant
3	tomatoes (early)
3	tomatoes (midseason)
3	tomatoes (late)
3	sweet corn, early midseason late
3	sweet corn, early midseason late
3	plant early midseason
3	plant early midseason ⎱ late varieties
	⎰ at same time
3	pole beans
3	summer squash pumpkins
6	winter squash
6	cucumbers
3	

100 feet

* Cut outside leaves only inside out so as not to cut growing heart.
Vegetables listed in ( ) are second crops.

*Prepared by: E. C. Minnum, Extension Vegetable Specialist,
Connecticut Agricultural Extension Service*

Planting Table

CROP	VARIETY	Seed or plants per 100 feet of row	Depth to sow seed (inches)	Distance between rows* (feet)	Distance between plants in row	When vegetables can be used	Average days from planting to harvest	Average yield per 100 feet of row
CROPS THAT STAND SHARP FROST. PLANT AS SOON AS SOIL CAN BE WORKED.								
root crops								
beets	Crosby's Egyptian Detroit dark red	1 oz.	¾	2½	3 in.	1" diam. & up§	55	1½ bu.
carrots	Nantes - table Oxheart - heavy soils Chantenay - storage	1 oz.	½	2½	2-3 in.	½" diam. & up	65 by Nov. 1	1½ bu.
onions (sets)	yellow	2 lbs.	1	2½	3 in.	1½" stem diam.	50-120	1½ bu.
parsnips	Improved Hollow Crown	½ oz.	½	2½	3 in.	mature	110	1½ bu.
peas	World's Record, Little Marvel	1 lb.	1	2½	1 in.	3/16" & up	65	1½ bu. (pods)
radishes	Scarlet Globe	½ oz.	½	6"	½ in.	½" & up	30	100 bunches
rutabaga	Long Island Improved	2 pkts.	½	2½	4 in.	mature	by Nov. 1	2 bu.
turnip	Purple Top White Globe	2 pkts.	½	2½	3 in.	1½" & up	60	1½ bu.
greens and salad crops								
broccoli	Calabrese	50 plants	½	2½	18-24 in.	while buds are tight	100	30 bunches
cabbage	early - Golden Acre late - Danish Ballhead	50 plants 50 plants	....	2½	2 ft.	as heads become firm	80 120	35 heads
endive	green curled or broad-leaved Batavian	¼ oz.	½	2½	12 in.	whole plant§ 6-8" spread	90	80 plants
kale	Scotch curled Siberian (for wintering)	1 pkt.	½	2½	16 in.	leaves 6-8" long	70	60 bunches
lettuce (leaf)	Grand Rapids	1 pkt.	½	2½	12 in.	outside leaves§ 3-4" long	60	85 plants
spinach	Bloomsdale Savoy	½ oz.	½	2½	2-3 in.	4" spread of leaves	50	2 bu.
Swiss chard	Locullus	1 oz.	¾	2½	10-14 in.	outside leaves 4-5" long	65	60 plants

Planting Table

CROP	VARIETY	Seed or plants per 100 feet of row	Depth to sow seed (inches)	Distance between rows* (feet)	Distance between plants in row	When vegetables can be used	Average days from planting to harvest	Average yield per 100 feet of row
CROPS THAT STAND LIGHT FROST. PLANT WHEN DANGER OF SOIL FREEZING IS PAST.								
green, snap beans......	bountiful, stringless greenpod	1 lb.	1	2½	3 in.	pods 3-4″ long	60	1½ bu.
yellow, snap beans......	Pencil Pod, Golden Wax	1 lb.	1	2½	3 in.	pods 3-4″ long	60	1½ bu.
pole, snap beans......	Kentucky Wonder	½ lb.	1	2½	Poles - 3 ft.†	pods 3-4″ long	80	2 bu.
sweet corn......	Golden Cross Bantam	¼ lb.	1	2½	15-18 in.	kernels filled with milk	80-90	60 ears
squash......	Straight Neck (Summer Bush) / butter nut / green delicious (Winter)	1 oz.	1	5	4 ft. / 8 ft. / 8 ft.	fruits 4-5″ long / mature / mature	60 / before frost / before frost	150 fruits / 75 fruits / 50 fruits
CROPS THAT CANNOT STAND FROST. PLANT WHEN FROST NO LONGER EXPECTED.								
bush lima beans......	Fordhook, improved bush	1 lb.	1	2½	8-10 in.	when beans show in pod	85	1½ bu.
pole lima beans......	King of the Garden, challenger	1 lb.	.....	2½	Poles - 3 ft.†	when beans show in pod		2 bu.
peppers......	World Beater, Yolo Wonder	50 plants	.....	2½	2 ft.	green or red	July 25	3 bu.
tomatoes......	Rutgers, Marglobe, Queens	50 plants	.....	2½‡	2 ft.	green or red ripe	July 25	3 bu.

*Some vegetables such as peas, spinach, carrots, beets, onions, and lettuce may be sown in rows closer than distances shown. See Garden Plan or follow directions on seed packets or in seed catalogs. Time of outdoor planting is approximate, may vary 2 to 3 weeks from southern to northern New Jersey.

†6 beans around pole. Thin to four strong plants after second pair of leaves develops.

‡If not grown on stakes, 25 plants 4′ x 5′.

§Thinnings of beets can be used for greens, with small roots attached. Thinnings of lettuce, endive, and other salad plants sown in rows can be used as leaves are 3 to 4 inches long.

—*New Jersey Agicultural Extension Service*

Plan for a Farm Garden for a Family of Five Persons

1 { 4*	Asparagus, rhubarb, chives, horseradish, herbs, winter onions
4	onion sets to mature, thinnings used for green onions—April
2½	onion seed to mature, thinnings used for green onions—April
2½	early spinach, lettuce, turnips, cress, kohlrabi—April, followed by snap beans—June 15 - July 1
2½	early peas—April, followed by beets and late carrots—June 15 - July 1
2½	second early peas—April, followed by late celery, cauliflower, broccoli—June 15 - July 1
2 { 2½	late peas—April, followed by late endive, chinese cabbage, lettuce—July 1-15, or late turnips—July 15 - August 1
2½	early beets, early carrots—April, followed by late spinach, or snap beans—July 20
2½	early cabbage, broccoli, cauliflower—April, followed by spinach or kale—July 15 - August 1
2½	parsnips, salsify, Swiss chard, New Zealand spinach, parsley—April (Seeded with marker of early and second early radishes)
2½	cabbage, Brussels sprouts, early celery—May
2½	second plantings of beets, carrots, kohlrabi, lettuce—May
4	cucumbers, muskmelons, summer pumpkins, winter squash—May 15
4	

Plan for a Farm Garden for a Family of Five Persons (cont.)

	sweet corn
2½	sweet corn—May 1, May 20, June 15, July 1
2½	sweet corn
3 2½	snap beans—May 1 - 15
2½	green shell beans, dry shell beans—May 20
2½	lima beans—May 20
2½	lima beans—May 20
4	tomatoes, sweet and sharp peppers, eggplant—May 20
4	late cabbage—June 15
2½	late cabbage—June 15
2½	

Dates are for Central Pennsylvania.
Grouping shows:—1. Perennial crops. 2. Early maturing crops
followed by succession crops. 3. Crops occupying the
ground all season.

—*Pennsylvania Agricultural Extension Service*

* Distance between rows may depend upon type of cultivator to be used.

Plan for a 25 x 50-foot Garden

Practical row arrangements with companion and succession plantings and approximate dates for sowing seed or transplanting plants (Northeastern Area). Adjust size of plantings to fit needs and preferences of your family.

FEET 00	ROWS 25 FEET LONG (PLAN NOT DRAWN TO SCALE)
1	peas, double row, 6 in. apart — April 1, follow with 1 row snap beans — June 15
3½	peas, double row, 6 in. apart* — April 1, follow with 1 row snap beans — June 15
6	spinach, double row, 6 in. apart* — April 1, interplant with 12 staked tomato plants — May 15
8½	spinach, double row, 6 in. apart* — April 1, interplant with 12 staked tomato plants — May 15
9¾	carrots — April 1
11	carrots — April 1, follow with rutabagas — July 1
12¼	beets — April 1, follow with carrots — July 15
13½	beets — April 1, follow with carrots — July 15
16	Swiss chard, 15 ft. of row — April 1, peppers, 5 plants 2 ft. apart — May 15
18½	cabbage, 12 plants — April 1, interplant with lettuce, radish seed, or onion sets
21	broccoli, 12 plants — April 1, interplant with lettuce, radish seed, or onion sets
23½	snap beans — May 1, snap beans — July 10
26	corn, ½ row — May 1, other half — May 10, follow with 12 kale plants — Aug. 15
28½	corn, ½ row — May 1, other half — May 10, follow with late lettuce, radish, or endive — Aug. 15
31	lima beans — May 10
33½	snap beans — May 10, follow with cabbage, 12 plants — July 15

Plan for a 25 x 50-foot Garden (cont.)

36	snap beans—May 10, follow with snap beans—July 15
38½	snap beans—May 20, follow with beets, 2 rows, 15 in. apart*—July 15
41	lima beans—May 20
43½	lima beans—May 30
46	corn—½ row—May 20, other half—May 30, spinach—Aug. 20
48½	corn—½ row—May 20, other half—May 30, spinach—Aug. 20
50	

*Allow 2½ feet from center of double row.   —New Jersey Agricultural Experiment Station

Vegetable Planting Table and Requirements

PLANTING DIRECTIONS

VEGETABLE	TIME TO PLANT	DISTANCE BETWEEN PLANTS (INCHES)	DISTANCE BETWEEN ROWS (INCHES)	ROW-FEET AMOUNT OF SEED PER 100	YIELD PER 100 ROW-FEET
asparagus	spring	18	48 - 60	Roots	12 - 24 lb.
beans, bush	1 - 8 weeks after last spring frost	4 - 6	18 - 24	1 lb.	50 lb.
lima	2 - 6 weeks after last spring frost	6 - 10	24	1 lb.	60 - 75 lb.
beets, early	2 - 4 weeks before last spring frost	3	12 - 18	2 oz.	100 lb.
late	6 - 8 weeks before first fall freeze	3	12 - 18	2 oz.	100 lb.
broccoli	4 - 6 weeks before last spring frost	18 - 24	24 - 30	plants	50 lb.
cabbage, early	4 - 6 weeks before last spring frost	15 - 18	24 - 30	plants	100 lb.
late	3 months before first fall freeze	24 - 30	24 - 30	plants	175 lb.
carrots, early	2 - 4 weeks before last spring frost	3	12 - 18	1 pkt.	100 lb.
late	10 weeks before first fall freeze	3	12 - 18	1 oz.	150 lb.
cauliflower, early	2 - 4 weeks before last spring frost	18 - 24	24 - 30	plants	45 heads
late	3½ months before first fall freeze	18 - 24	24 - 30	1 pkt.	45 heads
corn, early	on frost-free date	12 - 18	24 - 36	4 oz.	100 ears
late	10 weeks before first fall frost	12 - 18	24 - 36	4 oz.	100 ears
cucumbers	1 week after last spring frost	36 - 60	36 - 60	½ oz.	150 lb.
eggplant	1 week after last spring frost	24 - 30	24 - 30	plants	125 fruit
lettuce, head	4 - 6 weeks before last spring frost	6 - 12	12 - 18	½ oz.	50 lb.
leaf	6 weeks before first fall freeze	6 - 12	12 - 18	½ oz.	50 lb.
muskmelons	1 - 2 weeks after last spring frost	48 - 72	48 - 72	½ oz.	50 fruit
onions	4 - 6 weeks before last spring frost	2 - 3	12 - 18	300 pl.	75 - 100 lb.
parsnips	2 - 4 weeks before last spring frost	3 - 6	18 - 24	¼ oz.	100 lb.
parsley	2 - 4 weeks before last spring frost	3 - 6	12 - 18	¼ oz.	50 lb.
peas	4 - 6 weeks before last spring frost	1 - 3	18 - 36	1 lb.	40 lb.

Vegetable Planting Table and Requirements (cont.)

		PLANTING DIRECTIONS			
VEGETABLE	TIME TO PLANT	DISTANCE BETWEEN PLANTS (INCHES)	BETWEEN ROWS (INCHES) DISTANCE	AMOUNT ROW-FEET OF SEED PER 100	YIELD PER 100 ROW-FEET
potatoes, white	4 - 6 weeks before last spring frost	12 - 15	24 - 30	6 - 10 lb.	75 lb.
sweet	1 - 2 weeks after last spring frost	12 - 18	30 - 48	plants	100 lb.
radishes	2 - 4 weeks before last spring frost	1	12 - 18	1 oz.	1,200
rutabaga	3 months before first fall freeze	6 - 10	18 - 24	¼ oz.	150 lb.
soybeans	on frost-free date	6 - 10	24	½ lb.	50 lb.
spinach	4 - 6 weeks before last spring frost	2 - 6	15 - 24	1 oz.	50 lb.
squash, summer	on frost-free date	36 - 80	36 - 80	½ oz.	100 fruits
winter	1-2 weeks after last spring frost	48 - 120	60 - 120	½ oz.	100 fruits
strawberries	spring	12 - 18	36	plants	varies
tomatoes	on frost-free date	24 - 48	24 - 48	plants	200 lb.
turnips	4 - 6 weeks before last spring frost	3	21 - 18	½ oz.	100 lb.

3. Make a Little Garden Do the Work of a Big One

A tiny garden is the best education that I know.

Each plant is just a few feet from all the others, so you notice things you'd overlook in a large garden. When something goes wrong, you realize it from the start, look for the cause, and take action.

Moreover, the tiny garden can be beautiful. Put to work, every square inch is fruitfully productive. But you must keep its nose to the grindstone. If enough growing season remains, never pull out a vegetable without planting a couple of seeds in its place. Always count on the weather being with you. You lose little if it isn't; and a long shot sometimes pays off, giving you besides food, that comforting feeling that your judgment is pretty good, after all.

Shade can be greatest problem

In your little garden, the greatest problem may be shade. Raise a lightloving plant a foot or two above the others and in some cases you'll double the light it receives. You can do that by planting it in a bottomless box set on top of the earth. Go around the garden with a light meter (borrowed from your camera-fan neighbor) and test light availability here and there. It will reveal interesting facts.

Space problems

Corn is not impossible in a small garden. True, the leaves should touch for pollination, but they will when planted in triangles of three. Quite a few of these triangles can be wedged in here and there for a vegetable that must be fresh to be real.

The best of all vegetables, asparagus, admittedly is a space-taker. But it makes such a lovely background for the summer flowers and vegetables that I slip one in wherever there are a few inches to spare. Give it room in the tiny garden if only to have a crop when other vegetables are scarce.

My space limitations started me growing tomatoes in large cans. A 2-gallon container with drainage filled with rich earth will hold a well trained and clipped tomato through its whole bearing period. It has always seemed regrettable to me that we should grow tomatoes into rich bearing plants only to have them destroyed when they reach their peak performance. Find a reasonably bright, cool place inside for these cans, and you can stretch your tomato season right through the winter. Start these winter-into-spring tomatoes later than the others, but have them bearing when you take them into the house.

—DOROTHY BAKER

The gardener who is really cramped for space might take a tip from big city designers. They've learned a long time ago that the best utilization of space is to make things go up. According to Brian Furner, vertical gardening can be the answer to a highly successful vegetable patch.

Vertical gardens

Your garden fence can be your most useful garden asset. Each summer sees my fences converted into attractive, fruitful, living walls. I invested in a few rolls of strong steel mesh which soon paid for itself and now continues to show a profit. The 6-foot-high fencing has to carry quite a load each season, so I'm glad that I secured it to strong steel poles when setting it up.

Squash and cukes decorate fence, too

One of the fences is devoted to vegetables. Hubbards and other vining squash give a remarkable flower display, crop well, and take up no valuable garden space. I give the plants an early start by sowing in peat pots filled with sifted garden compost in mid-April. Germination is good in the cold frame, and I have strong, healthy plants for setting out 15 inches apart alongside the fence in early June. Although squash plants have tendrils, I encourage the main shoots to climb to the top of my fence by tying in regularly until August. Squash plants are greedy feeders and they have a terrible thirst. They find all the nourishment they need in my organically rich soil, and to save precious water, I supply it directly to the roots via a clay flower pot sunk alongside each plant.

Although the flower display is not so gaudy, cukes may also be grown on the garden fence. Burpee F1 Hybrid is a rapid climber. I sow as for squash, but when setting out the plants in June, I plant them only 12 inches apart. The secret of success with cucumbers is to pick often. This encourages the plants to keep on cropping until temperatures get a bit low in the fall.

In some summers, most of the "vegetable fence" is devoted to pole beans; the cukes are then trained on a trellis. The bean seeds are sown at 8-inch spacing, which some people say is too close, and the plants quickly climb the mesh and make a thick stand of junglelike greenery and loads of tender pods from late July until October. Here again, regular harvesting is the secret of long cropping. Although I'm a great one for mulching, I do find it necessary to flood the bean plants now and then when they are in full bearing.

Not all neighbors take kindly to 6-foot-high fences, but I see no reason at all why the fruit and vegetables I grow on my own tall fences could not be grown on the more conventional 4-foot fencing, although you'd lose two feet of vertical space and yields would be somewhat less. In addition to the crops I have mentioned, I'm sure that tomatoes would do well alongside a 4-foot fence. I know how well my tomato plants crop train each season to a 4-foot trellis.

Bamboo sticks

Bamboo tepees are a must in vertical gardening—they're so spectacular that you can place them in the flower garden and mingle flowers and vegetables in a startling way. You need 4 long, strong bamboo canes (tall poles will do). After pushing the supports into the soil a few inches to anchor them, tie them together somewhere near the top. Then link the supports together—from base to apex—with soft wire. You then have an openwork wigwam on which squash, cucumbers, or pole beans can be grown. If the climate permits, muskmelons and watermelons should do fine on tepees, too. It doesn't matter whether you plant inside or outside the tepee. The important thing is to position the plants so that they will be able to climb up the legs of the tepees.

If space is not your problem, pass on these tips to friends and neighbors who say they just can't grow any food crops because of lack of garden space. Make sure, though, that they understand that good, healthy crops like yours and mine aren't produced by waving magic wands or sprinkling chemicals around the garden. Some work has to be done (but not too much), and the soil must get its annual quota of organic matter.

—BRIAN FURNER

Starting Plants from Seed

1. What Seeds Are

Seeds are embryo plants with enough food stored around them to last until they can make their own food. If you soak a bean seed in water for a day or two, then carefully open it along the seam, you can see the young plant at one end of the bean seed. It will be very small and delicate. You'll easily be able to see the first few leaves, as well as the small round, pointed root.

All seeds are alike in that they have a small plant in them. The rest of the seed contains stored food for the young plant. This little plant needs certain conditions in order for it to grow; these are air, warmth, light, plant food, and moisture. Given these conditions, the plant should become well established.

As soon as the plant has a root and *green* leaves, it can start to make its own food. This usually takes from 10 to 30 days. The root takes up water and minerals from the soil. These *raw materials* are carried in the stream of water or sap up to the *green leaves,* where they are made into plant food. The water and minerals in the soil, carbon dioxide in the air, and light must all come together in a green leaf before they can be used by the plant as food.

The green color in the leaf is caused by chlorophyll, which has the ability to transform raw materials into starch in the presence of light. Without light, true plants cannot continue to grow because plant foods cannot be manufactured. Both chlorophyll and light are necessary.

Leaves turn green in the light. Seeds germinated and kept dark will have white sprouts which will turn green when brought into the light for a few days.

The leaves and other green parts of the plant are a sort of kitchen or manufacturing plant for preparing the plant food.

131

After the green parts have prepared the food, it is sent back to the roots and other parts of the plant and is used for growth. The leaves or "plant kitchen" must have sunlight in order to work.

On the following pages, you'll learn how to grow your own plants from seeds and how to provide seedlings with the best growing conditions.

2. Growing Your Own Plants

Plant growing was once an art and a must with gardeners throughout the land. They knew their work, did it well and, as a result, reaped a bountiful harvest.

Today, it is surprising how few gardeners and farmers do grow their own plants. Even those who stand to profit greatly by doing so, turn their backs on the cold frame. They have come to depend upon outside sources for their needs, in turn, they are gambling their entire crop upon another's method of growing the all important item.

In the opinion of G. J. Raleigh of Cornell University's Department of Horticulture:

> Plants of similar quality usually can be grown cheaper than they can be purchased. Moreover, the grower who produces his own plants is much less likely to be troubled by such diseases as clubroot and yellows of cabbage which are commonly introduced by purchasing plants from infested soils. Southern grown and inferior locally grown plants may sell at low prices, but too often results with such plants are disappointing.
>
> When early maturity is of importance, as in most market-garden sections, the kind of plants used often determines whether or not the crop will be profitable. Large, sturdy plants with good root systems commence growth quickly after careful transplanting and produce crops earlier than do poorly grown plants.

Another great advantage in growing your own plants in hotbeds and cold frames is that you can send off for seeds from any part of the world, and thus raise and experiment with varieties and with new plants unobtainable from local seedmen. Nurseries usually limit themselves to a few good selling varieties of plants. If you want to experiment with some new hybrids, or with new varieties developed abroad or elsewhere in the United States, you should by all means learn to grow your own plants.

3. Starting Out

Vermiculite gives renewed hope to all home gardeners who want to grow their own vegetable and flower plants, but who have neither the time, place, nor funds for a cold frame. Vermiculite can also be a solution to the damping-off problem for those who do maintain a cold frame, but have trouble with this and other diseases caused by contaminated soil. A ½-inch layer of vermiculite is simply spread evenly over the entire surface in the cold frame, just as in the flat, and the seeds are then planted.

If just a small number of plants is desired, the vermiculite seed flat is your best bet. Plants growing in such a flat have less chance of being stunted by insufficient water, improper temperatures, or lack of good air circulation.

Seeds can be germinated well just in damp vermiculite—especially the tiny, hard-to-sprout ones such as double petunias. If only vermiculite is used, the seedlings must be transplanted to good soil as soon as they are large enough to handle. If transplanting is inconvenient at the time, the plants must be fed a liquid fertilizer high in nitrogen, such as one made by dissolving 3 tablespoons of dehydrated cow manure in one quart of water. When 2 inches tall, the plants should be transplanted to soil to prevent crowding. When feeding, saturate the flats well with liquid.

A combination of vermiculite on top of a mixture of organically enriched soil is best, however, for all-around seed germination. Even before sprouting seeds develop top growth, they send a long taproot down through the vermiculite into the rich soil below. This gets them off to a good start and develops strong plants for transplanting.

Vermiculite is heat-expanded mica, which is a form of rock. While in the process of being treated, it becomes sterile, thus rendering itself to good seed germination. Other reasons, such as fine water-holding capacity, good aeration, and lightness in weight, also make it an excellent medium with which to work.

Some organic gardeners have a mistaken impression that vermiculite is not acceptable in the natural method. Since it is formed from a rock-based, naturally occurring mineral without the application or addition of chemicals, there is nothing objectionable about its use for starting seeds or for improving the air- and water-holding capacity of soil. (It will hold several times its own weight of water, and even when thoroughly soaked will permit ample air circulation around plant roots, helping to avoid damping-off.)

Vermiculite does not supply plant-growth nutrients, and should not be counted on to do this. It's an excellent seed-germinating material, and can also be used to store bulbs and winter vegetables, or provide a base for flower arrangements. But it cannot substitute for humus or for any of the food needs of growing plants. Neither is it as good for mulching as organic matter, which lightens, aerates, and helps hold moisture in soils—along with feeding plants and aiding topsoil.

Another wonderful thing about vermiculite is its cost. The small amount needed to grow enough plants for the average garden costs no more than a dozen tomato plants at your garden shop. You can purchase it in small as well as in large amounts, depending upon your needs.

Damping-off

If you have been troubled with damping-off, your soil is most likely contaminated. If you like, you can sterilize your soil at this time by pouring boiling water slowly through the soil. One gallon of boiling water is sufficient for a standard-sized flat. If you would rather, you can add one cup of white (5 percent) vinegar to one quart of water and pour this slowly through the prepared soil. Although it is not as effective as the boiling water in stamping out damping-off, it does help to control it. Allow the soil to rest for 24 hours, then place a ½-inch layer of vermiculite over it. Apply loosely without tamping with your hand.

4. Building a Cold Frame and Hotbed

What is the difference between a hotbed and a cold frame? If you want to grow peppers, tomatoes, eggplants, or any of the other heat-loving plants, a hotbed is best to grow them in. A cold frame has the same construction as a hotbed, except that there is no heat used inside it. In a cold frame, you can propagate such cold-loving plants as cabbage, the broccoli family, cauliflower. Or you can use your cold frames to taper off and harden plants that have been moved into them from the hotbeds, to get them hardened between the hotbed and setting out into open garden or field.

There are two types of hotbeds. One is heated by a great deal of fermenting straw or fresh manures (preferably horse or chicken), which has been placed in a pit 2½ feet deep. The manure is packed down to a depth of 18 inches, well watered to soak. Then you shovel into the pit 5 to 6 inches of composted soil or good rich top soil. This soil—which will make the seedbed—must be sieved fine.

Manure hotbeds

The making of a manure hotbed is described by New Mexico extension horticulturists as follows:

The first essential in preparing a manure hotbed is to have fresh horse manure, preferably from grain fed animals. The manure should contain ⅓ straw or other similar litter. Sometimes there is insufficient straw in the manure for proper heating. If it does not have sufficient straw in the manure, it may not ferment or, if fermentation does take place, the heat may be evolved rapidly and be of only short duration. About 10 to 12 days before the manure is to be put in the pit, it should be placed in a flat pile 4 to 5 feet high. If it is dry, it should be dampened with water, but not made soggy. The manure should begin to heat in 3 or 4 days after which it should be turned, placing the inside of the pile on the outside of the new one. In 3 or 4 more days, the manure should be ready to be placed in the pit. The manure is filled into the pit in successive layers of 4 to 6 inches and tamped firmly to secure uniform heating and prevent excessive settling. It is also desirable to place the soil on top of the manure at the same time, since higher temperatures that develop when the bed is first made up tend to kill some of the weed seeds that may be present in the soil. Since a high temperature is likely to develop the first few days after the bed is made up, the planting should be delayed until the temperature drops to about 85 degrees or slightly lower.

If the seeds are planted when the bed is first made up, the

high temperature is likely to kill the seeds or at least injure them. Manure heated hotbeds are usually economical to operate after the initial construction costs are paid. Temperature cannot be properly controlled in the manure heated hotbed because the rate of fermentation, and hence the rate of heat formation, is more or less the same on warm days as on the colder days. Thus the bed may be too hot or too cold depending upon the weather. The only means of controlling temperature is by ventilation, but unless much time is spent regulating the ventilation, the temperature is likely to vary considerably from the optimum for the growth of the seedlings.

5. Starting in Flats

In a flat, the bottom ¼ to ½ should be sphagnum moss. Soil which is added to cover these layers should be moist, not wet or dry. Seed should be thinly sown in rows or in circles in the pot, and in rows in the flat. If more than one kind of seed is planted in a container, the seeds should be chosen to germinate in about the same length of time, and to grow at the same rate so that all will be ready for transplanting together. After the seed has been placed in its rows, sand or fine compost is sifted over it to the correct depth. The soil may then be firmed and watered, either with a very fine misty spray from above, or by plunging the container into water almost as deep as the soil. When wet patches begin to appear on top of the soil, the container should be removed from the water and drained.

Seed flats may be covered to preserve surface moisture until germination starts. Temperature for germination of seed may usually be somewhat higher than the plants will bear after growth has started. (Exceptions are the seeds which need a period of frost before they will germinate.) Soil should be kept moist, but not wet, during this period. If the top of the container is covered with glass or paper, the cover should be lifted occasionally to permit air to circulate. At the first sign of fungus growth, the cover should be removed.

As soon as the first green begins to appear, covering should be removed from the seed pot and it should be placed in a southern window. Gradually, as the seedlings sprout and the roots stretch down into the pot, watering may be lighter and less frequent, but the container should never be permitted to become dry. If seedlings are too thick, they must be thinned immediately. Occasionally when fine seed is planted, it will come up unevenly, with thick patches in places in the pot. These patches should be thinned by means of tweezers, because crowding at this stage will almost inevitably result in damping-off.

Watering

Water the beds daily after planting. Use a fine can sprinkler and *tepid* water. Don't muddy the seedbed; just water it enough to be nicely damp. One gallon sprinkling can to a 6-foot section is generally adequate. For added moisture, beds can be opened to a warm, quiet rain.

Once the plants have sprouted and are several weeks old— and there is the delightful feeling of their crowding one another—lift the lids more and more. As the growing season progresses, and the bedding plants grow faster, there will be nice days when you should take the lids off and get the full benefit of the sun.

First transplanting: When your plants have grown to a size large enough to be handled, they are ready to transplant over into the cold frame beds. There they will grow rapidly and harden off so that the shock of final planting into the open garden won't hurt them.

About the only thing that can harm growing plants in the hotbeds or cold frames is overheating, drying out for lack of water, or being attacked by the fungus disease known as *damping-off*. This damping-off or "black root" or "wire stem" in the seedbed is caused by about a half dozen or more fungus parasites. They usually grow near the surface, and enter the tiny plants at the point where they emerge from the ground. All of these fungus parasites require a high moisture content of soil and air for quick growth.

To prevent trouble from *damping-off,* the best defense is to keep the air and surface of the seedbed as dry as is consistent with good growth of the plants. Getting the beds heated without proper ventilation, and not allowing the moisture to escape, is what causes damping-off.

6. Proper Soil for Plants

Make a mixture of 2 parts good garden loam, 1 part fine, but sharp sand, and 1 part leaf mold, peat, or old decayed compost or manure. Mix well and put 8 inches of it into the bed. It's a good idea to let it age for several months before seeding. Sift the soil mixture through a ¼ inch mesh screen to get it in condition for planting. When screening the mixture, place coarse screenings in the bottom of the flats to provide better drainage.

There is enough plant food in this mixture without adding manure or organic fertilizers high in nitrogen. Used too soon, these often cause the young plants to grow too rapidly, unbalancing their natural growth.

When to plant

Two separate compartments are helpful in the cold frame. All vegetables do not require the same temperature for germination. Where some will sprout in the heat, others will rot. To get the maximum number of plants from the seed, the plants must be divided into two groups. Celery, cabbage, lettuce, cauliflower, and broccoli require low temperatures for germination. Plant these together in one section of the cold frame, dropping the seeds evenly in rows 2 inches apart. Plant about the first week in April or 8 weeks before transplanting time. An inch of fine mulch may be spread evenly over the seeded area to keep the ground moist and to discourage early weeds. The growing plants will push their way through as they grow. Water lightly, then close the frame.

About the middle of April, when the sun is warmer, plant tomatoes, peppers, eggplants, muskmelons, summer squash, and cucumbers. Plant these in the other half of the bed. The plants in the first half of the bed should have sprouted by now and need ventilation. Close the cover on the tomato bed until the plants sprout, then ventilate along with the other half.

Cucumbers, muskmelons, and summer squash are grown in parts of milk cartons and set out in the open after danger of frost. This is not absolutely necessary. It merely helps produce an earlier yield.

Ventilation

No matter what the germination temperatures had been, all growing plants do best around 70 degrees. Regulate the temperature each day by slightly lifting the two sashes. On cold days, allow the beds to remain closed. Never lift covers into the wind. A cold wind can damage the tender shoots. Open away from the draft, and secure the windows so they will not be broken.

Nevada's experiment station points out that flats, cold frames, and hotbeds will bring many plants into production a month to 6 weeks earlier than when they are sown outdoors.

The minimum maturity dates given here indicate the length of time required for maturing after the plants are set in Nevada's high altitude gardens. At elevations below 5,000 feet, and in favorable seasons, some fruit may ripen in a shorter period.

KIND	HEIGHT (INCHES)	MATURITY DATES	DEPTH TO COVER THE SEEDS
broccoli*	10–16	65 to 100 days	¼ to ½ inch
cabbage*	10–15	65 to 125 days	¼ to ½ inch
cauliflower*	10–15	90 to 150 days	¼ to ½ inch
celery*	8–12	115 to 150 days	¼ to ½ inch
eggplant	8–12	90 to 125 days	¼ to ½ inch
peppers	8–12	70 to 90 days	¼ to ½ inch
tomatoes	12–30	100 to 150 days	¼ to ½ inch

*Frost resistant and can be set out while weather is still cool.

Time, Spacing, and Temperature Recommended for Growing Plants in the Home or the Hotbed

VEGETABLE	WEEKS FROM SEEDING TO SETTING IN GARDEN	INCHES TO SPACE AFTER FIRST LEAVES ARE FORMED	DEGREES OF TEMPERATURE	
			DAY	NIGHT
broccoli brussels sprouts cabbage cauliflower head lettuce	5 to 7	2 x 2	65	55
tomato	5 to 7	3 x 3	75	65
eggplant pepper	6 to 8	3 x 3	75	65

—Virginia Polytechnic Institute

Approximate Dates for Sowing Vegetable Seeds Under Glass, and Ranges of Day Temperatures

VEGETABLE	LONG ISLAND AND SOUTHEASTERN NEW YORK	SOUTHERN-TIER COUNTIES	REMAINDER OF NEW YORK OTHER THAN MOUNTAIN REGIONS	APPROXIMATE TEMPERATURES (day)
beets	Feb. 15 - 28	March 15 - 31	March 1 - 15	60 - 65
broccoli	Feb. 10 - 20	March 1 - 15	Feb. 20 - 28	60 - 65
cabbage, early	Feb. 10 - 20	March 1 - 15	Feb. 20 - 28	60 - 65
cauliflower	Feb. 10 - 20	March 1 - 15	Feb. 20 - 28	60 - 65
celery	Feb. 10 - 20	March 1 - 15	Feb. 20 - 28	60 - 65
eggplant*	March 10 - 20	March 25 - April 5	March 15 - 25	70 - 75
endive	Feb. 10 - 20	March 10 - 20	Feb. 20 - 28	60 - 65
kohlrabi	Feb. 10 - 20	March 1 - 15	Feb. 20 - 28	60 - 65
leeks	Feb. 10 - 20	March 1 - 15	Feb. 20 - 28	60 - 65
lettuce	Feb. 10 - 20	March 1 - 15	Feb. 20 - 28	60 - 65
melons	April 10 - 15	April 25 - May 5	April 15 - 25	70 - 75
onions, sweet spanish	Jan. 20 - 31	Feb. 10 - 20	Feb. 1 - 10	60 - 65
peppers*	March 10 - 20	March 25 - April 5	March 15 - 25	70 - 75
squash	April 10 - 15	April 25 - May 5	April 15 - 25	65 - 70
tomatoes*	March 10 - 20	March 25 - April 5	March 15 - 25	65 - 70

* If to be transplanted twice or if transplanted once but grown in bands or pots, seeds should be two weeks earlier.

—Prepared by G. J. Raleigh, Cornell University

7. Using the Cold Frame for Winter Vegetables

A cold frame is really a protected seedbed and can be used in the first frosty days of autumn just as advantageously as in early spring. Tender lettuce and crisp endive can be enjoyed until after Thanksgiving by properly utilizing the cold frame.

Plant seeds in early autumn

For lettuce, endive, and parsley, plant seeds in one compartment in rows 3 inches apart and about ¼ inch deep, covering the seed with vermiculite to prevent damping-off. Then water the rows with a fine spray, and adjust the sash and place a covering of light boards over it. As soon as the seeds sprout, remove this cover and raise the sash several inches to allow good circulation of air.

Seedlings will grow rapidly, and when they begin to crowd each other, they are ready to transplant. Set the little plants in another compartment, about 3 inches apart each way. Mulch again with vermiculite and keep them shaded for a few days. As plants grow, they can be thinned and the thinnings used in salads. The remaining plants will then begin to form heads.

When nights grow frosty, close the frame tightly before sundown to hold the day's heat within, opening it again each morning. If nights are very cold, cover the frame with a blanket and bank leaves around the sides. If the day remains cold, remove the blanket to allow light to enter, but keep the frame closed.

You'll be amazed at how much cold the plants could stand under glass. As the season grows late, plants may be frozen occasionally, but by sprinkling with cold water and keeping in the dark for a while, they will revive and come back in good condition. It is possible to have fresh salads until winter.

You can also use the cold frame in winter for storing vegetables. Before the ground freezes, remove about 18 inches of soil and place in vegetables like turnips, rutabagas, beets, carrots, and celery on a layer of straw. Over the vegetables cover another layer of straw with sash boards. Vegetables should keep crisp and unfrozen all winter.

Time to Plant Seeds (For Earliness)

Name of Vegetable	Average Number of Seeds per Ounce	In Greenhouse or Hotbeds	In Cold Frames	In Open Ground
beans, dwarf	100		last of April	May - July
beans, pole	100		last of April	May - July
Brussels sprouts	6,500	mid-March	April	May - June
beet, garden	1,750	first of March	early April	April 5 - 15
cabbage (early)	5,000	last of Feb.	March 15 - 30	April 5 - 10
cauliflower (early)	14,000	last of March	April 20 - 25	May 1 - 5
celery (early)	100,000	first of March	April 25 - 30	May 5 - 10
cucumber	1,000		last of April	May 20 - 25
eggplant	5,000	April 1 - 10	May 1 - 15	June 1 - 5
endive	13,500	April 1 - 10	May 1 - 5	May 5 - 10
kohlrabi	7,000	April 1 - 10	last of April	May 5 - 10
leek	8,000	April 1 - 10	May 1 - 5	May 5 - 10
lettuce	16,000	March 1 - 10	April 1 - 10	April 5 - 15
melon, musk	1,200		April 25 - 30	May 25 - 30
melon, water	225		April 25 - 30	May 25 - 30
onion	12,500	March 10 - 15	April 15 - 20	May 1 - 5
parsley	17,500	March 10 - 15	April 20 - 25	May 1 - 5
pepper	4,000	March 10 - 15	April 25 - 30	May 20 - 30
squash (early)	300		last of April	May 10 - 20
tomato	7,500	March 10 - 15	April 25 - 30	May 15 - 25

—*University of Connecticut*

8. Saving Seeds

If you grow your own seeds, you can often develop highly productive and disease-resistant strains in your own back-yard. Here are a few simple rules that will help.

1. At the beginning of the season, prepare some stakes or strings to label the plants you select to keep for seeds. Make sure everyone who works in the garden knows the meaning of these markers.

2. Watch your plants as they develop and select a few, only a few, of the outstandingly healthy ones to preserve for seed. Make your selection on the basis of the *whole plant.* Seed development is an all-season job for you as well as the plant, not just a hurried trip through the frost-bitten garden to salvage the largest seed pods that happen to be left. Make a habit of observing your plants with seed selection in mind. You'll form new ideals of what the well balanced plant really can be.

3. Remember there are different characteristics to encourage in each kind of plant. In spinach or Chinese cabbage, for example, do not mark the first few nice ones which go to seed and consider the job done. Those are the very ones you do *not* want. The desirable plants are those which continue producing leafy growth longest and send up seed stalks *latest* in the season. On the other hand, with broccoli or cauliflower, we like best the plants that produce flower heads promptly. Likewise with radishes, save the plant you want most to eat, the first fat root. A healthy top growth should balance the root, but not a premature flower stalk. The same with carrots, beets, turnips, and the like, except that these are biennials and normal seed production takes place only the second year, adding the problem of how to keep your best plants safely through the winter. However, it's worth the trouble as over the years you have seed you can rely on and gradually you may find that you are developing new and valuable plant characteristics.

4. Hybrid plants are the result of crossbreeding of two pure-strain varieties. Seeds from these should not be saved as they will revert to the parent varieties and often be useless for your purposes, or may not even be fertile

at all. (Hybrid corn, for instance, is not fertile.) Cross-breeding, or crosspollination, means that the pollen of a flower has come in contact with the flower of a plant of another variety or species. The pollen can be blown by the wind, or carried by bees. The seed which results will not be true to type of either variety.

You will have to keep in mind, then, that many vegetables will crossbreed. Do not, for instance, plant seed from sweet corn that has been planted near field corn, or beets near chard or sugar beets.

Corn, cucumber, melon, squash, pumpkin, mustard, Brussels sprouts, collards, kale, kohlrabi, onion, radish, beet, turnips—all are vegetables which crosspollinate easily.

Less easily crossbred are tomatoes, eggplant, pepper, celery, and carrot.

Beans, okra, peas, and lettuce are generally selfpollinated.

It is necessary then, that you plant only one variety or strain of the vegetable you wish to seed. If you do plant more, be sure the plants are at least 100 feet apart, though even at this distance bees or wind may effect crosspollination.

5. Let the seeds ripen as long as possible in the garden, but not so long as to risk shattering out or feeding birds. Bring in the whole plant and hang it or lay it in a dry place until the pods are brittle and the seed comes out easily.

6. The easiest homemade way to clean seed is to keep a collection of pieces of wire screening of various sizes of mesh. With one size or another you can sift out either the seed or the chaff sufficiently for storage purposes.

7. Keeping seed safely over the winter requires consideration, as mold or insects can spoil it. Store in a dry, cool place, covered but *not* in airtight containers. To prevent insects from taking hold in wheat or bean seed, stir the seed frequently. Also look it over occasionally, removing any spoiling material.

8. To make sure your seed is fertile, test it long enough before planting time so that you can buy more if necessary. Take about 30 seeds and place in a shallow dish on a piece of blotting paper or raw cotton that is kept

moist. Do not let the seed actually stand in water, but on the other hand if it once dries out, the test will have to be started again with fresh seed. Best cover the container to shut out light and prevent evaporation, but not so as to keep out air, or mold may develop. *Keep in a warm place.* Record the date and see how long germination takes, also what proportion of seeds grow. Naturally some will be slower, like parsley; some will need more heat, like tomatoes, peppers, and eggplant. Any batch from which the test seeds mold without sending out shoots is, of course, not fit to plant.

There are different things to watch for and do in connection with the culture of each type of vegetable for seed.

The cabbage family

Remember that all types of cabbage cross with one another. If it is not possible to grow different varieties at great distance from one another, then one kind only is grown for seed. The firmest heads are selected and stored very carefully over winter. These are set out early in the following April. They must be set quite deeply with support provided for the seed stalks. The seed must be protected from the birds. The mature seed stalks are hung indoors and allowed to dry until it is possible to thresh them or remove the seed by hand.

Carrots

Carefully keep the best developed roots with medium tops and small cores over the winter. Set these out in March, 12 to 20 inches apart, according to the variety. The cultural directions are the same as those given under summer care. (Regular weeding and shallow cultivating is necessary. A mulch of composted oak leaves and bark rich in tannin is helpful if the carrots are attacked by root lice.) Seed stock must not be forced! Cut the ripe umbels, dry them in the shade, rub the chaff out by hand. Seed propagation only makes sense if the area is not surrounded with meadow land, since wild carrot (Queen Anne's Lace) crosses with garden carrot.

Cucumbers

Let the earliest maturing well formed fruit from healthy plants hang until ripe. The seeds are then scraped out of the fully ripened cucumbers and put into a warm place in a little water to ferment. The next steps are to sieve them, wash them, dry gently with a cloth, and spread out on a blotting paper to dry.

Beets

The perfectly formed beets, showing no white markings inside, are kept over winter and set out early in April about 20 inches apart. Cut the ripe stalks and hang in the shade to dry. Later, seeds can be rubbed out by hand.

Head lettuce

Select 2 or 3 of the firmest heads from among those that are slowest to bolt to seed, and leave them in the garden to blossom. The large flowering stalks should be well staked. When most of the seeds are already developed, pull the plants out and hang them in the shade to dry. The removing and cleaning of the seed can be done in winter.

Leeks

Seed bearers are hilled very high to protect them from freezing in the winter. The plant should stand at least a foot and a half apart in all directions. The blossom stem will need supporting. The seeds mature fully only in favorable summers and in a warm situation. Keep in mind that leeks cross easily with pearl onions.

Onions

Select solid, well ripened onions which were grown from sets the year before. These should be set out as early as possible in a sunny, protected location. It's a good idea to apply a compost mulch. Support the blossom stems. Seeds ripen slowly and must be dried under cover since they fall out easily. Ripe seeds are coal black.

Peas and beans

Mark a few of the finest plants with a bit of cloth at the beginning of the harvesting season. Allow entire crop of these plants to ripen. It is best to choose plants most alike in variety and earliness.

Potatoes

For a seed stock, choose only perfectly scabfree potatoes from healthy plants surrounded by other healthy plants. The chosen ones should be marked beforehand, and the potatoes dug before harvesting the others. Store these carefully over the winter in a frost-free dry cellar or pit. They require good ventilation too. Burying in dry sand is one of the best ways to store them.

Radishes

Seed culture occasionally succeeds with early radishes. The plants which bolt to seed *quite late* are left standing. The blossoming plants are very brittle and must be carefully staked. Harvested seed stalks ripen completely when hung in shade, but protect them from finches!

Sweet corn

The earliest, best developed, full-grained ears are allowed to ripen on the stalk. (Hybrid varieties do not produce fertile seed.) When the husks are bleached and strawlike, pick the ears, pull the husks back, tie 2 ears together, and hang up to dry.

Tomatoes

Choose healthy, well formed fruit. Allow tomatoes to ripen beyond the edible stage but do not let them become rotted. Pick off and scrape out the seeds. Set these in a little water and allow them to ferment several days. Then place them in a sieve and wash under a faucet. Spread on blotting paper to dry. The fermentation process is effective in preventing the seed distribution of the bacterial canker disease. Tomatoes intercross only to a small extent, so more than one variety may be planted within a few yards of each other.

Early turnips and rutabagas

The chosen plants should be lightly covered and left to remain in the ground over the winter. In the spring uncover early. Further treatment is the same as for beets. Turnips should be harvested early in the morning to avoid shattering by noon heat.

—EVELYN SPEIDEN

Seeding, Planting, and Transplanting Outside

1. When to Plant Outside—With Tables of Outside Dates

Getting plants off to an early start outside in the garden is an objective of every gardener. All of us want to make the first planting of each vegetable as soon as it can be safely done—as soon as there's little chance of its being damaged by cold. There's good reason for this early planting. In many cases, it will mean that a second crop can be planted later in the season in the same spot. And—just as important—the latent gardening energy must find its release.

Many vegetables are so hardy to cold that they can be planted a month or more before the average date of the last freeze or about 6 weeks before the frost-free date. (According to th USDA's Victor Boswell, the frost-free date in spring is usually 2 to 3 weeks later than the average date of the last freeze in a locality and is approximately the date that oak trees leaf out.)

It should also be remembered that most, if not all, of the cold-tolerant crops actually thrive better in cool weather than in hot weather and should not be planted late in the spring in the southern ⅔ of the country where hot summers occur. Therefore, the gardener should time his planting not only to escape cold but, with certain crops, also to escape heat. Some vegetables that will not thrive when planted in late spring in areas having rather hot summers may be sown in late summer. Thus, they will make most of their growth in cooler weather.

Some Common Vegetables Grouped According to
the Approximate Times They Can Be Planted and Their
Relative Requirements for Cool and Warm Weather

COLD-HARDY PLANTS FOR EARLY-SPRING PLANTING		COLD-TENDER OR HEAT-HARDY PLANTS FOR LATE-SPRING OR EARLY-SUMMER PLANTING			
Very hardy (plant 4 to 6 weeks before frost-free date)	Hardy (plant 2 to 4 weeks before frost-free date)	Not cold hardy (plant on frost-free date)	Requiring hot weather (plant 1 week or more after frost-free date)	Medium heat tolerant (good for summer planting)	Hardy plants for late-summer or fall planting except in the North (plant 6 to 8 weeks before first fall freeze)
broccoli	beets	beans, snap	beans, lima	beans, all	beets
cabbage	carrots	cucumbers	eggplant	chard	collards
lettuce	chard	okra	peppers	New Zealand	kale
onions	mustard	New Zealand	sweet	spinach,	lettuce
peas	parsnips	spinach,	potatoes	soybeans	mustard
potatoes	radishes	soybeans		squash	spinach
spinach		squash		sweet corn	turnips
turnips		sweet corn			
		tomatoes			

Earliest Safe Planting Dates and Range of Spring-Planting Dates for Vegetables in the Open

Planting dates for localities with average last freeze on -

CROP	Jan. 30	Feb. 8	Feb. 18	Feb. 28	Mar. 10	Mar. 20	Mar. 30
asparagus[1]	(1)	Feb. 10 - May 1	Mar. 1 - May 1	Mar. 15 - June 1	Jan. 1 - Mar. 1	Feb. 1 - Mar. 1	Feb. 15 - Mar. 20
beans, lima	Feb. 1 - Apr. 15	Feb. 1 - May 1	do.	Mar. 15 - June 1	Mar. 20 - June 1	Apr. 1 - June 15	Apr. 15 - June 20
beans, snap	Feb. 1 - Apr. 1	Feb. 1 - May 1	do.	Mar. 10 - May 15	Mar. 15 - May 15	Mar. 15 - May 25	Apr. 1 - June 1
beets	Jan. 1 - Mar. 15	Jan. 10 - Mar. 15	Jan. 20 - Apr. 1	Feb. 1 - Mar. 1	Feb. 15 - June 1	Feb. 15 - May 15	Mar. 1 - 20
broccoli, sprouting[1]	Jan. 1 - 30	Jan. 1 - 30	Jan. 15 - Feb. 15	Feb. 1 - Mar. 1	Feb. 10 - Mar. 15	Feb. 15 - Mar. 15	Feb. 15 - Mar. 10
Brussels sprouts[1]	do	(1)	(1)	do.	(1)	(1)	Mar. 15 - Apr. 10
cabbage[1]	(1)	Jan. 1 - Mar. 1	Jan. 15 - Mar. 1	Feb. 1 - Mar. 1	Feb. 10 - Mar. 1	Feb. 15 - Mar. 10	Mar. 20 - Apr. 10
cabbage, Chinese	Jan. 1 - Mar. 1	Jan. 10 - Feb. 10	Jan. 10 - Feb. 20	Jan. 20 - Feb. 1	Feb. 1 - Mar. 20	Feb. 20 - Apr. 1	Mar. 15 - Apr. 15
carrots	Jan. 1 - Feb. 1	Jan. 1 - Feb. 1	Jan. 15 - Mar. 1	Feb. 1 - Mar. 1	Feb. 15 - Mar. 1	Feb. 20 - Apr. 1	Mar. 15 - Apr. 15
cauliflower[1]	do.	Jan. 10 - Feb. 10	Jan. 20 - Feb. 20	Jan. 20 - Feb. 20	Feb. 15 - Mar. 20	Mar. 15 - Apr. 15	Mar. 15 - May 25
celery and celeriac	Jan. 1 - Apr. 1	Jan. 10 - Apr. 1	Jan. 20 - Apr. 15	Feb. 1 - May 1	Feb. 15 - May 15	Feb. 20 - May 15	Feb. 15 - May 15
chard	Jan. 1 - Feb. 1	Jan. 10 - Apr. 1	Jan. 20 - Apr. 15	Feb. 1 - May 1	Feb. 15 - May 15	Feb. 20 - May 15	Mar. 15 - May 15
chervil and chives	Jan. 1 - Feb. 15	Jan. 1 - Feb. 1	Jan. 1 - Feb. 1	Jan. 15 - Feb. 15	Feb. 1 - 15	Feb. 10 - Mar. 15	Feb. 15 - Mar. 15
chicory, witloof	Feb. 1 - Mar. 15	Jan. 1 - Feb. 15	Jan. 1 - Mar. 15	Jan. 15 - Mar. 15	June 1 - July 1	June 1 - July 1	June 1 - July 1
collards[1]	Jan. 1 - Feb. 15	Jan. 1 - Mar. 15	Jan. 1 - Mar. 15	Jan. 1 - Mar. 1	Jan. 1 - Apr. 1	Feb. 1 - May 1	Jan. 15 - June 1
corn salad	Jan. 1 - Feb. 1	Jan. 1 - Feb. 1	Jan. 1 - Mar. 15	Jan. 15 - Mar. 1	Jan. 1 - Apr. 15	Feb. 1 - May 1	Mar. 25 - May 15
corn, sweet	Feb. 1 - Mar. 15	Feb. 10 - Apr. 1	Feb. 20 - Apr. 15	Mar. 1 - Apr. 15	Mar. 10 - Apr. 15	Mar. 15 - May 1	Apr. 10 - Apr. 1
cress, upland	Jan. 1 - Feb. 1	Jan. 1 - Feb. 1	Jan. 15 - Feb. 15	Feb. 1 - Mar. 1	Feb. 15 - Apr. 1	Mar. 1 - Apr. 1	Feb. 20 - May 20
cucumbers	Feb. 15 - Mar. 15	Jan. 1 - Feb. 1	Feb. 15 - Apr. 15	Mar. 1 - Apr. 1	Mar. 15 - Apr. 15	Apr. 1 - May 1	Apr. 15 - May 15
dandelion	Jan. 1 - Feb. 1	Jan. 1 - Feb. 1	Jan. 15 - Feb. 15	Mar. 10 - Apr. 15	Mar. 15 - Apr. 1	Apr. 1 - May 1	Mar. 10 - Apr. 10
eggplant[1]	Feb. 1 - Mar. 1	Feb. 10 - Mar. 15	Feb. 20 - Apr. 1	Mar. 10 - Apr. 15	Mar. 15 - Apr. 15	Apr. 1 - May 1	Feb. 10 - Mar. 10
endive	Jan. 1 - Mar. 1	Jan. 1 - Mar. 1	Jan. 15 - Mar. 1	Feb. 1 - Mar. 1	Feb. 15 - Mar. 1	Apr. 1 - May 1	Mar. 1 - 20
Florence fennel	....	....	....	....	....	Feb. 1 - Mar. 1	Mar. 1 - 20
garlic	(1)	do.	do.	(1)	do.	do.	Feb. 15 - Mar. 15
horseradish[1]	....	....	....	....	....	Feb. 20 - Mar. 10	Feb. 1 - 20
kale	Jan. 1 - Feb. 1	Jan. 10 - Feb. 1	Jan. 20 - Feb. 10	Feb. 1 - 20	Feb. 10 - Mar. 10	do.	Feb. 10 - Mar. 10
kohlrabi	do.	do.	do.	Jan. 15 - Feb. 15	do.	Jan. 25 - Mar. 1	Mar. 1 - 20
leeks	do.	Jan. 1 - Feb. 1	Jan. 1 - Feb. 1	Jan. 15 - Feb. 15	Jan. 25 - Mar. 1	Feb. 1 - 20	Feb. 15 - Mar. 15
lettuce, head[1]	do.	do.	Jan. 1 - Feb. 1	do.	Feb. 1 - 20	Feb. 15 - Mar. 10	Mar. 1 - 20
lettuce, leaf	do.	do.	Jan. 1 - Mar. 15	Jan. 1 - Mar. 15	Jan. 15 - Apr. 1	Feb. 1 - Apr. 1	Feb. 15 - Apr. 15

Earliest Safe Planting Dates and Range of Spring-Planting Dates for Vegetables in the Open (cont.)

CROP	Planting dates for localities with average last freeze on -						
	Jan. 30	Feb. 8	Feb. 18	Feb. 28	Mar. 10	Mar. 20	Mar. 30
mustard	Jan. 1 - Mar. 1	Jan. 1 - Mar. 1	do.	Feb. 1 - Mar. 1	Feb. 10 - Mar. 15	Feb. 20 - Apr. 1	Mar. 1 - Apr. 15
okra	Feb. 15 - Apr. 15	Feb. 15 - Apr. 15	Mar. 1 - June 1	Mar. 10 - June 1	Mar. 20 - June 1	Apr. 1 - June 15	Apr. 10 - June 15
onions¹	Jan. 1 - 15	Jan. 1 - 15	Jan. 1 - 15	Jan. 1 - Feb. 1	Jan. 15 - Feb. 15	Feb. 10 - Mar. 10	Feb. 15 - Mar. 15
onions, seed	do.	do.	do.	Jan. 1 - Feb. 15	Feb. 1 - Mar. 1	do.	Feb. 20 - Mar. 15
onions, sets	do.	do.	do.	Jan. 1 - Mar. 1	Jan. 15 - Mar. 10	Feb. 1 - Mar. 20	Feb. 15 - Mar. 20
parsley	Jan. 1 - 30	Jan. 1 - 30	Jan. 1 - 30	Jan. 15 - Mar. 1	Feb. 1 - Mar. 10	Feb. 15 - Mar. 15	Mar. 1 - Apr. 1
parsnips			Jan. 1 - Feb. 1	Jan. 15 - Feb. 15	Jan. 15 - Mar. 1	Feb. 15 - Mar. 15	Feb. 20 - Mar. 20
peas, garden	Jan. 1 - Feb. 15	Jan. 1 - Feb. 15	Jan. 1 - Feb. 1	Jan. 15 - Mar. 1	Jan. 15 - Mar. 15	Feb. 1 - Mar. 15	Feb. 10 - Mar. 20
peas, black-eyed	Feb. 15 - May 1	Feb. 15 - May 15	Mar. 1 - June 15	Mar. 10 - June 20	Mar. 15 - July 1	Apr. 1 - July 1	Apr. 15 - July 1
peppers¹	Feb. 15 - Apr. 15	Feb. 15 - Apr. 15	Mar. 1 - May 1	Mar. 15 - May 1	Apr. 1 - June 1	Apr. 10 - June 1	Apr. 15 - June 1
potatoes	Jan. 1 - Feb. 15	Jan. 1 - Feb. 15	Jan. 15 - Mar. 1	Jan. 15 - Mar. 1	Feb. 1 - Mar. 1	Feb. 10 - Mar. 15	Feb. 15 - Mar. 15
radishes	Jan. 1 - Apr. 1	Jan. 1 - Apr. 1	Jan. 1 - Apr. 1	Jan. 1 - Apr. 1	Jan. 1 - Apr. 15	Jan. 20 - May 1	Feb. 15 - May 1
rhubarb¹			do.	do.	do.	do.	do.
rutabagas¹		Jan. 1 - Feb. 10	Jan. 15 - Feb. 20	Jan. 15 - Mar. 1	Jan. 15 - Mar. 1	Jan. 15 - Mar. 15	Feb. 1 - Mar. 1
salsify	Jan. 1 - Feb. 1	Jan. 1 - Feb. 10	Jan. 15 - Feb. 20	Jan. 15 - Mar. 1	Feb. 15 - Mar. 1	Feb. 15 - Mar. 15	Mar. 1 - Mar. 15
shallots	do.	Jan. 1 - Feb. 10	Jan. 15 - Feb. 15	Jan. 1 - Mar. 1	Feb. 15 - Mar. 15	Feb. 10 - Mar. 10	Feb. 20 - Apr. 1
sorrel	Jan. 1 - Mar. 1	Jan. 1 - Mar. 1	Jan. 15 - Mar. 1	Feb. 1 - Mar. 1	Feb. 10 - Mar. 10	Feb. 10 - Mar. 10	Mar. 1 - Apr. 1
soybeans	Mar. 1 - June 30	Mar. 1 - June 30	Mar. 10 - June 30	Mar. 20 - June 30	Mar. 20 - June 30	Apr. 10 - June 30	Apr. 20 - June 30
spinach	Jan. 1 - Feb. 15	Jan. 1 - Feb. 15	Jan. 1 - Mar. 1	Jan. 1 - Mar. 1	Jan. 15 - Mar. 1	Feb. 1 - Mar. 1	Feb. 15 - Mar. 15
spinach, New Zealand	Feb. 1 - Apr. 15	Feb. 15 - Apr. 15	Mar. 1 - Apr. 15	Mar. 15 - May 15	Mar. 20 - May 15	Apr. 1 - May 20	Apr. 10 - June 1
squash, summer		Mar. 1 - Apr. 15	Mar. 10 - June 30	Mar. 15 - May 15	Mar. 20 - May 15	Apr. 1 - May 20	Apr. 10 - June 1
sweet potatoes¹	Feb. 15 - May 15	Mar. 1 - May 15	Mar. 20 - June 1	Mar. 20 - June 1	Apr. 1 - June 1	Apr. 10 - May 20	Apr. 20 - June 1
tomatoes¹	Feb. 1 - Apr. 1	Feb. 20 - Apr. 10	Mar. 1 - Apr. 20	Mar. 10 - May 1	Mar. 20 - May 10	Apr. 1 - May 20	Apr. 10 - June 1
turnips	Jan. 1 - Mar. 1	Jan. 1 - Mar. 1	Jan. 10 - Mar. 1	Jan. 20 - Mar. 1	Feb. 1 - Mar. 1	Feb. 10 - Mar. 10	Feb. 20 - Mar. 20

¹Plants planted in the fall only

Earliest Safe Planting Dates and Range of Spring-Planting Dates for Vegetables in the Open (continued)

Planting dates for localities with average last freeze on -

CROP	Apr. 10	Apr. 20	Apr. 30	May 10	May 20	May 30	June 10
asparagus[1]	Mar. 10 - Apr. 10	Mar. 15 - Apr. 15	Mar. 20 - Apr. 15	Apr. 10 - Apr. 30	Apr. 20 - May 15	May 1 - June 1	May 15 - June 1.
beans, lima	Apr. 15 - June 30	May 1 - June 20	May 15 - June 15	May 25 - June 15	May 15 - June 30	May 25 - June 15	
beans, snap[2]	Apr. 10 - June 30	Apr. 25 - June 30	May 10 - June 30	May 25 - June 30	May 15 - June 30	May 1 - June 15	May 15 - June 15.
beets	Mar. 10 - June 1	Mar. 20 - June 1	Apr. 1 - June 15	Apr. 15 - June 1	Apr. 25 - June 15	May 1 - June 15	May 20 - June 10.
broccoli, sprouting[1]	Mar. 15 - Apr. 15	Mar. 25 - Apr. 20	Apr. 1 - May 1	Apr. 15 - June 1	May 1 - June 15	May 1 - June 15	May 20 - June 10.
Brussels sprouts[1]	do.	do.	do.	do.	do.	Do.	Do.
cabbage[1]	Mar. 1 - Apr. 1	Mar. 10 - Apr. 1	Mar. 15 - Apr. 10	Apr. 1 - May 15	do.	May 10 - June 15	May 20 - June 1.
cabbage, Chinese			(²)	do.	do.	do.	Do.
carrots	Mar. (²) - Apr. 20	Apr. 1 - May 15	Apr. 10 - June 1	Apr. 20 - June 15	May 1 - June 1	May 10 - June 1	June 1 - June 15.
cauliflower[1]	Mar. 1 - Mar. 20	Mar. 15 - Apr. 20	Apr. 10 - May 10	Apr. 15 - May 15	May 10 - June 15	May 20 - June 1	Do.
celery and celeriac	Apr. 1 - June 20	Apr. 1 - May 1	Apr. 15 - May 1	Apr. 20 - June 1	do.	do.	June 1 - June 15.
chard	Mar. 15 - June 15	Apr. 1 - June 15	Apr. 15 - July 1	Apr. 15 - June 1	Apr. 15 - May 15	May 1 - 15	May 15 - June 1.
chervil and chives	Mar. 1 - Apr. 1	Mar. 1 - June 1	Mar. 20 - Apr. 20	Apr. 1 - May 1	June 1 - 15	June 1 - 15	May 15 - June 1.
chicory, witloof	June 10 - July 1	June 15 - July 1	June 15 - July 1	June 1 - 20	June 1 - 15	June 1 - 15	June 1 - 1-15.
collards[1]	Mar. 1 - June 1	Mar. 1 - June 1	Apr. 1 - June 1	Apr. 15 - June 1	Apr. 15 - June 1	May 10 - June 1	May 20 - June 1.
corn salad	Feb. 1 - Apr. 1	Feb. 15 - Apr. 15	Mar. 1 - June 1	Apr. 1 - June 1	Apr. 15 - June 1	May 20 - June 1	May 15 - June 15.
corn, sweet	Apr. 10 - June 1	Apr. 25 - June 15	May 10 - May 20	Apr. 20 - June 20	May 1 - June 1	May 15 - June 1	May 15 - June 15.
cress, upland	Apr. 20 - June 1	Mar. 20 - May 1	May 10 - May 20	May 20 - June 15	May 15 - May 15	May 15 - June 1	May 1 - 30.
cucumbers	Mar. 1 - Apr. 1	May 1 - June 15	May 20 - May 20	Apr. 1 - May 1	June 1 - 15	May 15 - June 1	May 1 - 30.
dandelion	Mar. 1 - Apr. 1	Mar. 20 - May 1	Mar. 20 - Apr. 20	Apr. 1 - May 1	Apr. 15 - May 15	May 1 - 30	May 15 - June 1.
eggplant[1]	May 1 - June 1	May 1 - June 1	May 15 - June 15	May 20 - June 1	June 1 - 15	May 1 - 30	Do.
endive	Mar. 15 - Apr. 15	Mar. 25 - Apr. 15	Apr. 1 - May 1	Apr. 15 - May 15	May 1 - 30	May 1 - 30	May 15 - June 1.
Florence fennel	do.	do.	do.	do.	do.	do.	Do.
garlic	Feb. 20 - Mar. 20	Mar. 10 - Apr. 1	Mar. 15 - Apr. 15	Apr. 15 - May 1	Apr. 15 - May 15	do.	Do.
horseradish[1]	Mar. 10 - Apr. 10	Mar. 20 - Apr. 20	Apr. 1 - 30	Apr. 15 - May 15	Apr. 20 - May 20	do.	Do.
kale	Mar. 10 - Apr. 1	Mar. 20 - May 10	Apr. 1 - 20	Apr. 10 - May 15	Apr. 20 - May 20	do.	Do.
kohlrabi	Mar. 10 - Apr. 10	Mar. 20 - May 1	Apr. 1 - May 10	Apr. 10 - May 15	Apr. 20 - May 20	do.	Do.
leeks	Mar. 1 - Apr. 1	Mar. 15 - Apr. 15	Apr. 1 - May 1	Apr. 15 - May 15	May 1 - May 20.	May 1 - 15	May 20 - June 30.
lettuce, head[1]	Mar. 10 - Apr. 1	Mar. 20 - Apr. 15	do.	do.	do.	do.	May 1 - 15.
lettuce, leaf	Mar. 15 - May 15	Mar. 20 - Apr. 15	Apr. 1 - June 1	Apr. 15 - June 15	May 1 - June 30	May 10 - June 30	May 20 - June 30.

Earliest Safe Planting Dates and Late Range of Planting Dates for Vegetables in the Open (cont.)

CROP	Apr. 10	Apr. 20	Apr. 30	May 10	May 20	May 30	June 10
				Planting dates for localities with average last freeze on -			
mustard	Mar. 10 - Apr. 20	Mar. 20 - May 1	Apr. 1 - May 10	Apr. 15 - June 1	...do...	...do...	Do.
okra	Apr. 20 - June 15	May 1	May 10 - June 1	May 20 - June 10	June 1 - 20	May 1 - 30	
onions[1]	Mar. 1 - Apr. 1	Mar. 15 - Apr. 10	Apr. 1 - May 1	Apr. 10 - May 1	Apr. 20 - May 15	May 1 - 30	May 10 - June 10.
onions, seed	...do...	Mar. 10 - Apr. 1	Mar. 15 - Apr. 15	Apr. 10 - May 1	...do...	...do...	Do.
onions, sets	...do...	Mar. 10 - Apr. 1	Mar. 15 - Apr. 10	Apr. 10 - May 1	...do...	...do...	Do.
parsley	Mar. 10 - Apr. 10	Mar. 20 - Apr. 20	Apr. 1 - May 1	Apr. 15 - May 15	May 10 - June 1	May 10 - June 1	May 20 - June 10.
parsnips	...do...	...do...	...do...	Apr. 1 - May 15	May 15 - June 1	...do...	Do.
peas, garden	Feb. 20 - Mar. 20	Mar. 10 - Apr. 10	Mar. 20 - May 1	Apr. 1 - May 15	Apr. 15 - June 1	May 1 - June 15	May 10 - June 15.
peas, black-eyed	May 1 - July 1	May 10 - June 15	May 15 - June 1	...do...			Do.
peppers[1]	May 1 - June 1	May 10 - June 1	May 15 - June 10	May 20 - June 10	May 25 - June 15	June 1 - 15	May 15 - June 1.
potatoes	Mar. 10 - Apr. 1	Mar. 10 - May 10	Mar. 20 - May 10	Apr. 1 - June 1	Apr. 15 - June 15	May 1 - June 15	Do.
radishes	Mar. 1 - May 1	Mar. 10 - May 10	Mar. 20 - May 10	...do...	...do...	...do...	Do.
rhubarb[1]	Mar. 1 - Apr. 1	Mar. 10 - Apr. 10	Mar. 20 - Apr. 15	Apr. 1 - May 1			Do.
salsify	Mar. 10 - Apr. 15	Mar. 20 - May 1	Mar. 20 - Apr. 15	Apr. 1 - May 1	Apr. 15 - May 10	May 10 - 20	May 20 - June 1.
shallots	Mar. 1 - Apr. 1	Mar. 15 - Apr. 15	Apr. 1 - May 15	Apr. 15 - May 15	May 1 - 20	May 10 - June 1	Do.
sorrel	Mar. 1 - Apr. 1	Mar. 15 - Apr. 15	Apr. 1 - May 15	Apr. 15 - June 1	Apr. 20 - June 10	May 10 - June 1	May 10 - June 1.
soybeans	May 1 - June 30	May 10 - June 20	May 15 - June 15	May 25 - June 10	Apr. 15 - May 10	May 10 - June 10	May 20 - June 10.
spinach	Feb. 15 - Apr. 1	Mar. 1 - Apr. 15	Mar. 20 - May 1	Apr. 1 - June 15	Apr. 10 - June 15	Apr. 20 - June 15	May 1 - June 15.
spinach, New Zealand	Apr. 20 - June 1	May 1 - June 15	May 1 - June 15	May 10 - June 10	May 20 - June 15	June 1 - 15	June 1 - 20.
squash, summer	...do...	...do...	May 1 - 30	May 10 - June 10	...do...	June 1 - 20	June 10 - 20.
sweet potatoes[1]	May 1 - June 1	May 10 - June 10	May 20 - June 10	May 15 - June 10	May 25 - June 15	June 5 - 20.	June 15 - 30.
tomatoes[1]	Apr. 20 - June 1	May 5 - June 10	May 10 - June 15	May 15 - June 10	May 25 - June 15	June 5 - 20	May 15 - June 15.
turnips[1]	Mar. 1 - Apr. 1	Mar.10 - Apr. 1	Mar. 20 - May 1	Apr. 1 - June 1	Apr. 15 - June 1	May 1 - June 15	May 15 - June 15.

[1]Plants   [2]Planted in fall only

Latest Safe Planting Dates and Late Range of Planting Dates for Vegetables in the Open

CROP	Aug. 30	Sept. 10	Sept. 20	Sept. 30	Oct. 10	Oct. 20
			Planting dates for localities with average last freeze on -			
asparagus[1]					Oct. 20 - Nov. 15	Nov. 1 - Dec. 15.
beans, lima				June 1 - 15	June 15 - July 15	June 15 - 30.
beans, snap			June 1 - July 1	June 1 - July 10	June 15 - July 20	July 1 - Aug. 1.
beets	May 15 - June 15	May 15 - June 15	May 1 - July 1	do.	June 15 - July 25	July 1 - Aug. 5.
broccoli, sprouting	May 1 - June 1	do.	do.	do.	June 15 - July 15	July 1 - Aug. 1.
Brussels sprouts	do.	do.	do.	do.	June 15 - July 15	do
cabbage[1]	do.	do.	May 1 - July 1	June 1 - July 10	June 1 - July 15	July 1 - 20.
cabbage, Chinese	May 15 - June 15	May 15 - June 15	do.	June 1 - July 10	June 15 - Aug. 1	July 15 - Aug. 15.
carrots	do.	do.	May 1 - July 1	June 1 - July 10	June 1 - July 20	June 15 - Aug. 1.
cauliflower[1]	May 1 - June 1	May 1 - July 1	May 15 - July 1	June 1 - July 10	June 1 - July 25	July 1 - Aug. 1.
celery and celeriac	do.	May 15 - June 15	May 15 - July 1	May 10 - July 15	June 1 - July 15	July 1 - Aug. 5.
chard	May 15 - June 15	May 15 - July 1	May 15 - July 1	June 1 - July 15	June 1 - July 20	June 1 - Aug. 1.
chervil and chives	May 10 - June 10	May 15 - June 15	May 15 - July 1	do.	(²)	do
chicory, witloof	May 15 - June 15	May 15 - June 15	May 15 - June 15	June 1 - July 1	June 1 - July 1	(²)
collards[1]	do.	May 15 - June 15	do.	June 15 - July 15	June 1 - July 1	June 15 - July 15.
corn salad	do.	May 15 - July 1	do.	July 15 - Sept. 1	Aug. 15 - Sept. 15	July 15 - Oct. 15.
corn, sweet	May 15 - June 15	May 15 - July 1	June 1 - Aug. 1	June 1 - July 1	June 1 - July 10	Sept. 1 - Oct. 15.
cress, upland	June 1 - 15	May 15 - July 1	June 1 - Aug. 1	July 15 - Sept. 1	Aug. 15 - Sept. 15	Sept. 1 - Oct. 15.
cucumbers		June 1 - July 1	June 1 - Aug. 1	June 1 - July 1	June 1 - July 1	June 1 - July 20.
dandelion	June 1 - July 1	June 1 - July 1	June 1 - 15	June 1 - Aug. 1	July 15 - Sept. 1	Sept. 1 - Oct. 15.
eggplant[1]	May 15 - June 15	May 15 - July 15	June 1 - July 1	May 20 - June 10	May 15 - June 15	June 1 - July 15.
endive	(²)	June 1 - July 1	June 15 - July 15	June 15 - Aug. 1	July 1 - Aug. 15	Aug. 1 - Sept. 15.
Florence fennel	May 15 - June 15	June 1 - July 1	June 1 - July 1	June 1 - July 1	July 1 - Aug. 1	Aug. 1 - Sept. 1.
garlic	do.		(²)	(²)	(²)	June 15 - July 1.
horseradish[1]	(²)	(²)	(²)	(²)	(²)	July 15 - Sept. 1.
kale	May 15 - June 15	May 15 - June 15	June 15 - July 1	June 15 - July 15	July 1 - Aug. 1	June 15 - Aug. 1.
kohlrabi	May 1 - June 1	June 1 - July 1	June 1 - July 15	do	do	July 15 - Aug. 15.
leeks	May 1 - June 1	May 1 - June 1	(²)	(²)	(²)	do
lettuce, head[1]	May 15 - July 1	May 15 - July 1	June 1 - July 15	June 15 - Aug. 1	July 15 - Aug. 15	Aug. 1 - 30.
lettuce, leaf	May 15 - July 15	May 15 - July 15	June 1 - Aug. 1	June 1 - Aug. 1	July 15 - Sept. 1	July 15 - Sept. 1.

Latest Safe Planting Dates and Late Range of Planting Dates for Vegetables in the Open (cont.)

CROP	Planting dates for localities with average last freeze on –					
	Aug. 30	Sept. 10	Sept. 20	Sept. 30	Oct. 10	Oct. 20
mustard	do	do	do	June 15 - Aug. 1	July 15 - Aug. 15	Aug. 1 - Sept. 1.
okra¹	May 10 - June 10	May 1 - June 1	June 1 - 20	(²)	June 1 - July 10	June 1 - Aug. 1.
onions¹	May 1 - June 1	do	(²)	(²)	(²)	(²)
onions, seed	May 1 - June 1	do	(²)	(²)	(²)	(²)
onions, sets	do	do	(²)	(²)	(²)	July 15 - Aug. 15.
parsley	May 15 - June 15	May 1 - June 15	June 1 - July 1	June 1 - July 1	June 15 - Aug. 1	July 15 - Aug. 15.
parsnips	May 15 - June 15				June 1 - July 1	June 1 - July 1.
peas, garden	May 10 - June 15	May 1 - July 1	May 20 - June 20	May 20 - June 10	May 20 - June 10	June 1 - July 1.
peas, black-eyed			June 1 - June 20	June 1 - July 1	do	June 1 - July 10.
peppers¹	May 15 - June 1	May 1 - June 15	June 1 - June 20	May 1 - June 15	May 15 - June 15	June 1 - July 1.
potatoes¹	May 1 - July 15	May 1 - Aug. 1	May 1 - Aug. 15	July 1 - Sept. 1	July 15 - Sept. 15	June 15 - July 15.
radishes	May 1 - Aug. 1	May 1 - Oct. 15	Sept. 15 - Nov. 1	Oct. 1 - Nov. 1	Oct. 15 - Nov. 15	Oct. 15 - Dec. 1.
rhubarb¹	Sept. 1 - Oct. 15	Sept. 15 - Oct. 15	Sept. 15 - Nov. 1	Oct. 1 - Nov. 1	Oct. 15 - Nov. 15	July 10 - 20.
rutabagas	May 15 - June 15	May 10 - June 10	May 20 - June 20	June 1 - 20	June 15 - July 15	June 1 - July 1.
salsify	May 15 - June 1		May 20 - June 20	June 1 - July 1	June 1 - July 1	(²)
shallots	(²)			(²)	(²)	July 15 - Aug. 15.
sorrel	May 15 - June 15	May 1 - June 15	June 1 - July 1	June 1 - July 15	July 1 - Aug. 1	June 1 - July 5.
soybeans	May 15 - July 1	June 1 - 20	June 1 - July 1	May 25 - June 10	June 1 - 25	Aug. 20 - Sept. 10.
spinach		June 1 - 20	June 1 - Aug. 1	July 1 - Sept. 1	Aug. 1 - Sept. 1	June 1 - July 20.
spinach, New Zealand	june 10 - 20		May 15 - July 1	May 15 - July 1	June 1 - July 15	June 1 - July 20.
squash, summer	June 1 - 20	June 1 - 20	May 15 - July 1	June 1 - July 1	June 1 - July 1	June 1 - 15.
squash, winter			May 20 - June 10	June 1 - 15	do	— 15.
sweet potatoes¹	June 20 - 30	June 10 - 20	June 1 - 20	june 1 - 20	May 20 - June 10	June 1 - July 1.
tomatoes¹	June 20 - 30	June 1 - July 1	June 1 - 20	June 1 - 20	June 1 - 20	June 1 - July 1.
turnips	May 15 - June 15	June 1 - July 1	June 1 - July 15	June 1 - Aug. 1	July 1 - Aug. 1	July 15 - Aug. 15.

¹Plants   ²Generally spring planted only

Latest Safe Planting Dates and Late Range of Planting Dates for Vegetables in the Open (continued)

CROP	Planting dates for localities with average last freeze on -					
	Oct. 30	Nov. 10	Nov. 20	Nov. 30	Dec. 10	Dec. 20
asparagus[1]	Nov. 15 - Jan. 1	Dec. 1 - Jan. 1	July 15 - Sept. 1	Aug. 1 - Sept. 15	Sept. 1 - 30	Sept. 1 - Oct. 1
beans, lima	July 1 - Aug. 15	July 1 - Aug. 15	July 1 - Sept. 10	Aug. 15 - Sept. 20	do	Sept. 1 - Nov. 1
beans, snap	July 1 - Sept. 1	July 1 - Sept. 1	July 1 - Sept. 1	Sept. 1 - Dec. 15	Sept. 1 - Dec. 31	Sept. 1 - Dec. 31
beets	Aug. 1 - Sept. 1	Aug. 1 - Oct. 1	Aug. 1 - Sept. 15	Aug. 1 - Oct. 1	Aug. 1 - Nov. 1	do
broccoli, sprouting	July 1 - Aug. 15	Aug. 1 - Sept. 1	do	do	do	do
Brussels sprouts	do	do	do	do	do	do
cabbage[1]	Aug. 1 - Sept. 1	Sept. 1 - 15	Sept. 1 - Dec. 1	Sept. 1 - Dec. 31	Sept. 1 - Dec. 31	Sept. 1 - Dec. 1
cabbage, Chinese	Aug. 1 - Sept. 15	Aug. 15 - Oct. 1	Sept. 1 - Oct. 15	Sept. 1 - Nov. 15	Sept. 1 - Nov. 15	Sept. 15 - Dec. 1
carrots	July 1 - Aug. 15	Aug. 1 - Sept. 1	Sept. 1 - Nov. 1	Sept. 15 - Dec. 1	Sept. 15 - Oct. 20	Sept. 15 - Nov. 1
cauliflower[1]	July 15 - Aug. 15	Aug. - Sept. 1	Aug. 1 - Sept. 15	Aug. 15 - Oct. 10	Sept. 1 - Dec. 31	Oct. 1 - Dec. 31
celery and celeriac	June 15 - Aug. 15	do	July 15 - Sept. 1	Aug. 1 - Dec. 1	Sept. 1 - Dec. 31	Oct. 1 - Dec. 31
chard	June 1 - Sept. 10	July 1 - Aug. 15	June 1 - Oct. 1	Aug. 1 - Nov. 1	June 1 - Dec. 31	June 1 - Dec. 31
chervil and chives	(²)	June 1 - Sept. 15	Nov. 1 - Dec. 31	Nov. 1 - Dec. 31.	Nov. 1 - Dec. 31	Nov. 1 - Dec. 31.
chicory, witloof	July 1 - Aug. 10	July 10 - Aug. 20	July 20 - Sept. 1	Aug. 15 - Sept. 30	Aug. 15 - Oct. 15	Aug. 15 - Oct. 15.
collards[1]	Aug. 1 - Sept. 15	Aug. 15 - Oct. 1	Aug. 25 - Nov. 1	Sept. 1 - Dec. 31	Oct. 1 - Dec. 31	Oct. 1 - Dec. 31.
corn salad	Sept. 15 - Nov. 1	Oct. 1 - Dec. 1	Oct. 1 - Dec. 1	Oct. 1 - Dec. 31	Oct. 1 - Dec. 31	Oct. 1 - Dec. 31.
corn, sweet	June 1 - Aug. 1	June 1 - Aug. 1	June 1 - Sept. 1	July 15 - Sept. 15	Oct. 1 - Dec. 31	Oct. 1 - Dec. 31.
cress, upland	Sept. 15 - Nov. 1	Oct. 1 - Dec. 1	Oct. 1 - Dec. 1	Sept. 15 - Dec. 15	Oct. 1 - Dec. 31	Aug. 15 - Oct. 1.
cucumbers	June 1 - Aug. 1	June 1 - Aug. 15	June 1 - Aug. 15	July 1 - Nov. 15	Aug. 1 - Sept. 30	Oct. 1 - Dec. 31.
dandelion	Aug. 15 - Oct. 1	Sept. 1 - Oct. 15	Sept. 1 - Nov. 1	Sept. 1 - Nov. 15	Oct. 1 - Dec. 31	Aug. 1 - Sept. 30.
eggplant[1]	June 1 - July 1	June 1 - July 15	June 1 - Aug. 1	do	Sept. 1 - Dec. 31	Sept. 1 - Dec. 1.
endive	July 15 - Aug. 15	Aug. 1 - Sept. 1	Sept. 1 - Oct. 1	Sept. 1 - Nov. 15	Sept. 1 - Dec. 31	Sept. 1 - Dec. 1.
Florence fennel	July 1 - Aug. 1	July 15 - Aug. 15	Sept. 1 - Sept. 15	Sept. 1 - Nov. 15	Sept. 15 - Nov. 15	Sept. 15 - Nov. 15.
garlic	(²)	Aug. 1 - Oct. 1	Aug. 15 - Sept. 15	Sept. 1 - Dec. 1	Sept. 1 - Dec. 31	Sept. 1 - Dec. 31.
horseradish[1]	(²)					do
kale	July 15 - Sept. 1	Aug. 1 - Sept. 15	Aug. 15 - Oct. 15	Sept. 1 - Dec. 1	Sept. 1 - Dec. 31	Sept. 1 - Dec. 31.
kohlrabi	Aug. 1 - Sept. 1	Aug. 15 - Sept. 15	Sept. 1 - Oct. 15	do	Sept. 15 - Dec. 31	do
leeks	(²)	(²)	Sept. 1 - Nov. 1	Sept. 1 - Nov. 1	Sept. 15 - Nov. 1	Sept. 15 - Nov. 1.
lettuce, head[1]	Aug. 1 - Sept. 15	Aug. 15 - Oct. 15	do	Sept. 1 - Dec. 1	Sept. 15 - Dec. 31	Sept. 15 - Dec. 31.
lettuce, leaf	Aug. 15 - Oct. 1	Aug. 25 - Oct. 1	do	do	do	do

Latest Safe Planting Dates and Late Range of Planting Dates for Vegetables in the Open (cont.)

CROP	Planting dates for localities with average last freeze on -					
	Oct. 30	Nov. 10	Nov. 20	Nov. 30	Dec. 10	Dec. 20
mustard	Aug. 15 - Oct. 15	Aug. 15 - Nov. 1	Sept. 1 - Dec. 1	do	Sept. 1 - Dec. 1	Sept. 15 - Dec. 1
okra	June 1 - Aug. 10	June 1 - Aug. 20	June 1 - Sept. 10	June 1 - Sept. 20	Aug. 1 - Oct. 1	Aug. 1 - Dec. 31
onions¹	(²)	(²)	Oct. 1 - Dec. 31	Oct. 1 - Dec. 31	Oct. 1 - Dec. 31	Oct. 1 - Dec. 31
onions, seed	(²)	(²)	Sept. 1 - Nov. 1	Sept. 1 - Nov. 1	Sept. 1 - Nov. 1	Sept. 15 - Nov. 1
onions, sets	(²)	Oct. 1 - Dec. 1	Nov. 1 - Dec. 31	Nov. 1 - Dec. 31	Nov. 1 - Dec. 31	Nov. 1 - Dec. 31
parsley	Aug. 1 - Sept. 15	Sept. 1 - Nov. 15	Sept. 1 - Dec. 31	Sept. 1 - Dec. 31	Sept. 15 - Dec. 31	Sept. 1 - Dec. 31
parsnips	(²)	(²)	Aug. 1 - Sept. 1	Sept. 1 - Dec. 1	Sept. 1 - Dec. 1	Sept. 1 - Dec. 1
peas, garden	Aug. 1 - Sept. 15	Sept. 1 - Nov. 1	Oct. 1 - Dec. 1	Oct. 1 - Dec. 31	Oct. 1 - Dec. 31	Oct. 1 - Dec. 31
peas, black-eyed	June 1 - Aug. 1	June 15 - Aug. 15	July 1 - Sept. 1	July 1 - Sept. 10	July 1 - Sept. 20	July 1 - Sept. 20
peppers¹	June 1 - July 20	June 1 - Aug. 1	June 1 - Aug. 15	June 15 - Sept. 1	Aug. 15 - Oct. 1	Aug. 15 - Sept. 15
potatoes	July 20 - Aug. 10	July 25 - Aug. 20	Aug. 10 - Sept. 15	Aug. 1 - Sept. 15	Aug. 1 - Sept. 15	Aug. 1 - Sept. 15
radishes	Aug. 15 - Oct. 15	Sept. 1 - Nov. 15	Sept. 1 - Dec. 1	Sept. 1 - Dec. 31	do	Oct. 1 - Dec. 31
rhubarb¹	Nov. 1 - Dec. 1					
rutabagas	July 15 - Aug. 1	July 15 - Aug. 15	Aug. 1 - Sept. 1	Sept. 1 - Nov. 15	Oct. 1 - Nov. 15	Oct. 15 - Nov. 15
salsify	June 1 - July 10	June 15 - July 20	July 15 - Aug. 15	Aug. 15 - Sept. 30	Aug. 15 - Oct. 15	Sept. 15 - Oct. 31
shallots	(²)	Aug. 15 - Oct. 1	Aug. 15 - Oct. 15	Aug. 15 - Nov. 15	Sept. 15 - Nov. 1	Sept. 15 - Nov. 1
sorrel	Aug. 1 - Sept. 15	Aug. 15 - Oct. 1	Aug. 15 - Oct. 15	Sept. 1 - Nov. 15	Sept. 1 - Dec. 15	Sept. 1 - Dec. 31
soybeans	June 1 - July 15	June 1 - July 25	June 1 - July 30	June 1 - July 30	June 1 - July 30	June 1 - July 30
spinach	Sept. 1 - Oct. 1	Sept. 15 - Nov. 1	Oct. 1 - Dec. 1	Oct. 1 - Dec. 31	Oct. 1 - Dec. 31	Oct. 1 - Dec. 31
spinach, New Zealand	June 1 - Aug. 1	June 1 - Aug. 15	June 1 - Aug. 15	June 1 - Sept. 1	June 1 - Sept. 15	June 1 - Oct. 1
squash, summer	do	June 1 - Aug. 10	June 1 - Aug. 20	July 15 - Aug. 15	June 1 - Sept. 15	Aug. 1 - Oct. 1
sweet potatoes¹	June 1 - July 10	June 20 - July 20	July 1 - Aug. 1	July 15 - Aug. 15	Aug. 1 - Sept. 1	Aug. 1 - Sept. 1
tomatoes¹	June 1 - 15	June 1 - July 1	July 1 - Aug. 1	June 1 - July 1	June 1 - July 1	June 1 - July 1
turnips	June 1 - July 1	June 1 - July 15	June 1 - Aug. 1	Aug. 1 - Sept. 1	Aug. 15 - Oct. 1	Sept. 1 - Nov. 1
	Aug. 1 - Sept. 15	Sept. 1 - Oct. 15	Sept. 1 - Nov. 15	Sept. 1 - Dec. 31	Oct. 1 - Dec. 1	Oct. 1 - Dec. 31

2. Seeding

Mark the corners of the garden with permanent stakes or pipes. Carefully set up a line for the first row and mark it out with your rake handle or the corner of the hoe. Keep this line handy and always use it for laying out rows for sowing seed or setting plants. The handle may open up a furrow sufficiently deep for small seeds. A deeper furrow can be made with a hoe or regular furrower for planting larger seed.

Straight rows in the garden may be obtained by stretching a string between stakes set up at the ends of the row. Stretch the string tight enough to lift it above the surface of the soil or it will not be straight.

Most vegetable seeds should be planted very shallow. The smaller seeds, such as lettuce and radishes, should not be planted more than ¼ inch deep. For such small seeds, the hoe or rake handle is an excellent tool for opening the shallow seed furrow. For the larger seeds, such as peas and beans, the proper depth is from ½ to 1 inch. Late plantings may be somewhat deeper than early plantings.

As a general rule, plant seeds somewhat less than the recommended depth if the soil is heavy or the temperature low, and a little deeper in light soil or during warm weather. Bear in mind that more than one vegetable can be planted in a row, if necessary, for frequent small sowings to insure a continuous supply of tender vegetables.

It seldom pays to use a seed planter in the backyard garden, as it will not handle small quantities of seed efficiently. Sow your seeds by hand—it is one of the most pleasurable experiences of gardening. Sow the seed thick enough to get an even stand. Too much seed is wasteful and means twice the work of thinning.

Sow the seed thinly by shaking it from a cut corner of the package or individually dropping the seeds from the fingers. Many gardeners waste seed and make extra work by sowing seed too thick. After seeding, the soil is drawn over the seed, using the corner of the hoe. In case the soil is somewhat cloddy, try to draw in the finer soil to cover the seed.

Sandy soils should be firmed above the seed in order to hasten germination. On heavy soils, where crusting is likely, packing of the soil above the seed increases the danger of crusting. On such soils, a shower or irrigation may be neces-

sary to facilitate germination, and crusts will be less severe
if the soil is not packed.

Late planted seeds sown during the summer may not germinate unless provisions are made to retain moisture. When
sowing late-seeded crops, water along the rows and cover
with a board or a light mulch. To water such seeds without
protection against evaporation usually will result in failure,
as the soil will dry rapidly, and the young seedlings die before
emerging. Uncover the rows when the first plants appear.

The question of how long seeds remain viable often arises.
This will depend greatly upon the particular vegetable involved as well as conditions under which the seed is stored.
Seed will retain viability much longer when stored under cool,
dry conditions as compared with storage that is warm and
moist.

Vegetable seeds may be divided into the following general
groups:

1. Comparatively short-lived, usually not good after 1 to 2
   years: sweet corn, leek, onion, parsley, parsnip, and
   salsify
2. Moderately long-lived, often good for 3 to 5 years under favorable conditions: asparagus, bean, Brussels
   sprouts, cabbage, carrot, cauliflower, celery, chicory,
   cress, endive, kale, kohlrabi, lettuce, okra, peas, pepper,
   radish, spinach, turnip, and watermelon
3. Comparatively long-lived under favorable conditions,
   may be good for more than 5 years: beets, cucumber,
   muskmelon, mustard, and tomato.

You can plant seeds in drills, in hills, or by broadcasting.
Following is a description of these three methods, prepared
by members of the Nevada Horticultural Department.

The drill method usually is the best. Using the corner of
the hoe, make a straight drill or trench down each row. It
should be deep enough to reach into moist ground. The seeds
then are dropped into the drill row by hand. Directions
usually are found on seed packages indicating the right depth.
It is not necessary to fill the drill with soil when covering
small seeds. Simply cover the seeds to the right depth and
leave the rest of the drill unfilled. Large seeds, such as peas
or beans, should be planted from 2 to 4 inches apart. Very
small seeds should be mixed with about 3 times their bulk of
dry sand so they will not fall too thickly. This is helpful

especially with such small seeds as those of turnips and carrots, which are lost easily out of the hand between the fingers. Seeds should be covered with fine, moist soil, which should be firmly pressed down over the seeds with the back of the hoe. This prevents drying out around the seeds.

Hills frequently are used for plants that spread on the ground. A hole about a foot across and a foot deep is made and a 4- to 6-inch layer of *well rotted* manure is put in the bottom of the hole. Don't use fresh manure, since it injures the plants. The manure is covered wtih 4 to 6 inches of fine soil, packed down, and the seeds are planted in it. Hills are used because they afford a convenient way to give the plants food material, and because one may know where the roots are after the vines have covered the ground. The distance apart to make the hills will depend upon the size of the vines. Hills for vine squash or pumpkins may be 8 to 12 feet apart, while cucumber hills may be only 3 to 6 feet apart. Unless extra fertilizer is used under the hills, there is little advantage to the hill method. Corn usually is planted in hills because of convenience in planting and because it saves the labor of making a drill.

When the broadcasting method is used, the seeds are scattered thinly over the top of the soil and are then covered by light raking and packing with the back of a hoe. The seedbed should be well prepared first. This method is used with many small seeds, such as those of turnips, lettuce, etc. It is well adapted to use in small vegetable gardens where the sprinkling method of irrigation is to be used. It eliminates the need for irrigation furrows. It makes hand weeding necessary because the plants are not in rows and cannot be cultivated with power equipment or tools.

3. Thinning

Most gardeners sow too much seed. Consequently, plants are too close if seed has good germination. The natural tendency is to seed crops like beets, carrots, radishes, lettuce, turnips, and endive too thickly. This is because it is difficult to sow small seeds thinly enough to eliminate hand thinning, says E. C. Wittmeyer, Ohio State University extension horticulturist. Beet seeds, for example, are actually fruits containing several seeds. If root crops are not thinned, poorly shaped roots will result.

The easiest time to do the thinning job is when the plants are small and the soil is moist. Turnips should be thinned before their taproots become fleshy. They need 3 inches between plants for best development. Radishes, on the other hand, can be left in the ground until those that are to be thinned are large enough to eat unless they have been seeded very thickly. If this is the situation, thinning should be done early.

Surplus beet plants can be pulled when they are 4 to 5 inches tall and used for greens. Beets should have 3 inches between plants. Carrots should be thinned early and allowed to stand 1 inch apart. Later alternate carrots can be pulled and used.

Lettuce, Swiss chard, endive, kohlrabi, and similar crops also may need thinning. With lettuce, however, thinning at harvest will help produce high quality lettuce for a long time.

Here are some general rules regarding thinning:

1. Thinning should be done while plants are small and when the soil is moist, so they can be pulled out easily without injuring those that are left.

2. Root crops should be thinned before their taproots become fleshy. Onions from seeds, and radishes can be left in the ground until those that are thinned out are large enough to eat.

3. Carrots should be thinned first when they are 2 to 3 inches tall, so as to stand about 1 inch apart. They can then be left to develop until large enough to be eaten, when alternate plants can be pulled and used, leaving more room for those that are left.

4. Swiss chard can be thinned at first to 3 inches, then, as plants develop, harvest alternate ones. Cucumbers and melons should be thinned to 2 or 3 plants per hill or to stand 12 to 15 inches apart in the row.

5. Thinning is rarely practiced with beans, peas, corn, and some other large-seeded plants which produce vigorous seedlings, for a good stand usually is obtained by planting only a few more seeds than the number of plants required.

4. Transplanting Vegetables

The few minutes spent transplanting are the most important minutes in the life of the plant.

Some plants are more resistant to shock than others, but all react to some degree. Among the easiest plants to transplant are broccoli, cabbage, cauliflower, lettuce, and onions. Some loss may be expected with beans, eggplant, peppers, tomatoes, and celery. Among the very difficult to transplant successfully are carrots, corn, cucumber, melons, squash, and all other plants with taproots.

The idea in transplanting, of course, is to lessen the shock as much as possible. The plant is an amazingly well integrated mechanism in which each function of each cell is interdependent on the actions of other cells. Water and soil materials are moving constantly through the roots, stems, and leaves, feeding the cells of the leaves which manufacture the plant food. When transplanted, some of the vital roots and tiny root hairs are almost always torn away, the entire water chain system may be disrupted, and changed light conditions and temperature may disrupt other normal plant functions. It's up to you to help the seedling make as smooth an adjustment as possible.

If possible, try to transplant on a cloudy, moist day, when light and heat shock will be small. Before beginning to transplant, loosen soil in the new location, and about an hour or two before removing seedlings, thoroughly water soil in the flats to make loosening roots easier.

When taking up seedlings, take plenty of soil along. Some root damage is almost inevitable, but it can be kept to a minimum by special care in handling. Root damage can be virtually eliminated by use of special little containers made of dried manure. The seedling is usually placed in the container —or the seed is germinated therein—and when ready, the entire container is set into the soil. This method not only lessens transplanting shock, but also preserves roots intact and provides an initial stimulus for developing roots.

When making the final transplant, make sure roots are in good firm contact with the soil. A great deal depends on this, as roots depend on firm contact for absorption of essential soil ingredients. After the transplant, water well and shade seedlings for a few days; if the weather is hot and sunny, keep them shaded for as long as a week.

If tender seedlings were to be transplanted from indoor flats directly into the open ground, the inevitable result would be serious injury, often fatal. Therefore, to lessen the shock of temperature, wind, and sun, a hardening-off process is used, in which seedlings are gradually exposed to the natural elements.

Usually, the hardening-off process takes about 2 weeks, and should be timed so that the young seedlings end the 2 weeks in a period warm enough for them to be planted outside safely. The best way to harden off seedlings (or cuttings, for that matter) is to move them, flats and all, from their indoor location to the cold frame. (The cold frame should be an essential piece of equipment for any gardener. It is inexpensive, not difficult to construct, and provides a perfect medium for the hardening-off process.)

The frame should be closed for the first 2 days of the period. On the third day, the top should be opened just a crack, and over the remainder of the period, the air space should be widened more each day until, on the last day, the top is removed.

If you haven't gotten around to constructing a cold frame, you can use your imagination to stimulate the same conditions it provides. On the first day of the period, place flats outside for only a few minutes during the warmer part of the afternoon. Cover them with a burlap screen or preferably something more closely knit and place flats in a sheltered place. Then, gradually expose them more each day until the process is completed.

There have been scores of gadgets, most of which work pretty well, marketed to protect seedlings during the hardening-off process. In England, most popular are cloches—little glass tents—which are set over seedlings planted in open ground. In America, bell jars and various other similar coverings are used for the same purpose. The cloche idea allows you to place seedlings in permanent location one step sooner, cutting out the last transplanting which is the most dangerous to growing roots. And, if a late unexpected frost is announced during an afternoon, you can save your seedlings by setting up the protectors again.

If plant protectors made of plastic, waxed paper, etc., are used to cover plants when first set out, hardening off is not as important. Also, you'll be able to plant earlier. Tomato and strawberry baskets, as well as glass cloches are effective in shielding plants from sun or windburn. You can place them to cover the plants entirely or tilt them to allow air to circulate underneath.

To support the plastic or other cover material, gardeners often use such a variety of materials as branches (bent back with both ends in the ground), metal coat hangers, or a "stand" that can be purchased along with a plastic cover.

Tennessee University experimenters have found hill covers made of paper cloth are good for melons, cucumbers, squashes, and even tomatoes. They were able to plant seeds 2 weeks earlier than would be ordinarily safe in open ground; the covers also kept insects away for a longer time.

Cloth covers can be made of squares of cheese cloth, supported on 2 or 3 arches made from wire or pieces of veneer wood out of old baskets. The ends of these are stuck in the ground 2 inches deep. Cover cloth edges with soil. Since the edges decay in 3 or 4 weeks, the cloth as well as the paper covers cannot be used again.

About a week before it is safe to have plants in the open air uncovered, cut or tear open the paper cover tops for ventilation. The usual practice is to cut a slit on the south side first, then later enlarge the hole. If the plants grow through the holes, it's all right to leave the cover in place. Here are a list of points to remember when using plant covers:

1. Use early varieties of vegetables for planting under covers since your objective is to harvest as soon as possible.
2. Cabbage, onions, and other hardy crops will not be helped very much by covers.
3. A garden that has rather sandy or "early" soil that is protected from strong winds and perhaps slopes to the southeast, would be the very best place to use hill covers. Clay soil in a naturally cold spot, would seldom produce profitable gains from use of hill covers.

Some Basic
Vegetable—Growing Advice

1. Tables for Rotation Planting—Getting the Most from the Space Available

Plants Occupying the Ground All of the Growing Season

PERENNIAL

asparagus
chives
horseradish

onion, perennial
rhubarb

ANNUAL

beans, pole, snap
beans, pole, lima
chard, Swiss
cucumbers
eggplant
muskmelon
okra
onions
parsley
parsnip

peppers
potatoes, Irish late
potatoes, sweet
pumpkins
salsify
spinach, New Zealand
squash, winter
tomatoes
watermelons

Plants Occupying Ground Part of Season May be Followed by Others

beans, bush
beets

lettuce
mustard

cabbage
cabbage, Chinese
carrots
cauliflower
corn, early
kale
kohlrabi

onions, green
peas
potatoes, early
radish
rutabaga, spring
spinach
turnip, spring

Plants Which May Follow Others

beans, bush
beets
cabbage
cabbage, Chinese
carrots
celery
corn
kale

lettuce
mustard
potatoes, late
radish
rutabaga, fall
spinach
turnips, fall

Plants which May be Utilized in Interplanting
Early, Quick Maturing, Narrow Spaced

beans, bush
beets, early
carrots, early
lettuce
mustard

onions, sets
peas, early
radish
spinach

Later, Slower-growing, Wider-spaced Plants

broccoli
Brussels sprouts
cabbage
corn
cucumbers
muskmelons

pumpkins
spinach, New Zealand
squash
tomatoes
watermelons

Plants which May be Planted Together in the same row
Quick Germinating and Maturing

lettuce, leaf
mustard

radish
spinach

Slower Germinating and Maturing Plants

beets
carrots
chard
leek
parsley

parsnips
salsify
spinach, New Zealand
onions, seed

Plants which Can be Cut More Than Once

asparagus	mustard
chard	parsley
cress	rhubarb
kale	spinach, New Zealand

Plants of which Only a Few Are Needed for Average Family

asparagus	parsley
chard	peppers
herbs, various	rhubarb
horseradish	

Plants which Can be Staked or Trellised

beans, pole, snap	pumpkins
beans, pole, lima	squash
cucumber	tomatoes
muskmelon	watermelons
peas, pole	

Sun-Loving Plants

corn	pumpkins
cucumbers	squash
eggplant	tomatoes
muskmelon	watermelons
peppers	

Shade-Loving Plants

Lettuce is a cool weather crop and will thrive in partial shade.

Garden peas will thrive in partial shade.

Cucumbers require a cool, moist, even slightly shaded location.

Kohlrabi must be well drained, not overly exposed to excessive sunlight.

Scallions will tolerate a slight amount of shade but prefer open, moist, sunny conditions.

Mint will grow, if much moisture and a little shade is available, even on lawns.

2. Asparagus

Soil—Rich, deep loam, preferably free from stones.

Location—Asparagus should be planted along one side of the garden where its continued existence does not interfere with the cultivation of the garden.

Fertilizer—Just as soon as it is possible to work the ground, a heavy application of lime should be made over a 2-foot-wide strip along each side of the rows. This should be well raked into the surface. An inch deep layer of compost humus should then be well worked in over the same area. Well rotted manure should be substituted but not raw manure.

Soil type—Asparagus is rank growing, it demands an adequate supply of lime to assist in making available needed plant nutrients.

Depth of planting—Seed: ½″; Roots: 10″.

Width apart in the row—18″.

Distance between rows—5 feet.

How much seed—1 ounce of seed for 100 feet of row, 70 plants for 100 feet of row.

Planting instructions—Seed: Seed should be planted very early in the spring. When the roots are 1 or 2 years old, they should be transplanted to a permanent location. Plants: Dig a trench along the side of the garden about 2 feet from its edge. This trench should be 14″ wide and 14″ deep. In the bottom of the trench, place a 1″ layer of crushed limestone, and dig this material into the subsoil. Then place mature compost humus to bring the bottom of the trench to within 10″ of the surface. Water thoroughly and set the roots 18″ apart. Then fill the trench with compost humus and firm.

Date of planting—April–May.

Types—Martha Washington, rust resistant; Mary Washington, a light cropping can be secured from 2-year-old plants the same season.

Harvesting—When the shoots begin to grow, a ridge of mature compost humus should be drawn up toward them. For a period of about 2 weeks in the spring, the shoots may be harvested. After that, cutting should be discontinued and the plants permitted to bolt and flower.

The first winter, the rows should be well mulched with straw, etc., for protection. The following spring, this protection may be removed, and the ground well raked. The shoots may then be harvested from early spring until midsummer.

Yield—100 feet of row will yield about 30 pounds of shoots.

Note—Asparagus plants drive roots 4 feet down. If the surface of the ground is given a light dusting of salt, surface weeds will be kept under control without damage to the plants.

3. Beets

Soil—Loose, fresh, clean, and slightly sandy.

Location—Beets require an open well drained site, free from shade.

Fertilizers—Plenty of mature compost humus should have been dug in before planting. Because the taproot of the beet will penetrate several feet, plant nutrients placed near the surface are often of little value. Well rotted manure may be dug in, but the ground should be deeply dug and well prepared.

Soil—Acid or Alkaline: Beets are used as an indicator for the acidity of the soil. They will not tolerate a very acid soil. It is best, then, to use limestone very liberally. If crushed limestone is not available, a 2″ layer of hydrated lime should be deeply dug into the soil before planting time.

Depth of planting—Early: 1″; Late: 2″.

Width apart in the row—4″–6″.

Distance between rows—12″–15″.

How much seed—1 ounce of seed will plant 50 feet of row.

Planting instructions—Beet seed should be soaked for 24 hours in compost water, that is water which has been poured into a container holding a quantity of sifted compost humus and allowed to stand over night. Necessary because beet seed, as sold, is a small dried fruit containing real seeds.

Watering—After planting, the seed should be adequately watered to insure germination. If necessary during dry weather, burlap or boards may be placed above the planted seed to prevent the soil from drying out. These should be removed just as soon as there are signs of the growing seeds.

Date of planting—Early: March–April; Late: April–June.

Succession planting—Early beets may be followed by late broccoli, cabbage, etc.

Thinning—Plants removed in thinning may be used to form new rows in the garden. If the young beets which are pulled at thinning are fairly well matured, they are also very valuable for kitchen use, the small roots and the leaves being cooked complete.

Types—Early: Red Ball, 60 days to maturity; Egyptian: 53 days to maturity. Late: Detroit Dark Red, 59 days to maturity; Winter Keeper, 80 days to maturity.

Harvesting—Early beets are usually gathered and used at or before maturity. Winter storage types are allowed to remain until just before the arrival of the first fall frosts.

Storage—After the beets are gathered, the tops are removed allowing about an inch of the stalks to remain; take care not to break the skin. The roots can then be removed for storage to a root cellar, or they may be stored in pits as explained under "White Potatoes."

Yield—100 feet of row should yield about 2 bushels.

4. Broccoli

Soil—Rich, moist, friable loam.

Location—Cool, well drained, open.

Fertilizer—Early broccoli: About a pound of sifted compost humus should be placed around the roots of the plants when setting them out. Late broccoli: Along the line where the row is to stand, form a trench about 3″ deep and fill this trench with a 50–50 mixture of sifted topsoil and mature compost humus. If manure has to be substituted, it should be well rotted. Raw manure should be used only if dug in the previous fall.

Soil type—Broccoli will mature satisfactorily only if grown in soil rich in natural calcium. If a layer ½″ deep of crushed limestone can be applied the fall before planting, so much the better. Hydrated lime may be applied liberally in the early spring and well raked into the surface.

Depth of planting—Seed: ½"; Plants: 3".

Width apart in the row—Early: 18"; Late: 24"–36".

Distance between rows—Early: 24"; Late: 24"–36".

How much seed—Early: 35 plants for 50 feet of row; Late: 40 seeds for 50 feet of row.

Planting instructions—The young broccoli plants should be carefully set out in holes dug large enough to admit the supply of sifted compost humus and still have enough room for the roots to be well spread out. Water thoroughly and firm well. Transplants should be given temporary shade by the use of inverted boxes, baskets, etc., if the weather is very hot.

Watering—Broccoli requires plenty of moisture for its successful growth. This is best supplied during dry spells by placing the hose on the ground in the evening and thoroughly soaking the ground for several hours. The plants respond to mulching during hot weather.

Date of planting—Early: March–April; Late: April–May.

Succession planting—Broccoli, may be planted to fill areas in which early garden peas, etc., have been grown.

Companion cropping—Broccoli plants may be set out in rows of low growing vegetables such as onions, carrots, etc.

Thinning—When broccoli is seeded directly into the garden it is often best to seed rather quickly and later thin to 18" to 24" in the row. This should be done after the seedlings have attained several leaves. The seedlings should be protected from drying out from the direct action of sunlight on the roots, and may be used to form other rows.

Types—Early: Propageno, 80 days to mature; Late: Calabrese, 85 days to maturity.

Harvesting—Broccoli has a central head and several side heads. When some of these are gathered, the plant forms many more small edible clusters. Like chard, where the side leaves are gathered, the flower clusters of broccoli should be cut as needed in the kitchen and the plant left to form more edible clusters.

Yield—45 medium-sized heads for 100 feet of row.

Note—Broccoli is much easier to grow than cauliflower. It is almost as satisfactory as a kitchen delicacy.

5. Cabbage

Soil—Rich, moist, friable loam.

Location—Cool, moist, well drained.

Fertilizer—About a pound of mature compost humus should be placed around the roots of the plants when setting them out. Raw manure should be dug in as long as possible before planting. Well rotted manure is better.

Soil Type—Cabbages thrive only on soil which has its full quota of natural calcium. Use lime as liberally as possible. After the ground has been dug, the lime should be spread and well raked into the surface.

Depth of planting—Seed: ½"; Plants: 3".

Width apart in the row—Early cabbage: 15" to 18"; Late cabbage: 18" to 24".

Distance between rows—30".

How much seed—¼ ounce (10¢ packet) for 100 feet of row.

Number of plants needed—Early: 70 plants per 100 feet of row; Late: 60 plants per 100 feet of row.

Planting instructions—Cabbage plants should be carefully set out in holes wide enough to spread the roots. Enough water should be applied to insure proper contact between rootlets and soil. After setting, the soil should be well firmed. Late cabbage plants should be protected against the summer sun by inverted baskets, paper bags, etc.

Watering—Growing cabbages are gross feeders. They need drenching moisture during dry spells to insure rapid growth and fine flavor.

Dates of planting—Early varieties: April-May 15: Late varieties: June 15–July 30.

Succession planting—Late cabbages may be planted to follow early peas, sweet corn, etc.

Companion cropping—Cabbage plants may be set between rows of early radishes, lettuce, etc., or in the same rows for later harvesting.

Types—Early: Golden Acre (Yellows Resistant), 64 days to maturity; Late: Danish Roundhead, 105 days to maturity.

Harvesting—Early cabbage may be cut as needed. Late cabbage should be allowed to stand until cured by the first fall frosts.

Storage—In a trench 2' wide and 6" deep, which has been lined with a few inches of straw or dry weeds, place sound heads, roots up. Cover them with a few inches of straw, or similar material. Over this place a 6" layer of topsoil.

Another method is to quarter and shred the heads. Place them in a sterilized container made of wood or crockery. A handful of salt should be spread and pressed by hand into every 4" layer of shredded cabbage. When the container is filled it should be covered with a clean piece of muslin. The material should be allowed to ferment for a period of 6 weeks, after which it will be available for kitchen use as sauerkraut.

Yield—Early: 100 pounds to 100 foot of row; Late: 175 pounds to 100 foot of row.

Note—Cabbage plants benefit by a sprinkling of salt water before they form heads. The salt water hinders the growth of cabbage caterpillars.

6. Cantaloupes (Muskmelons)

Soil—Light, rich, fertile, warm.

Location—Sunny, well drained, preferably where considerable humus is found mixed with sandy soil.

Fertilizer—Whether planting in hills or rows, a liberal supply of mature compost humus should be provided. If the supply of compost humus is insufficient, well rotted manure may be substituted. Raw manure should be avoided.

Soil type—Cantaloupes will not tolerate a heavy, acid soil. Even though a light soil may be slightly acid, they will thrive.

Depth of planting—½".

Width apart in the row—14".

Distance between hills—60" apart each way (3 seeds to a hill). The hills should be 60" apart in the row, and the rows of hills 60" apart.

Distance between rows—60".

How much seed—½ ounce of seed for 100 feet of row.

Planting instructions—Rows: Dig a trench 1 foot deep, fill with sifted compost humus, cover lightly with top soil. Plant the seed 9" apart, cover with ½" of sifted compost humus, water and firm. Hills: Dig a hole 18" deep and 24" wide. Fill the holes full of sifted, mature compost humus, water. Then cover lightly with topsoil, place the seed and cover with ½" of sifted compost humus, water again and firm.

Watering—Cantaloupes contain a very large percentage of water, both in the fruit and in the vine. Plenty of water is urgently needed for their proper growth. This supply is best given them by placing the hose on the ground and allowing the water issuing from it to flood them late in the day.

Date of planting—Seed should not be sown before the ground has warmed up, usually about the middle of May.

Companion cropping—Although cantaloupes, because of the extensive growth of their vines, require much ground space, they may be successfully grown with plantings of sweet corn, much as pumpkins and squashes are grown.

Thinning—Plants should be thinned to stand 14" apart in the row, and not more than 3 plants should be permitted to each hill. It is best to wait until the seedlings are about 4" high before thinning. If this is done, the stockiest may be easily left and the spindling and the weak seedlings removed.

Types—Netted Gem (Green Flesh), 85 days to maturity; Hale's Best (Orange Flesh), 88 days to maturity; Hearts of Gold (Salmon Flesh), 90 days to maturity.

Harvesting—To determine whether a cantaloupe is ripe and fit for picking, a little pressure of the thumb upon the stem where it joins the fruit should be applied. If the stem parts readily from the fruit, the fruit is fit for harvesting. If considerable pressure is necessary, the fruit is still unripe.

Yield—100 feet of row should yield 60 cantaloupes.

7. Carrots

Soil—Well prepared, fertile loam, preferably one rich and sandy.

Location—Open, sunny, well drained.

Fertilizer—Carrots require an abundance of well broken down material. A 2″ layer of mature compost humus should be placed along the line where the row is to stand before the shallow trench is formed. Avoid the use of raw manures. These burn off the first root of the seed so that, forked, valueless carrots result.

Soil type—Carrots succeed in almost any reasonably good garden soil. However, it should be well dug and pulverized and free from stones. The generous addition of compost humus will do much to improve its condition.

Depth of planking—¼″. Carrot seed is very fine. One ounce should be mixed with a teacupful of dry, well sifted compost humus and this mixture planted.

Width apart in the row—3″ to 4″.

Distance between rows—12″.

How much seed—1 ounce of seed for 100 feet of row.

Watering—Root crops require adequate moisture for their proper growth. During dry spells, it is best to supply this water by placing the hose on the ground and flooding the area.

Dates of planting—Early: March–April, Late: April–May.

Succession planting—Carrots may be planted between rows of lettuce, radishes, etc.

Companion cropping—In the rows of carrots, it is very practicable to set plants of cabbage, Brussels sprouts, even staked tomato plants, with the earliest and latest dates for planting being April 1 and July 1.

Thinning—Carrots should be seeded rather thickly and thinned when they have attained the size of a man's thumb. The young roots are then of great value as a kitchen delicacy.

Types—Imperator and Chantenay (coreless), 75 days to maturity; Nantes and Danvers, 70 days to maturity.

Harvesting—Carrots should be dug in the fall shortly after the first fall frosts. The tops should be removed.

Storage—Dig a hole about a foot deep in a well drained spot. Place an apple box in this hole and in its place a couple of inches of straw or dried weeds. Fill the box with sound carrots and place a 6″ layer of straw upon them. Then invert another box over the first and cover the structure with about a foot of dry weeds. Over this place a layer of topsoil, 6″ deep. Smooth this with the shovel to form a steeply sloping roof. Several of these small pits are more convenient than one large one.

Yield—100 pounds to 100 feet of row.

8. Cauliflower

Soil—Rich, moist loam.

Location—Open, well drained, free from shade.

Fertilizer—Cauliflowers require a plentiful supply of organic matter. Fertile humus may be supplied by adding a heavy layer of compost humus along the lines where the plants are to stand. This should be lightly dug in. Well rotted manure may also be added if necessary. Raw manure, if used, should be dug in the previous year.

Soil type—Soil even slightly lacking in its natural amount of calcium should be corrected by the addition of crushed limestone the season before planting. If this is not possible, hydrated lime–100 pounds to 1,000 square feet of garden space–should be applied and well raked into the surface as early as possible.

Depth of planting—Seed: ¼″; Plants: Slightly deeper than they stood in the seed bed.

Width apart in the row—20″.

Distance beween rows—30″.

How much seed—A packet of seeds will produce enough plants to fill 100 feet of row.

Planting instructions—Because cauliflower is a coolweather crop, the seed should be sown very early in the spring in flats in the house, or during the summer in the open. When the plants are about 5 weeks old, they should be transplanted to their permanent location. In moving the seedlings, leave a ball of earth around the roots. Avoid disturbing the roots. A good plan is to run a knife around the plant, and prepare to remove the plant a week before it is moved. This will cut the extensive, spreading roots and cause the formation of a new bunch of root hairs at the base of the plant.

Watering—Cauliflowers are rapid growers and demand abundance of plant food and the moisture to make this food available. Seedlings, when transplanted, should be watered liberally and the roots shaded and kept from drying out. They should be well watered and shaded after a planting by the use of inverted baskets, etc. During its whole life, the plant should not be permitted to suffer from lack of water, this is especially important during the week or so that is required for the plant to form its flower, the edible head. Place the hose on the ground and flood the area thoroughly each evening during dry spells.

Date of planting—For spring crop, plant seed in flats in the house during March. For fall crop, plant seed in open during June or July. Transplant when the plants are 6″ tall.

Succession planting—Late cauliflower may be planted to follow early lettuce, radishes, etc.

Companion cropping—Onions may be planted in the same rows with the cauliflower, or some other low-growing vegetable such as carrots, etc.

Types—Ideal Snowball, 90 days to maturity; Danamerica, 85 days to maturity.

Harvesting—When examination shows the formation of a small flower head, the surrounding leaves of the plant should be promptly bent and tied over it to darken it. About a week after the leaves have been tied over it, the head should be developed and ready for cutting.

Storage—Fall cauliflower may be held for about a month by pulling the entire plant and placing it in a cold outhouse or vegetable cellar. It will stand moderate freezing.

Yield—100 feet of row should yield about 50 heads.

Note—There are varieties of the Cauliflower-broccoli type which are very useful and which form large heads: St. Valentines, 150 days to maturity.

9. Celery

Soil—Very fertile with an abundant moisture.

Location—Level, well drained, and open.

Fertilizer—Celery requires an abundance of plant food and the moisture to make this material available. Compost humus should be dug into the soil to a depth of about 14″. This is best done by digging a trench about a foot deep, afterward removing several inches of the soil at the bottom of the trench and replacing it with sifted compost humus. Well rotted manure may be used in a 50–50 mixture with compost humus if necessary.

Soil type—Celery will not thrive in a very acid soil. It is necessary, on very rich muck soils to correct this acidity by the application of large quantities of crushed limestone.

Depth of planting—Seed: Cover with a thin sprinkling of washed sand; Plants: Not deeper than the plants stood before being transplanted.

Width apart in the row—6″.

Distance between rows—28″.

How much seed—One packet of seed will produce enough plants for 100 feet of row.

Planting instructions—Plant the seed thinly as soon as the ground can be worked. Transplant the seedlings into specially prepared and heavily composted ground early in July.

Watering—Just as soon as the seedlings are transplanted, they should be given a thorough soaking, and a steady supply of moisture should insure the rapid, early growth.

Special care—When the plants begin to mature, the stalks may be blanched, and larger, crisper heads produced by placing boards about 12″ wide on each side of the plants to cover all except about 6″ of the leafy tops. Blanching should be complete in 10 days. Much celery is produced without blanching. It is probable that the green stalks have much greater food value than the blanched material.

Date of planting—Seed in open: March-April, Transplants: July.

Types—Golden Plume, 115 days from setting out of plants to maturity; Utah, 130 days from setting out of plants to maturity.

Harvesting—When the plants are about ⅔ mature, they may be harvested as required.

Storage—Celery may be stored in the ground where it grew by placing the blanching boards along the rows and covering the plants with a good layer of dry straw, weeds, etc., followed by a 6" layer of topsoil. If sufficient winter protection is given in this way, the plants will be available until after New Year's Day. If a small number of roots are to be stored, they may be dug with plenty of soil around the roots and replanted closely in boxes. These boxes may be placed in an unheated building. The roots should be kept moist to prevent drying out.

Yield—100 feet of row should yield about 200 plants.

Note—Celeriac, or root celery, is grown much like ordinary celery except that its leaves have no food value. Instead, it produces a turnip shaped, celeryflavored root, high in food value and used extensively as a flavoring.

10. Chinese Cabbage

Soil—Rich, moist loam.

Location—Open, temperate, with a tendency toward coolness, as on the northern slope of a slight elevation.

Fertilizer—Chinese cabbage requires an abundance of available plant food, the moisture to make the food easily assimilated, and coolness, if the soil is reasonably rich, a 3" layer of mature compost humus should be lightly dug in along the line where the rows are to stand. If necessary, well rotted manure may be substituted using a 6" layer.

Soil type—A reasonable amount of lime, if this material is available, should be well raked into the soils known to be acid. A better plan is to lay down about a ½" layer of crushed limestone, and dig this in the season before.

Depth of planting—½".

Width apart in the row—16".

Distance between rows—30".

How much seed—One packet of good grade seed will plant a 100 ft. row.

Planning instructions—Using a guideline, form a trench about 1" deep with the corner of the hoe. Fill this trench about half full with sifted compost humus. Place the seeds carefully, about 6″ apart, and cover with more sifted compost. Water well and firm.

Watering—Chinese cabbage requires an abundance of moisture as well as coolness and plant food. This is most easily supplied by giving the area where the plants grow a thorough drenching every evening during hot weather. This is especially necessary for summer-planted seed which is to mature during the fall.

Date of planting—In the vicinity of Philadelphia, Chinese cabbage is usually planted early in August to mature a full fall crop. It may also be planted early in the spring for an early crop, although the success of this plan depends much upon the lateness and coolness of the summer in that locality.

Succession planting—Chinese cabbage planted for fall crop may conveniently be used to follow spring crop which matures by the end of July.

Thinning—If care is taken to provide moisture, avoid sunlight, and keep as much soil as possible around the roots of the plants removed at thinning time, these may be used to form other rows.

Types—Chihli, 73 days to maturity; Pe-Tsai, 78 days to maturity; Wong Bok, 78 days to maturity.

Harvesting—When the heads reach maturity, cut them. The outer leaves are customarily removed although these may contain very valuable vitamins. The centers, young and tender and blanched, are generally used for salads or passed on for use in the kitchen. It may be that these are quite lacking in vitamin value.

Storage—A brief storage is possible by taking the untrimmed heads and placing them in the refrigerator. These will be preserved for about a month.

Yield—100 feet of row should yield about 70 heads.

11. Cucumbers

Soil—Warm, rich, sandy.

Location—Cucumbers require a cool, moist, even slightly shaded location.

Fertilizers—An abundant supply of easily available food is essential. This is best supplied by using mature compost humus. Directions for its application are given under the heading "Planting Instructions."

Soil type—Cucumbers thrive in a moderately acid soil but will not do well on a very acid soil.

Depth of planting—Seed should be covered with ½" of sifted compost humus.

Width apart in the row—48".

Distance between rows—48".

How much seed—½ ounce of seed will sow 100 feet of row.

Planting instructions—Cucumbers demand plenty of moisture and plenty of natural plant nutrients. This may be supplied in a number of ways.

Planting in hills—Make a hole about 2 feet in diameter, and 2 feet deep. Place about a pound of mature compost humus in this hole, water, and cover with topsoil so that a slight elevation is formed. Plant from 6 to 9 seeds in this mound. After the plants are 4" tall, thin to 4 plants.

Planting in rows—Dig a trench 8" deep, place a 2" layer of sifted compost humus in the bottom. Plant the seeds 6" apart in a ridge made by the addition of top soil.

Watering—Although water may be supplied by various means to fill the demands of a plant which requires very urgently large quantities, it is also advisable to lay down a 3" mulch around the plant. This mulch is best supplied by compost humus. But in the absence of it, dry straw, weeds, etc., will suffice—even boards or burlap bags will help.

Special care—Cucumbers are most economically grown by supplying some support. If they are grown in the open, a good plan is to construct an inverted V trellis with an apex about 5 feet high and a base 48" wide. This trellis will supply support for 2 rows, and the vines climbing on it will produce their fruits so that they are clear of the ground.

Date of planting—May.

Types—Black Diamond, 54 days to maturity; Extra Early White Spine, 55 days to maturity.

Harvesting—Cucumbers are gathered at almost any stage of growth before they turn a yellow-green. For table use the fruits should be a deep green.

Storage—Cucumbers are customarily pickled.

Yield—1½ bushels for 100 feet of row.

Note—A very good way to grow cucumbers is to take a butter tub, make several holes in its sides near the bottom, and fill it with mature compost humus. Around the tub, plant the seed and fill the tub with water. A bucket of water is daily poured into the tub, and it in time leaks out to supply the plants with the steady supply of moisture and natural plant food they so urgently require.

12. Dill

Soil—Any average garden soil.

Location—Open and unshaded, free from tree roots.

Fertilizer—A very small amount of mature compost humus dug in along the rows will render the soil sufficiently fertile to produce a good growth.

Soil type—Dill will tolerate a moderate amount of acidity, but it is well to have the soil well prepared and free from stones. Definitely sour soil should be corrected by an application of crushed limestone or shell lime.

Depth of planting—½".

Width apart in the row—15".

Distance between rows—3 feet.

How much seed—½ ounce will seed 100 feet of row.

Planting instructions—When the plants are about 5" tall, they should be thinned to 15" apart in the row. The plants removed may be used to form new rows and to fill gaps in the original row.

Watering—During transplanting, a plentiful supply of moisture should be available. Plants removed should be shaded and prevented from drying out, and when replanted should be well watered and firmed.

Date of planting—March–April, Oct.–Nov.
Seed may be planted early in the spring, and when the plants have attained 6″ in height, they may be transplanted for an early crop. Or the seed may be planted late in the fall and the young plants which come up early in the spring may be transplanted when they have attained sufficient growth.

Types—Dill—70 days to maturity—has not been developed into types. It is still very close to its wild ancestors.

Harvesting—Customarily, when the seed heads have developed, they are gathered and used for flavoring. The seed heads are usually dried in the shade. The young stems are often gathered and used also for flavoring soups, stews, and the like. Minced young dill stems are often mixed with lettuce in the salad.

Storage—The entire plant is gathered and hung in bunches until dry. This is best done by partially drying the plants in an airy, open shed and later placing the bunches to hang in a warm attic. These dried stalks are greatly prized for flavoring dill pickles.

Yield—100 feet of row should produce about 70 large bunches.

Note—The dill plant is quite hardy. It is usually grown as an annual but is sometimes considered as a biennial because seed planted in the fall will produce seedlings which are capable of surviving the winter and growing to maturity the following season.

13. Eggplant

Soil—Good, rich.

Location—Well drained, sunny, warm location.

Fertilizers—Eggplants are gross feeders. They demand a heavy supply of easily assimilated plant nutrients. These demands are best filled by supplying mature compost humus liberally. Well rotted manure may be substituted if necessary.

Soil type—Slightly on the acid side.

Depth of planting—Seed: ⅓", Plants: Slightly deeper than they grew in the flat.

Width apart in the row—48".

Distance between rows—48".

How much seed—A 10¢ packet of seed for 100 feet of row; Plants: 25 plants for 100 feet of row.

Planting instructions—Seeds: A trench about 6" deep should be formed and filled with good quality compost humus. The seeds of a 10¢ packet should then be mixed with a teacupful of finely sifted, dry compost material. This mixture should be laid down on the drill and later sprinkled lightly with a very thin layer of sifted compost humus. Plants: Holes should be dug large enough to permit the placing of about 2 pounds of sifted compost humus after the plants have been set, the roots well spread and watered. The plants should be well firmed and again watered. Shade should be supplied for the first 24 hours if necessary to prevent serious wilting.

Watering—Because eggplants are gross feeders, they require plenty of moisture flooded around them during dry weather to enable them to use the plant food they require.

Date of planting—May.

Companion cropping—Eggplants are conveniently placed in the garden by substituting every fourth or fifth tomato plant by an eggplant. Or they may be planted alternately with peppers.

Thinning—Eggplants raised from seed in the garden should be thinned to stand 48" apart in the row. It is sometimes possible to move the crowded seedlings to another part of the row where germination was poor. This should be done carefully, retaining as much soil as possible around the roots of the seedlings, avoiding direct sunlight, and supplying plenty of moisture and adequate shade.

Types—Black Beauty, 73 days to maturity; New Hampshire Hybrid, 60 days to maturity; White Beauty, 76 days to maturity.

Harvesting—Eggplants are usually gathered when ripe for immediate use in the kitchen. The fruits should be gathered when the surface is very glossy, and before it begins to assume a dull finish.

Yield—100 feet of row should yield well over 100 fruits.

14. Endive

Soil—Good, rich, fertile loam.

Location—Open, well drained.

Fertilizer—Endive demands an adequate supply of natural plant food located near the surface. If 2″ of mature compost humus are dug in over the area where the plants are to grow, this should suffice. If the plants appear poor when they are half grown, it is well to give them a side-dressing of sifted compost humus which will also act as a mulch. Well rotted manure may be substituted.

Soil type—Any reasonably good garden soil will suffice.

Depth of planting—Like lettuce, place the seed in a shallow trench and cover with a light sprinkling of sifted compost humus or mix the seed with sand and plant the mixture entire. The seed should not be covered more than ⅓″ deep.

Width apart in the row—12″.

Distance between rows—18″.

How much seed—1 ounce of seed should sow 100 feet of row.

Planting instructions—The seed should be sown directly into the garden and the seedlings thinned to stand 12″ apart in the row.

Watering—Being largely composed of water, sufficient moisture should be available to the plant. If considerable compost humus has been incorporated in the soil, its water-holding capacity will favor the steady growth of the plant. During excessively dry spells, it is sometimes necessary to flood the area where the plants grow for several hours during the evening.

Date of planting—Endive is usually grown as a fall crop. It is hardy to frost. What lettuce is in the spring, endive is in the fall—an essential salad crop. Seed for fall crop: June–July.

Succession planting—Fall endive may be sown to follow

such early crops as early peas, etc. March–April for spring crop; June–July for fall crop.

Types—Green Curled, 65 days to maturity; Deep Heart, 70 days to maturity; Broad Leaved Batavian, 90 days to maturity.

Harvesting—Mature heads are usually gathered when they are about 15″ in diameter. The outer soiled leaves are removed, leaving the heart which should be crisp and creamy white.

Storage—Because endive is hardy to frost, it is possible to protect plantings by using a mulch of dry straw applied as freezing weather approaches. During the winter, the plants thus protected are available for cutting.

Yield—1 ounce of seed will sow 100 feet of row.

Note—Endive is customarily blanched to reduce the pungent bitterness of the leaves and to improve their flavor. When the plants are about ⅔ grown, gather the outer leaves together in a bunch at the top of the plant and tie with string. The heads should be gathered 2 weeks later to prevent rotting which might be brought about through the limitations of the plant's growth.

15. Kale

Soil—Rich, fertile loam, preferably one in which cabbages, or related plants, have not been grown the previous year.

Location—Sunny, well drained, with some shelter, if possible, on the southern end.

Fertilizer—Kale requires a reasonably large amount of mature compost humus to supply its demands for plant food. The matter of its application will be explained under "Planting Instructions." Well rotted manure may be substituted if necessary. The use of raw manure is inadvisable because of its tendency to act as a carrier of plant disease.

Soil type—Lime is essential for the good growth of all members of the cabbage family. Kale requires it. A liberal application of crushed calcium limestone or shell limestone applied to the area at the time of digging will do much to assure good growth and make the plant food supplied by the compost applied readily available.

Depth of planting—½".

Width apart in the row—15".

Distance between rows—20".

How much seed—1 packet of good grade seed will sow 100 feet of row.

Planting instructions—Using a guideline, construct a trench about 6" deep and 6" wide. Line the bottom of this trench with crushed limestone—if this is not available, hydrated lime will have to suffice—then fill the trench to within 1" of the place of the seed and cover with ½" of the same material. Water again and firm.

Surface with mature compost humus, water well, and apply another layer of dry, sifted humus.

Date of planting—Aug. 1st.

Succession planting—Kale may be very conveniently used to follow almost any crop which matures by midsummer. It is often regarded as winter or cold weather cabbage.

Companion cropping—Kale is often sown in the same rows with late cabbage, storage potatoes, etc.

Thinning—The seedlings should be allowed to acquire some size before thinning even though they crowd a little. Thus, when pulled to thin the row, the material removed will have considerable value in the kitchen.

Types—Dwarf Green Curled, 55 days to maturity; Tall Green Curled Scotch, 60 days to maturity; Blue Curled Scotch, 55 days to maturity.

Harvesting—Although the outer leaves may be gathered and the heart of the plant allowed to remain, it is customary to cut the whole plant.

Storage—Kale is often planted very late in the fall and left to stand all winter in the garden. It is very hardy. It will continue to grow until very late in the fall. Before very severe cold approaches, it is best to mulch the plants with a heavy, loose covering of dry straw, weeds, etc., so that they may survive to produce a large and early supply of edible material.

Yield—100 feet of row should yield about 2 bushels.

16. Kohlrabi

Soil—Rich, moist, friable loam.

Location—Well drained, not overly exposed to excessive sunlight.

Fertilizer—Along the line where the seed is to be planted, place a 3″ layer of mature compost humus. This should then be dug in lightly, the drill lined up, and the seed planted. Well rotted manure may be substituted or even raw manure, if necessary, provided this material is free from waste material of plants of the cabbage family.

Soil type—Kohlrabi is a member of the cabbage family. It thrives only in soil in which the natural calcium is present in abundance. Calcium is chalk or lime. It is best to spread at the rate of 75 pounds to the 1,000 square feet, a good grade of lime. This material should be well raked in before planting.

Depth of planting—½″.

Width apart in the row—4″.

Between rows—15″.

How much seed—10¢ packet will sow 100 feet of row.

Planting instructions—The seed has to be planted ½″ deep. An easy method is to first soak the seed in rainwater, or, preferably, compost water, which is water saturated with plant food through being allowed to stand in a container partially filled with mature compost humus, for twenty-four hours.

Watering—Like all members of the cabbage family, kohlrabi is a gross feeder and demands plenty of water for its rapid growth. If sufficient water is lacking, the enlarged root stalk which it forms will be small, hard, and woody.

Date of planting—For Spring crop: March–April; For Fall crop: August 1.

Succession planting — Kohlrabi may be planted early to mature before late corn, potatoes, etc., or it may be planted to follow early crops.

Types—Early White Vienna, 55 days to maturity; Early Purple Vienna, 60 days to maturity.

Storage—Kohlrabi plants may be stored in the same manner as cabbage plants.

17. Leeks

Soil—Rich, deep loam.

Location—Well drained and reasonably free from stones.

Fertilizer—Leeks will respond to heavy applications of mature compost humus. Well rotted manure may be substituted, if necessary. Avoid the use of raw manure.

Soil type—Leeks will tolerate a moderately acid soil but it must be one rich in nitrogen. This is especially essential during early growth.

Depth of planting—Seed: ½"; Plants: ½".

Width apart in the row—Seeds: ½"; Plants: 6".

Distance between rows—18".

How much seed—½ ounce will sow 100 feet of row.

Planting instructions—Seed is planted thickly, ½" deep. When the seedlings are 8" high, they should be carefully dug up, about half the tops removed, and replanted 6" apart. Trenches 6" deep and 3" or 4" wide should be dug, and the seedlings planted in the bottoms of these trenches. As the plants grow, the sides of the trenches should be broken down to blanch the edible stems. A heavy supply of sifted compost humus should be incorporated with the soil in the bottoms of the trenches. (After the trenches have been filled, or if the leeks have not been set in trenches, it is possible to draw up earth to the plants to form ridges 3" high to cover the stems.)

Watering—During the early stages of their growth, leeks require an abundance of plant food. A plentiful supply of moisture is necessary to make this available to them.

Date of planting—Seed: March–April; Transplant: April–May.

Thinning—If the supply of seedlings is in excess of the garden requirements, those not needed at time of transplanting may be used in the kitchen.

Types—Broad London (Large American Flag), 130 days to maturity; Elephant, 125 days to maturity.

Harvesting—Leeks are customarily dug at maturity or when required in the kitchen, sometimes slightly before they reach maturity.

Storage—Young leeks may be left to overwinter in the garden if given some protection by mulching with salt hay, straw, or similar material. They will begin growing very early in the spring and furnish a valuable early crop.

Yield—100 feet of row should produce about 200 plants.

18. Lettuce

Soil—Loose, rich loam.

Location—Cool, temperate. Lettuce is a cool weather crop and will thrive in partial shade.

Fertilizer—Lettuce is very shallow rooted. An inch of mature compost humus raked into the surface of the garden before planting time greatly benefits the plants. After the plants are up, additional sifted compost should be placed along the rows as a side-dressing. If raw manure is used, it should be well incorporated with the soil during the digging.

Soil type—Lettuce will thrive on almost any type of well drained garden soil.

Depth of planting—¼".

Width apart in the row—8" to 12".

Distance between rows—12" to 15".

How much seed—10¢ packet for 100 feet of row.

Planting instructions—Care should be taken not to cover the seed too deeply. It is best to form a very shallow trench along the line where the row is to stand. Plant the seed in the bottom of this trench to prevent it being washed away during rain.

Watering—For its rapid growth, lettuce requires the addition of water during dry weather.

Date of planting — Early crop: March–April; Fall crop: August–September.

Succession planting—Make sowings 2 weeks apart until the end of May.

Thinning—When the young plants have formed 4 leaves, they should be thinned to stand 8" to 12" apart in the row.

The young plants removed in the thinning may be set out in other rows. Water generously and do the thinning and transplanting late in the day to avoid heat.

Types—Early: Big Boston, 80 days to maturity; Midseason: Iceberg, 85 days to maturity; Late: Butterhead, 78 days to maturity.

Note—Head lettuce will not usually form heads during warm weather. However, late spring plantings are often successfully headed up by setting the plants in a cool, partially shaded spot.

19. Lima Beans

Soil—A good loam that is not lacking in its natural amount of humus, and which warms up quickly.

Location—Open, sunny, well drained, quite free from shade. Limas require a long period of sunshine.

Fertilizer—Lima beans require more sun then fertilizer. However, if a couple of inches of matured compost humus is laid down along the drill where the plants are to stand, and lightly dug in, they will benefit greatly. (A drill is the line along which the seeds are to be planted.)

Soil type—Limas will succeed in almost any type of soil although they prefer a soil very slightly acid.

Depth of planting—1".

Width apart in the row—8".

Distance between rows—30".

How much seed—1 pound of seed will plant 100 feet of row.

Planting instructions—Bush limas: It is best to form a trench after the narrow layer of compost humus has been laid down. This trench should be about 2" deep. In the bottom of it, place 1" of sifted compost humus, place the seed 8" apart, and cover with 1" of the same material, then firm. The pole limas should be planted first. These should be about 10 feet high and should be planted in holes formed by driving a stake into the ground about 3 feet. The poles should be rough surface. After the poles are in position, the seed should be planted around the poles, 6 seeds to a pole, later thinned to 3 plants. Pole beans should be planted at the north end of the garden so as to protect the garden rather than to shade and hinder the growth of low growing plants. (Pole limas are excellent for covering a fence or trellis. Plant them along any boundary fence where there is adequate sunshine and save the garden space.)

Date of planting—Late May, after the soil has warmed up.

Types—Bush types: Fordhook, 76 days to maturity; Philadelphia Bush Limas, 68 days to maturity. Pole types: Giant Podded, 90 days to maturity; Sunnybrook, 84 days to maturity.

Harvesting—Lima beans should be picked as rapidly as they mature. Unlike pole snap beans, they come into maturity at very definite dates. They should be gathered promptly.

Storage—If the crop of fresh limas is too great for the immediate use in the kitchen, they may be allowed to remain on the vine in the fall and ripen. The dry pods should be gathered before they open. A better plan is to pull up the vines and place them in piles to dry. When the vines are quite dry, thresh them by walking over them and later gather the seed beans left after removing the dry vines. (The dry beans should be stored in airtight containers and are best freed from weevils by suspending muslin bags filled with dry seed for about one minute in boiling water.)

Yield—2 bushels for 100 feet of row.

20. Mint

Soil—Moist, fairly rich loam, having plenty of moisture.

Locality—Mint will grow if much moisture and a little shade is available, even on lawns.

Fertilizer—For best results, mint should be supplied with a very moderate amount of mature compost humus. This is best done by placing a 1″ layer on the surface of the area where the mint is to be planted and raking in. Raw manure is not recommended.

Soil type—Mint will thrive on a moderately acid soil. One type of mint is known as brook-mint and grows in its natural state in the very acid soil which borders small streams of water.

Depth of planting—Mint is usually propagated by the use of cutting, seldom by seed. Cuttings are easily made to form roots by setting them in water and later planted ½″ deeper than the roots which have formed.

Width apart in the row—3 feet.

Distance between rows—3 feet.

How much seed — About 35 rooted clippings, or young plants for 100 feet of row. Mint is customarily grown in beds, that is, the 100 feet of row is formed by 10 rows 10 feet long in a block.

Planting instructions—If rooted clippings or young plants are used, it is advisable to form a shallow and wide trench, 3″ deep by 12″ wide. This trench should be well watered and then covered with a 1″ layer of mature sifted compost. The clippings should be kept moist and laid in this trench and covered with about 2″ of top soil or compost material.

Watering—Mint requires much moisture. In nature, it grows readily along the banks of running streams. It will thrive in a damp shady place, but in the open it is best to give it a good soaking now and then by flooding the area by placing the hose on the ground and allowing the water to run for several hours.

Date of planting—April–May or Aug.–Sept.

Types—Peppermint, spearmint, both types grow very fast under normal conditions. Clippings planted in the spring should afford a valuable crop in the fall.

Harvesting—Mint should be picked when required. It is used in the kitchen for jellies and as a flavoring of drinks. Roast lamb and mint sauce are not to be separated. Customarily, the shoots are picked as required in the kitchen.

Storage—Mint is seldom stored except in the form of mint jellies and the like. But the material cut from the growing plants to prevent it reaching too high—2 feet—may be dried by hanging in a shady place, where there is good air circulation. Mint dried in the open may be later crushed or ground and stored safely in tight cans or jars.

Note—For best flavor, the tips of the tall stalks are picked before the plant has bolted, that is, run up a seed stalk. When the plant goes to seed, much of its aromatic value is lost.

During the winter, it is very convenient to grow a supply of mint by using indoor window boxes, etc. Cuttings may be rooted in water at any time.

21. Mushrooms

Soil—A good, soft loam especially rich in new humus.

Location—Any open fairly well drained lawn.

Fertilizer—Before planting, it is best to place a large supply of mature compost humus. Well rotted manure may be substituted if used in abundance, see "Planting Instructions."

Soil type—Mushrooms will thrive in any soil in which grass will grow.

Depth of planting—1".

Width apart in the row—2 feet.

Distance between rows—2 feet.

How much seed—Mushrooms are customarily propagated by using spawn—the root mass of the healthy plant. Because this plant is a fungoid growth, its roots, mycellium, form a tightly packed mass. One pound should be enough to plant 100 feet of row. (There are two types of spawn, bottle spawn, which is spawn produced under laboratory supervision, and manure spawn, which is produced under something like natural conditions.)

Planting instructions—If planting for permanence in a lawn, dig a large hole 2 feet wide by 2 feet deep and fill with mature sifted compost humus. In this hole, place a small part of the brick, a piece about as large as a walnut. If bottle spawn is used, a chunk about the same size is necessary. Cover 1" deep with finely sifted compost and water well.

Watering—Mushrooms depend very largely upon climatic conditions for their successful formation. Generally they produce their stools above ground when cool nights follow warm days. They require plenty of moisture and will not thrive in

dry areas, although they will survive much competition from
grass roots, etc.

Date of planting—March–April, or for next year, Sept.–
Nov.

Harvesting—Mushrooms are customarily pulled each day.
Their growth is very largely dependent upon the immediate
breakdown of the material in which they grow. They illus-
trate the value of mature compost humus more than any
plant. If ideal conditions exist, even on a common lawn, the
number of mushrooms to be pulled will be prodigous.

Storage—Mushrooms may be dried, or more commonly
canned. Canning should be done according to conditions very
thoroughly explained under canning, and the drying of mushrooms is easily accomplished with an ordinary kitchen drying
outfit.

Yield—Mushrooms are customarily used fresh, although they
are also sold in the dehydrated form. Under ideal conditions,
a 50 foot row will yield a very large quantity of fine grade
edible mushrooms. The amount of the yield depends very
largely upon the skill of the picker.

Note—Much publicity has lately been given to the production of mushrooms through the use of sawdust, or some other
media, used as a base, and synthetic material being supplied
as a plant food. Avoid this method of production. The available food value of mushrooms is very slight. The flavor value
is very great. Mushrooms produced by the use of artificial
chemicals not only have little or no food value, but may be
positively poisonous.

22. Onions

Soil—Rich, moist loam, preferably with a subsoil of clay.

Location—Onions thrive in a moist (not wet) location which
is also well drained. Any place in the garden where rainwater
tends to form a pool long after the rain is not well drained.

Fertilizer—Onions demand an abundance of moisture and
plant nutrients, especially during the early stages of their
development. They require much nitrogen, and this is best
supplied by a heavy layer of manure compost humus layed

down over the area where they are to grow. Well rotted manure may be substituted if necessary.

Soil type—Onions prefer a moderately acid soil.

Depth of planting—Seed: ½"; Sets (small onions): 1"; Plants: slightly deeper than they grew in the flat.

Width apart in the row—2" although in very rich soil they will succeed if grown closer.

Distance between rows—12" to 18".

How much seed—½ ounce of seed will sow 100 feet of row, 2 pounds of sets will sow 100 feet of row, 600 plants will sow 100 feet of row.

Planting instructions—Seed: Seed should be planted quite thickly and covered with ½" of sifted compost humus. It should be well watered after planting. Sets: Sets should be covered with 1" of sifted compost humus. Sets larger than a dime should not be used, if possible, as they have a tendency to go to flower instead of developing an onion. Plants: Plants should be carefully set out and shaded if necessary against summer heat. Onions formed by transplants are excellent for winter storage.

Watering—It is a good plan to lay the hose down on the ground near a planting of onions and allow the water to flood them during dry spells. If the subsoil is of clay, this has a tendency to prevent the too rapid passing away of the water.

Companion cropping—Onions are a low growing crop, and they may very conveniently be planted to fill the row space between such widely spaced plants as broccoli, late cabbage, etc.

Types—Seed: Sweet Spanish, 110 days to maturity; Southport Yellow Globe, 115 days to maturity; Yellow Globe Danvers, 112 days to maturity. Sets: Ebenezer, 100 days to maturity. Plants: The maturity of onion plants depends very greatly upon many elements and cannot be accurately estimated. But they produce fine onions.

Harvesting—As the plants mature, the tops will fall to the ground. Those still standing should be broken down with a rake to allow the bulbs to mature. After a day or two, pull the bulbs and spread out on the ground in the sun and allow them to remain there for 2 days. Then cut off the tops an inch above the bulbs.

Storage—Harvested bulbs should be placed in net bags and placed where there is free circulation of air until freezing weather approaches when they may be moved to a storage cellar. The place of storage should be cool, dry, and dark.

Yield—1½ bushels to 100 feet of row.

Note—Scallions: White Welsh, which matures in 95 days, does not form a bulb but the thick shoots are used for bunching and for early green onions. It is quite hardy, mild, and very early. Scallions are perennial, that is they continue to grow so long as a portion of the plant is allowed to remain. Plants continue to increase in size as they grow older. They should be thinned to 12″ between plants during the second year. They should be given a light mulch during severe winters.

23. Parsley

Soil—Fertile, rich, loam.

Location—Open, well drained, and not shaded excessively by tall growing plants.

Fertilizer—Parsley requires large quantities of nitrogen for its successful growth. This is best supplied by 2 ways. First, a trench about 3″ deep should be dug where the row is to stand. This trench should be filled with mature, sifted, compost and the seed sown, watered, and firmed. Later, a sidedressing of sifted compost humus should be applied. This is especially necessary during the second year of growth.

Soil type—Any ordinary garden soil, preferably one that does not dry out too rapidly and is not excessively alkaline.

Depth of planting—Place seed in shallow trench, cover with about ¼″ of sharp sand or mix seed with cupful of sifted compost humus, and spread the mixture along the trench.

Width apart in the row—2″.

Distance between rows—16″.

How much seed—1 packet of seed should sow 100 feet of row.

Date of planting—March–April.

Companion cropping—Parsley may be grown successfully in the same rows with such tall growing plants as corn or staked tomatoes. It is a biennial which does well either in open sun or partial shade. It will fit in between such widely spaced plants as cabbage, kohlrabi, and peppers.

Thinning—Seed should be planted thickly to allow for lack of germination and the inability of many of the shoots to force their way through the surface. The plants should later be thinned to stand 2″ apart in the rows.

Types—Extra Curled Dwarf, 70 days to maturity; Plain or Single, 60 days to maturity; Parsnip-Rooted or Hamburg Parsley, 90 days to maturity, has plain leaves which may be used as with ordinary parsley. It also produces a parsnip shaped root which is much valued in the kitchen especially as a flavoring, although it may be prepared and used as an edible root vegetable.

Harvesting—Customarily, the outer leaves only are gathered. This practice permits the hearts of the plant to continue to grow and produce more leaves.

Storage—The leaves may be picked and spread out in the shade until partially dried. They should then be moved to a very dry place, and completely dried. When the dried leaves crumble easily, the flakes may be stored in sealed cans. Or a few plants grown in pots may be moved to a sunny windowsill in the house. These will supply much fresh material during the severe winter weather.

Yield—100 feet of row should yield about 100 bunches.

Note—For kitchen use, small crops of parsley are often produced by planting seed in pots, boxes, etc. About 15 plants will produce enough material for the average family. Fifteen plants at 2″ apart require only 30″ of row space. Parsley, if given the protection of a light mulch during severely cold weather, will survive the winter and be one of the earliest green plants to show in the spring. During the second year of its growth, the plant will go to seed, and arrangements should be made to replace it the following spring by a new plant.

24. Parsnips

Soil—Good, rich, very deeply dug, and pulverized to a depth of at least 2 feet.

Location—Open, sunny, preferably with a clay subsoil.

Fertilizer—Parsnips demand plenty of food for the formation of their roots. The fertilizer should be quite mature and deeply placed in the soil. Mature compost humus well dug in before planting is best. Avoid the use of raw manure especially in direct contact with the young roots as this causes pronging. An excessive amount of stones will also cause malformed roots.

Soil type—Parsnips will grow in any reasonably good soil not excessively acid.

Depth of planting — Seed should be placed in shallow trenches and covered with ½" of sifted compost humus, watered, and well firmed.

Width apart in the row—3".

Distance between rows—18".

How much seed—½ ounce of seed will plant 100 feet of row.

Planting instructions—Because parsnip seed is rather fine and difficult to handle, it is best to mix ½ ounce with 1 teacupful of finely sifted, dry compost material and plant the mixture. After the seed has been planted and watered, it is often a good plan to place planks or burlap bags along the rows to cover the seed, thus preventing drying out and aiding germination.

Watering—Parsnips should be supplied with adequate moisture while the plants are small, later this may be dispensed with.

Date of planting—March–April.

Thinning—Seed should be sown rather thickly and later the seedlings thinned to stand 3" apart in the row.

Types—Guernsey, 100 days to maturity; Long Smooth Hollow Crown, 105 days to maturity; Improved Short Thick, 85 days to maturity.

Harvesting—Parsnips are customarily left in the ground until after freezing weather. The cold weather is believed to cure them and improve their flavor. They may be left in the garden all winter and harvested in the early spring before growth begins. However, for a convenient supply during the winter, it is best to dig them before the ground freezes solid.

Storage—Since freezing improves rather than damages parsnips, their storage is a simple matter. If a shallow excavation is made in a well drained spot, and this covered with a layer of dry weeds, straw, etc., the parsnips may be placed in a conical pile upon it. A foot-thick layer of straw should then be used to cover the pile, and enough topsoil, branches, etc., be placed upon it to hold it in place against winds and rain. Parsnips may be stored in a cool cellar but not in a dry place as they wilt readily.

Yield—100 feet of row should yield about 2 bushels.

25. Peas

Soil—Light, rich, sandy.

Location—Enjoys moderate temperatures and will thrive in partial shade.

Fertilizer—Trenches 12″ to 16″ deep should be made where the rows are to stand. Three inches of mature compost humus should be placed in the bottom of each trench.

Soil type—Peas will tolerate a moderate amount of acidity, but the soil should not be over rich in nitrogen.

Depth of planting—Cover seed, place in bottom of trenches with 1″ to 2″ of sifted compost humus.

Width apart in row—2″ to 4″.

Distance between rows—35″.

How much seed—1 packet of seed, 20 feet; 1 pound, 100 ft.

Planting instructions—After the seedlings are about an inch high, the sides of the trench should be broken down gently until only the tips of the seedlings are exposed. This process should be repeated until the trenches are almost filled.

Watering—Peas suffer most from heat and drought. They require adequate moisture during dry weather.

Special care—Bush varieties require no support but the climbing varieties should be given brush or other material upon which to climb. This brush should be in place just as soon as the plants are out of the ground, should reach a bit higher than the estimated height of the plants, and should be securely fixed.

Date of planting—Early, midseason, and late varieties should be sown just as early as the group can be worked. Make successive sowings about 2 weeks apart until about the middle of May.

Succession planting—Late cabbage, or some other late crop may be planted just as soon as the peas are out of the way.

Companion cropping—If bush varieties of peas are used, onions, carrots, lettuce, etc., may be planted in between the bushes. The earliest and latest dates for planting are Early Crop: April 1; Fall Crop: August 30.

Thinning—If 12 to 15 seeds are planted per foot of row, thinning will be unnecessary.

Types—Dwarf type: Dwarf Alderman; Brush type: Hundredfold; Tall growing: Telephone; Edible podded: Mammoth Melting Sugar.

Harvesting—Pods should be harvested daily to prevent ripening pods holding up the formation of new ones.

Yield—Green peas, 1 bushel for 100 ft. of row; Edible podded peas, 2 bushels for 100 ft. of row.

Note—Mammoth Melting Sugar and the many other edible podded varieties produce pods which are about 4″ long, brittle, and tender when not fully matured, and which may be used as snap beans are used.

26. Peppers

Soil—Mellow, not over rich.

Location—Very sunny, well drained, and open.

Fertilizer—Peppers do best in a soil which does not contain an excess of nitrogen. Too much plant nutrient favors the excessive formation of leaf growth detrimental to the proper forming of the fruits. Mature compost humus should be supplied moderately, an inch layer being lightly dug in if the soil is very poor. Raw manure should be avoided.

Soil type—A loose, well matured loam, containing some gravel and having a gravel rather than a clay subsoil is best. It should not be acid.

Depth of planting—Seed: ½″; Plants: Slightly deeper than they grew in the flats.

Width apart in the row—24″.

Distance between rows—30″.

How much seed—A 10¢ packet will sow 100 feet of row. About 60 plants for 100 feet of row.

Planting instructions—Seeds: After a shallow layer of sifted compost humus has been laid down, a shallow trench should be formed and the seed planted in it and covered ½″ deep. Plants: The hole in which the plant is placed should be amply large so that the roots can be well spread out. During planting the roots of the young plants should be protected against direct sun and kept moist. The plants should be well watered and firmed and shaded for a day or so during very hot weather.

Watering—Pepper plants should be well watered during the early stages of their growth, later this is usually not necessary.

Date of planting—May–June.

Succession planting—Peppers may be planted to follow such early crops as garden cress, mustard, lettuce, early beets, etc.

Companion cropping—Onions and carrots are often sown in between the pepper plants in the same row.

Thinning—Although pepper plants are usually raised indoors, it is possible to thin out seedlings raised from seed planted directly into the drills to about 24″ apart and to use these seedlings to form other rows. If conditions are ideal, these transplants will grow fast enough to mature their fruits although they are often too late.

Types—Mild: California Wonder, 75 days to maturity; Chinese Giant, 79 days to maturity. Hot: Long Red Cayenne, 72 days to maturity; Large Cherry, 69 days to maturity.

Harvesting—Peppers are commonly picked when ripe for use in the kitchen.

Storage—Peppers are used in the making of pickles and condiments. A very old method was to fill a narrow-mouth jar almost full of a good grade of vinegar. Into this was dropped, one by one, peppers of the hot, cayenne type, after each pepper had been punctured several times with a needle. The mixture was capped and allowed to stand for some time after which it was used as a hot chile sauce.

Yield—100 feet of row should yield 4 bushels.

27. Potatoes

Soil—Fertile, garden soil, preferably a sandy loam.

Location—Well drained, moist. Potatoes thrive best during mild, cloudy weather. They are very sensitive to frost.

Fertilizer—Mature compost humus should be used. If raw manure is to be used, it should be dug in the previous fall. Avoid the use of raw cow manure, and the use of lime.

Soil type—Acid or alkaline, potatoes thrive in a slightly acid soil. Alkalinity, the use of lime, causes the rapid development of a potato disease known as *scab*.

Depth of planting—3″.

Width apart in the row—13″.

Distance between rows—28″.

How much seed—¼ peck of seed potatoes will plant 50 feet of row. (If seed potatoes are difficult to obtain, it is always possible to save the eyes with a small ball of plant material adhering to them, from the potatoes being used in the kitchen. These eyes should be collected daily, wrapped in wax paper, and stored in a cool place until enough have accumulated to plant a row.)

Planting instructions—Trenches from 8″ to 10″ deep are made and a 2″ layer of sifted compost humus laid down in the bottom. The seed is then placed in the trench. Two inches of sifted compost humus is then placed, and covered with enough fine topsoil to form a slight ridge. If single eyes are planted, they should be used at the rate of 3 eyes for each seed potato.

Watering—Potatoes enjoy moist, temperate conditions. They should be soaked with water, if necessary, during excessively hot, dry spells.

Date of planting—Early: March–April; Late: end of May.

Succession planting—Early potatoes may be harvested and followed by some late crop, such as late turnips.

Companion cropping—Early sweet corn, or late cabbage may be planted between rows of early potatoes.

Types—Early: Irish Cobbler, 80 days to maturity; Late: Green Mountain, 140 days to maturity; Kathahdin, 140 days to maturity.

Harvesting—Early potatoes are gathered during the summer for use in the kitchen. Late potatoes are allowed to remain in the ground until the vines die down, but are harvested before frost reaches them.

Storage—Early potatoes may be stored temporarily in a cool basement. Late potatoes are best stored in the garden. Dig out a circular place 7" to 8" deep and 6 feet in diameter. Fill this space with dry litter and make a conical pile of potatoes upon it. Cover this pile with a foot-thick layer of dry grass, etc., and over this place a foot-thick layer of topsoil, well smoothed. Then repeat the layers. Allow the straw layer to protrude at the peak. Several small piles are more convenient than one large one.

Yield—The average family requires about 15 bushels yearly. 100 feet of row will produce about 3 bushels.

28. Radishes

Soil—Light, sandy loam, one that drains rapidly.

Location—Temperate, fairly open.

Fertilizer—Radishes thrive with little plant food. Mature compost humus, a layer 1" deep dug into the drills before planting time, should suffice. A drill, as you know, is the line along which the seed is to be planted. Avoid using raw manure in direct contact with radish roots. Unhealthy soil conditions brought about by wrong fertilizers greatly encourage attacks of root maggots.

Soil type—Radishes do well if planted in any reasonably good garden soil.

Depth of planting—Cover with ½″ of sifted compost humus.

Width apart in the row—15 seeds per foot of row.

Distance between rows—12″.

How much seed—½ ounce of seed will sow 100 feet of row.

Planting instructions—If a 1″ layer of mature compost humus has been dug into the soil, a shallow trench should be formed with the hoe. In this trench, the seed should be sown, and covered with ½″ layer of sifted compost humus. The seed should be well watered, and well firmed after planting.

Watering—Radishes demand great quantities of water for their rapid and successful growth. Too much water cannot be furnished them, provided the drainage is adequate. Much of their fine flavor and their brittleness depend upon an adequate supply of moisture.

Date of planting—April 1st for early varieties; June 1st for late varieties.

Succession planting — Make succession plantings every week until early summer, then wait until a month before the first frost. Or plant early, midsummer, and late varieties.

Types—Early: Red Giant, 29 days to maturity; Midsummer: White Icicle, 28 days to maturity; Late: Round Black Spanish, 55 days to maturity.

Note—If radishes are lacking in the normal supply of moisture, they tend to fill out their roots very slowly, and these roots are apt to be woody and very hot flavored. Slow growth also favors the early bolting (the early formation of flowers and seed pods). A steady supply of moisture which has filtered through a heavy layer of mature compost humus placed as a sidedressing for the plants will do much to help them to form crisp, full flavored roots.

29. Rhubarb

Soil—Deep, rich loam.

Location—Rhubarb should be placed along one side of the

garden, preferably in a place where it will receive plenty of natural moisture.

Fertilizer—Being a gross feeder, rhubarb should be supplied with plenty of mature compost humus, both dug in and as a mulch. Well rotted manure may be substituted.

Soil type—Rhubarb will tolerate a moderately acid soil.

Depth of planting—Plants: 2½".

Width apart in the row—48".

Distance between rows—48".

Planting instructions—In a hole large enough to hold a pound of good, sifted compost humus, set the root about 2½" below the surface of the garden, water well, then fill the hole completely, water again, and firm.

Watering—Rhubarb plants require great quantities of moisture, especially during the rapid formation of their large leaves. Additional water supplied them by an occasional thorough soaking helps produce more tender, better flavored stalks. Heavy mulches of compost humus also help the roots retain the moisture and supply additional much needed plant food.

Date of planting—April–May.

Thinning—About every 5 years, it is usually best to dig up about ¼ of the row, divide the large clumps of roots, and reset the portions containing several small stalks. This is best done in the fall.

Types—MacDonald, Myatt's Victoria, Colossal. A light cropping is usually possible the second year after setting out the plants.

Harvesting—In the spring, the leaves as they mature should be pulled—not cut—from the plant. Careful harvesting of only mature leaves, so as not to strip the plant entirely, greatly encourages the growth of more leaves.

Yield—100 feet of row should yield about 200 stalks.

Note—The plants are benefitted by being given a little protection during severe winter. A light mulch of dry straw, weeds, etc., prevents the severe freezing of the roots and helps to produce an earlier crop of leaves. A very early crop, valuable in the kitchen, may be produced by baskets, boxes, etc., over strong plants as it forces the growth of shoots.

30. Rutabaga (Yellow Turnip)

Soil—Deep, moist, fertile, sandy.

Location—Well drained, open, preferably with a subsoil of clay.

Fertilizer—Rutabaga requires a rich, mellow soil containing a maximum of easily available plant nutrients. Mature compost humus may be used in abundance to promote its satisfactory growth, but the use of raw manure should be avoided. Lime should be supplied to correct lack of mellowness and any tendency toward acidity of soil.

Depth of planting—¼″.

Width apart in the row—3″.

Distance between rows—18″.

How much seed—One packet of seed should sow 100 feet of row.

Planting instructions—Rutabaga is most valuable as a fall corp. The seed should be sown directly into the garden during July–August, and the seedlings thinned to stand 3″ apart in the rows.

Watering—During the early stages of its growth, the rutabaga should be supplied with adequate moisture. To offset the lack of rainfall during July and August, it is often necessary to flood the seedlings during the evening. This is best done by placing the hose on the ground in the center of the planting and allowing it to run for several hours.

Date of planting—Plants for spring crop: April–May; Seed, for fall crop: July–August.

Succession planting—Late rutabagas may be planted on ground from which early salad crops, lettuce, radishes, etc., have been removed.

Companion cropping—Rutabagas may be planted with radishes to mature long after the radishes have been removed.

Thinning—Healthy seedlings removed during thinning may be used to fill new rows if they are taken carefully and an ample supply of water is used to prevent wilting and ensure their rapid placement in their new location. Shade should be supplied during the first day or two after transplanting.

Types—Golden Ball, 57 days to maturity; Large Yellow, 57 days to maturity.

Harvesting—Late in the fall the roots are usually gathered before frost.

Storage—Rutabagas are primarily grown for garden storage. They keep well. They may be stored in a sandbox in an unheated cellar but are best held in an outdoor pit. This pit is constructed by excavating a few inches of topsoil in a well drained place and covering the excavation with about 3″ of straw, dry weeds, or similar material. The rutabagas are then arranged in a conical pile on this foundation and covered with about a foot of the same material. Over this, a 6″ layer of topsoil is spread and smoothed. Additional material in the way of corn stalks, heavy brush, etc., may be added before the advent of very severe weather.

Yield—100 feet of row should yield about 2 bushels of fine roots.

Note—There are several varieties of foliage rutabagas, that is, rutabagas which produce edible foliage much like spinach. These also produce desirable roots. Seven Top, 50 days to maturity, Foliage or Shogoin, 70 days to maturity. Both of these types produce a very valuable leaf crop.

31. Salsify (Oyster Plant)

Soil—Light, mellow loam, fairly free from stones.

Location—Open, sunny, well drained.

Fertilizer—Mature compost humus should be deeply placed where the rows are to stand. Salsify roots penetrate to a depth of almost a foot. A trench about 13″ deep and 13″ wide should be made and filled with sifted compost humus. Raw manure, or even improperly rotted manure should be carefully avoided because of its tendency to cause the plants to form pronged and valueless roots.

Soil type—Crushed limestone should be applied—75 pounds to 1,000 square feet of garden space—if the soil is suspected of being sour.

Depth of planting—½″.

Width apart in the row—2″.

Distance between rows—16″.

How much seed—1 ounce for 100 feet of row.

Planting instructions—Seed should be placed thinly along the row and covered with ½″ of sifted compost humus, watered and firmed. When the seedlings have attained some growth, they should be thinned to stand 2″ apart in the row.

Watering—Except in the early stages of its growth, the plant seldom needs watering provided the soil in which it is growing is deep and well supplied with fertile humus.

Date of planting—March–April.

Types—Sandwich Island Mammoth, 120 days to maturity.

Harvesting—Roots may be dug as required by the time the plants are a little more than ⅔ grown. They are generally allowed to remain in the ground during the winter to be dug as required, provided the ground has not frozen hard. They may be harvested until they start growth the following spring. Freezing is believed to improve their flavor.

Storage—Salsify roots may be dug after the first fall frost and stored for convenience. For best results, an outdoor pit should be used. Since freezing does not damage the roots, only slight protection need be given. In a shallow trench lined with straw or dry weeds, place the roots after removing the tops. About 2″ of the leaf stems should be left attached to the roots. Pile the roots to form a ridge about a foot high and as long as may be required. Cover with a foot layer of straw and a light covering of topsoil to hold the straw in place. If a cool cellar is available, the roots may be packed in sand and stored in boxes placed upon an earthen floor.

Yield—100 feet of row should produce over 500 fine roots.

32. Scallions

Soil—Rich, moist loam containing an abundance of humus.

Location—Scallions will tolerate a slight amount of shade but prefer open, moist, sunny conditions.

Fertilizers—These plants are perennials and demand an -abundance of natural plant nutrients for the continued reproduction of the plant material which is, year in and year out, taken from them as a crop. The area in which they grow should be very heavily supplied with mature compost humus. See "Planting Instructions."

Soil type—Scallions will thrive in a moderately acid soil.

Depth of planting—½".

Width apart in the row—4".

Distance between rows—18".

How much seed—½ ounce of seed for 100 feet of row.

Planting instructions—Seed should be planted quite thickly and covered with ½" of sifted compost humus.

Watering—During dry weather sufficient water should be provided to supply the natural requirements of the plants. This is best done by a thorough, slow flooding of the area during the cool of the evening.

Date of planting—Sow in the spring or summer and harvest a moderate crop in the fall or the following spring. Fall sowing is recommended because this plant, being a perennial, needs time to become established.

Succession planting—Scallions may be planted to follow the harvesting of early carrots, beets, or any of the spring greens.

Thinning—After the first year, the plants should be thinned to about 10" apart because they increase in size as they grow. The material secured in thinning should be welcome in the kitchen.

Types—Long Bunching, 95 days to maturity; White Welsh, 95 days to maturity.

Harvesting—Scallions are customarily used in the very early spring and sometimes in the fall. They supply a needed kitchen delicacy when other plants fail.

Yield—Like all perennial plants the yield cannot be definitely stated, but you may be sure that a 50 foot row will yield, if properly cared for, much more than your family can consume.

Note—Scallions are a perennial but they should be given some protection to insure that they winter comfortably. This protection is easily arranged by throwing over the rows a loose mulch of dry weeds, leaves, straw, etc. For best results, scallions should be planted to one side of the garden where they will not interfere with the cultivation of annual plants.

33. Snap Beans

Soil—Sandy loam.

Location—Open, sunny, well drained.

Fertilizer—Snap beans produce a tremendous crop with little fertilizer. However, it is much the best plan to incorporate a moderate supply of mature compost humus in the area in which they are to grow. Any of the organic manures may be substituted although they may not be quickly available.

Soil type—Snap beans will succeed in almost any reasonable good garden soil.

Depth of planting—Cover with 1" of sifted compost humus.

Width apart in the row—Bush types: 3"; Pole types: 5 to 8 seeds to a pole.

Distance between rows—Bush type: 18"; Pole types: 4 feet.

How much seed—1 pound will sow 100 feet of row.

Planting instructions—Pole beans require adequate support. This is best supplied by rough-surfaced poles about 10 feet long. With rows 4 feet apart, it is a good plan to place every 4 poles so that they meet at the top and form a tepee. Where they meet, they should be secured by twine. In this way, the poles do not have to be driven into the ground but stand upon it and are later held securely by the growth of the vine. Pole snap beans, like pole limas, are excellent for planting to cover a boundary fence. They thrive under almost primitive conditions. Planted in this way, they do not encroach on the garden area and provide a fine crop.

Date of planting—May 1, or after the ground has warmed up.

Succession planting—Green pod bush beans may be sown a row every 2 weeks until the end of June.

Companion cropping—Snap beans may be planted in the same ground in which early spinach, radishes, lettuce, etc., have been grown.

Thinning—If 8 seeds are planted to a pole, the plants may be thinned to 3 or 4, and the seedlings removed may be carefully set to fill other poles. With bush beans, they may be used to form another row.

Types—Bush beans: Stringless Green Pod, 49 days to maturity; Tendergreen-Stringless, 53 days to maturity. Wax bush beans: Brittle wax, stringless, 52 days to maturity; Pencilpod, Black wax, 52 days to maturity. Pole beans: Kentucky Wonder, 65 days to maturity. Lazy Wife, 80 days to maturity.

Harvesting—Snap beans should be picked from the vines just as soon, or slightly before they mature. Beans left on the vines tend to prevent the formation of new ones. Never pick beans or work in them when they are wet. Many diseases of beans are spread through the movements of the cultivator during the time they are wet with rain or dew.

Yield—2 bushels for 100 feet of row.

Note—There are several types of unusual beans you will like to try. Edible Soy Bean, plants grow 24″ high and do not need support. They are grown and harvested much like bush limas. Scarlet Runner Bean, this is often grown for the ornamental value of its scarlet flower. It is of the vine type and produces a bean equal to any of the pole beans if gathered before it matures. It also provides a bright spot in the garden.

34. Spinach

Soil—Spinach requires an abundance of plant food, especially nitrogen.

Location—A northern exposure is best because this plant enjoys low temperatures.

Fertilizer—Because this plant requires plenty of nitrogen, it is a good plan to dig in a heavy layer of mature compost humus where the plants are to stand, 3" to 6" is not too much. If raw manures must be used, it is best to work it into the soil the year before or to use well rotted material.

Soil type—Spinach thrives in any reasonably good garden soil.

Depth of planting—Cover the seeds with ½" sifted compost humus and firm well.

Width apart in the row—3" to 4".

Distance between rows—12" to 15".

How much seed—1 packet, 25 feet; 1 ounce, 100 feet.

Planting instructions—Care should be taken to see that the seed is properly spaced and the soil firmed.

Watering—Spinach is a quick growing leafy plant. It requires adequate moisture. This should be done by thoroughly soaking the area late in the day.

Date of planting—Early: March–April; Late: August–September.

Succession planting—Spinach is a cool weather crop. It is not damaged by late spring frosts. Plant a row every 2 weeks until summer, and again in the early fall.

Companion cropping—Early spinach may be followed by later maturing bush or pole beans.

Thinning—The young plants should be thinned to stand 3" apart in the row. The plants removed may be used to form other rows.

Types—Bloomsdale Long Standing, 48 days to maturity; Summer Savoy, 50 days to maturity; Nobel, 49 days to maturity.

Harvesting—The outer leaves are gathered and the center of the plant left intact to continue growth and the production of new leaves.

Storage—When winter comes, strong plants may be mulched with a deep layer of dry straw, grass, weeds, etc. Under this mulch, they will survive the winter and be available for a very early spring crop.

Yield—A 100 foot row should yield about 3 bushels of edible material.

Note—New Zealand spinach, while not really a spinach, may be used as a substitute, will grow during the heat of the summer, and is excellent to fill the period between spring and fall crops.

35. Squash

Soil—Sandy loam, rich in natural humus.

Location—Squash thrives best in well drained sandy locations where the soil warms up quickly.

Fertilizer—An abundance of moisture and plant nutrients is essential. This is best supplied by using mature compost humus. If necessary, well rotted manure may be substituted.

Soil type—Acid or alkaline. Squashes succeed in a slightly acid soil. The texture of the soil is of greater importance. It is possible to improve the condition of very heavy soils by the incorporation of large quantities of a 50-50 mixture of mature compost humus and sharp sand.

Depth of planting — Summer squash: ½"–1"; Winter squash: 1".

Width apart in the row—Summer squash: 36"–72". Winter squash: 72"–96".

Distance between rows—48"–72", 72"–96".

How much seed—¼ ounce will plant 50 feet of row.

Planting instructions—If bush-type squashes are planted, they may be set out in the garden like bush beans. But if the vine types are used, care should be made to allow for the large area they will cover. A good plan is to plant vine squashes at the edge of the garden near an uncultivated area and cause them to climb over the weeds. Vine squashes may also be "pinched back" after they have attained some length to check their wandering.

Watering—Seedlings should receive adequate moisture during their early growth.

Date of planting — Summer squash: April–May; Winter squash: May–June.

Succession planting—It is a good plan to plant only a few short rows of Summer squash, and to save the greater part of the planting for Winter squashes, which may be stored and used when vegetables are scarce.

Thinning—Most squash seed is viable. Avoid seeding too thickly to have to thin later. Squash seed not used will retain its vitality for several years if properly stored.

Types—Summer squash: Golden Summer Crookneck, 53 days to maturity; Zucchini Bush, 56 days to maturity; Cocozelle Bush, 60 days to maturity. Winter squash: Blue Hubbard, 120 days to maturity; Buttercup, 105 days to maturity; Golden Delicious, 105 days to maturity.

Harvesting—Summer squash is picked during the summer as needed in the kitchen. It is usually taken before reaching maturity. Winter squash should be allowed to remain until just before the first frosts arrive in the fall.

Storage—Winter squash for storage should have a shell sufficiently hard so that pressure by the thumb nail will not mar it. It should be gathered and carefully washed and allowed to remain in a protected place for 24 hours to cure. Perfectly sound squashes may then be selected and brought into the house for storage in single layers on shelves in a moderately cool place. Wiping them every few weeks with an oily cloth prevents the formation of a very damaging mould.

Yield—Per hundred feet of row: Summer squash, 135 pounds; Winter squash: 30 pounds.

36. Sweet Corn

Soil—Fertile, medium loam, not overly rich.

Location—Well drained, sunny hillsides, in locations which are new and have not been previously cultivated. Corn is a tough plant. It will thrive in locations where most garden vegetables would fail to survive.

Fertilizer—Corn demands sufficient natural humus for its heavy growth. The soil may be rough but an adequate supply of plant nutrients should be there. If the ground is not already rich, this material is best furnished by digging about 1" layer of compost humus into the area where sweet corn is to grow. Well rotted manure may also be substituted.

Soil type—Acid or alkaline. For corn, the soil should contain its natural quota of calcium. If this is lacking, it should be replaced by the use of ground limestone, which will also make for the success of other garden crops.

Depth of planting—½"–1".

Width apart in the row—Early: 36"; Late: 48".

Distance between rows—Early: 36"–48"; Late: 48".

How much seed—½ pint will seed 50 feet of row.

Planting instructions—Plant the seed, after all danger of frost has passed and the ground has warmed up, about 6" apart in the row and thin later to 12", or plant in hills, as above, allowing 3 seeds to the hill. Any spot in the garden where more than one seed is planted is called a hill. The seed should be well firmed and no unused seed should be allowed to remain on the surface to attract crows who will thus be led to digging out the planted seed.

Date of planting—Early: April–May; Late: May–June.

Succession planting—It is a good plan to plant a row of sweet corn every week or so in the spring. In this way, the harvest is spread over a long period.

Companion cropping—Low-growing crops such as onions, carrots, etc., may be planted in the same row with the sweet corn. Lettuce of the heading type often does exceptionally well under these conditions because the corn supplies the slight shade necessary for the heading up of the lettuce. Be sure enough available plant food exists and that enough moisture is supplied.

Types—Early: Golden Bantam, 82 days to maturity; Golden Giant, 85 days to maturity. Late: Delicious, 91 days to maturity; Evergreen, 95 days to maturity.

Harvesting—It is best to have a large pot of water going at a rolling boil before you think of gathering any sweet corn ears. Secure the ears and shuck them rapidly and slip them one by one into the boiling water. The water should contain a little sweet milk.

Yield—100 feet of row should yield about 48 ears.

Note—Popcorn may be planted in small amounts but with very satisfactory results. Also there are various types of corn which produce multicolored ears which are valuable during the fall celebrations.

37. Sweet Potatoes

Soil—Warm, sandy, well drained, and well aerated.

Location—A warm, well drained, location, sheltered from northern cold winds.

Fertilizer—Sweet potatoes are famous for their ability to survive in soil lacking its quota of natural plant food. However, they do best in the north in sheltered locations and under conditions where the natural plant nutrients are easily available.

Depth of planting—4″–6″.

Width apart in the row—12″.

Distance between rows—41″.

How much seed—50 plants will fill 50 feet of row.

Planting instructions—Sweet potato slips are sprouted from sweet potatoes. These young plants should be set carefully. The shoots should be planted slightly lower than they were evidently grown in the cold frame and should be well supplied with compost water. There are two common methods of growing sweet potatoes, the first is to dig in a liberal quantity of mature compost humus before setting the slips and to apply an equal amount of compost humus as a side dressing after the plants are up. The second method requires that the total amount of humus be applied after the plant tips appear.

Date of planting—May.

Succession planting—Sweet potatoes may be planted to follow early spring crops, such as radish, lettuce, etc.

Companion cropping—Sweet potatoes may be planted in the same rows with bush beans, pole beans, etc.

Types—Nancy Hall, Yellow Jersey, Puerto Rico. Plants should be set out anytime between April 15 and July 1.

Harvesting—When they are large enough for use in the kitchen, the roots may be dug.

Storage—Sweet potatoes, after being dug, are best held for curing at a temperature of about 85° F. for about 10 days. The humidity should be high—90 percent. In this way, many injuries to the surface of the roots sustained during digging will be healed. After curing them, the sweet potatoes should be stored in a place having a temperature of about 55° F., and having a high humidity, that is quite damp.

Yield—100 feet of row should yield about 2 bushels of edible roots.

Note—Until recent years, the growing of sweet potatoes was unknown in the northern states. Today, however, young plants produced in the south are sent north in a condition favorable to the production of a good crop of tubers.

38. Swiss Chard

Soil—Swiss chard thrives on any garden soil containing natural mature humus. For best results, the soil should be supplied with lime—about 50 pounds per 1,000 square feet of garden space.

Location—Open, sunny, well drained.

Fertilizer—Along the line where the row of plants is to stand, a small ridge of compost humus should be laid down and then dug in. The ridge need not be more than 3″ by 3″. Well rotted manure may be substituted, if necessary.

Soil type—Swiss chard belongs to the beet family. It responds to the use of lime and the absence of great acidity.

Depth of planting—1″.

Width apart in the row—8″ to 12″.

Distance between rows—1½ feet.

How much seed—1 packet will sow 25 feet of row, 1 ounce 100 feet.

Planting instructions—It is best to form a shallow trench using the corner of the hoe. In this trench, place the seeds about 4" apart and cover with 1" of sifted compost humus, firm carefully.

Date of planting—March–May; Latest date, June.

Companion cropping—Although chard succeeds itself in its long growing season, it is possible to plant the seed in a row of low-growing, quick-maturing plants such as radishes or beats.

Thinning—If seeds are sown 4" apart, the plants may be thinned as soon as they start to crowd, until they finally stand 12" or 15" apart in the row. The thinned material may be used in the house.

Types—Fordhook Giant, 60 days to maturity; Rhubarb Chard, 65 days to maturity.

Harvesting—Only the outer leaves of the chard should be gathered. The inner, younger leaves should be allowed to remain so that the plant will continue to grow and thus form a steady supply of valuable greens throughout the summer.

Storage—Chard may be kept producing through all but the most severe winters by covering the plants with a deep layer of dry straw, weeds, or similar material.

Note—Because chard is a member of the beet family, it is best to soak the seeds for 24 hours before planting. The seed should be soaked in compost water, that is, water which has been placed in a container ⅔ full of sifted compost humus, allowed to stand for 24 hours, and then drained off.

39. Tomatoes

Soil—Light, porous, and well drained.

Location—Sunny and open.

Fertilizer—About a ½ pound of sifted compost humus should be worked in around the roots of the plants when setting them out. Tomatoes respond readily to a mulch of compost humus placed around each plant upon the arrival of warm weather.

Soil type—If the soil is excessively acid, ground limestone or oyster-shell lime should be raked in before planting time at the rate of 75 pounds per 1,000 square feet of garden space.

Depth of planting—Seed: ½"; Plants: 1" deeper than the plant stood before it was moved. A 3" square of wrapping paper rolled around the stem of each plant so as to cover the stem at slightly below surface level will prevent cutworms from doing injury.

Width apart in the row—36" to 48".

Distance between rows—48" to 60".

How much seed—10¢ packet of seed for 100 feet of row.

Planting instructions—The hole which is to receive the plant should be wide and deep enough for the roots to be well spread out. Enough water should be applied to secure proper contact between soil and roots. In warm weather, the young plants should be protected by inverted baskets, etc.

Watering—Except during excessively hot, dry weather, tomato plants seldom require watering.

Special care—For larger tomatoes, the plants should be pruned to 1 or 2 stems and tied to stakes. The stakes should be about the thickness of a broomstick. They may be smooth surfaced or rough finished. They should be about 6 feet long and driven into the ground 6" to 8".

Date of planting—May–June, after all danger of frost is past. Latest date, June 30.

Succession planting—Plant early and late varieties.

Types—Earliana, 58 days to maturity from time of setting out the plant; Marglobe, 73 days maturity from time of setting out the plant; Ponderosa, 81 days to maturity from time of setting out the plant.

Harvesting—Crop should be harvested before frost.

Storage—Sound green tomatoes which form on the vines too late to ripen, may be gathered, wrapped individually in pieces of paper, and stored in a cool, dark place. They will ripen without light and furnish a supply of fresh fruit for winter use.

40. Turnips

Soil—Sandy and not too rich in nitrogen.

Location—Cool-weather plant requiring a temperate climate, adequate moisture, and good drainage.

Fertilizer—Turnips require very little extra plant nutrients. They are especially valuable to the gardener in that they will thrive on the plant foods left unconsumed by the spring crop which they are planted to follow. With early turnips, however, it is best to dig in a liberal supply of mature compost humus, diluted with sand if the soil is very clayey.

Soil type—Turnips thrive in relatively poor soils. However, they do best in a soil only moderately acid.

Depth of planting—Early: ¼" to ½"; Late: ½".

Width apart in the row—Early: 4" to 6"; Late: 6" to 8".

Distance between rows—15".

How much seed—One packet of seed 50 feet of row, one ounce 250 feet.

Planting instructions—A shallow trench should be formed using the corner of the hoe and the seed sown thinly, not closer than 6" apart, and covered with finely sifted compost humus about ¼" deep. The seed should be watered and well firmed.

Watering—Turnips send down a taproot to some depth. However, they require plenty of moisture to mature their large roots. This should be applied when necessary by giving them a thorough soaking.

Date of planting—Usually considered as a fall crop, turnips may be matured during the cool months of early spring. Early crop: Just as soon as the ground can be worked; Late crop: From the middle of July to the middle of August.

Succession planting—Late turnips are very successfully grown to follow any crop which matures before the end of July. A very good plan is to look over the garden about this date, see how many rows are vacant, and plant turnips to grow using the plant nutrients left over by the crops which occupied these rows.

Thinning—Seedlings should be thinned to stand, at the most, not closer than 3" apart.

Types—Purple–Top–White Globe, 55 days to maturity; Golden Ball, 57 days to maturity; White Milan early, 48 days to maturity.

Harvesting—Turnips will withstand hard frost but they should be harvested before the ground freezes solid.

Storage—For storage, the turnips should be gathered and topped late in the fall. They may be then stored in a root cellar or in small pits built in the garden. A very simple method used to form a small pit is to dig a hole in a well drained place sufficiently large to admit an apple or orange crate after the hole has been lined with 3" of dry straw weeds, etc. Fill the box with sound turnips, cover with straw, and place over it an inverted box of about the same size. Cover this structure with a foot thick layer of straw, and upon this place about a foot of topsoil, well smoothed and built up to a ridge.

Yield—100 feet of row should yield about 2 bushels of fine quality turnips.

41. Watercress

(Many gardeners have access to little streams where an ample supply of watercress may be grown without encroaching on the garden area. These little places should be taken advantage of to provide the kitchen with a liberal supply of valuable salad material.)

Soil—Watercress is commonly grown in a shallow running stream of pure water with a clean, sandy bottom.

Location—Moist, shady soil, with plenty of water. Watercress is often grown commercially by digging in leaf mold or compost humus over meadows below river level, planting the cuttings, and flooding them sufficiently with river water to promote their rapid and succulent growth.

Fertilizer—On a small scale, it is advisable to fill pots or other receptacles with sifted, mature compost humus. These receptacles should be set in pans of running water, and the seed planted ⅛" deep. Avoid the use of any kind of raw manure, use compost or, if necessary, sharp sand, with a light admixture of leaf mold. It is essential that the water supply be pure and suitable for drinking purposes. Any fertilizing material which is likely to contaminate the plants is to be avoided.

Soil type—Watercress thrives best in water heavily loaded with a supply of natural calcium.

Width apart in the row—12″.

Distance between rows—18″.

How much seed—1 packet of seed should plant 100 feet of row. When it is not possible to secure seed, and seed of watercress is often scarce, it is very easy to buy a few bunches of watercress on the market and cause them to form roots by placing the bunches in jars of water. This water should be changed daily, and the plants kept in a cool, shady place. When the stalks are thick with roots, they may be transplanted.

Planting instructions—Where a clean area or shallow running fresh water is available, it is best to lay down about 2″ of mature compost humus and stir lightly to mix with the stream bottom. Just as soon as the seedlings are well grown they should be transplanted in groups to their permanent place. This plant grows especially well when planted near the edges of running water that is supplied by springs which issue from limestone rocks. When once established in a clear brook, it spreads with great luxuriance.

Date of planting—Seeds: March–April; Transplants: April–May.

Types—Watercress is still very near to nature. No special types have been developed, 50 days to maturity.

Harvesting—Watercress is a perennial, aquatic plant. It is frequently harvested quite early in the spring, and again in the cool of the fall.

Yield—100 feet of row should yield about 100 large bunches.

PART IV

PROTECTION AGAINST
THE BUGS—
SOME ALTERNATIVES TO
INSECTICIDES

Hundreds of thousands of gardeners in this country have made up their minds to grow fruits and vegetables, flowers, and lawns *without* using pesticides and weed killers. They realize the danger of poison spray residues—how the problem can eventually be more serious to mankind than fallout. They have read about the death of children from playing with pesticide containers; they know how bird populations and wildlife have been killed by indiscriminate use of sprays. They understand the futility of having to make continually more lethal substances in order to kill the new insect generations which have built up a resistance to the older types. They have no desire to pollute the portion of the earth which they own. They have made their decision *not to use poison sprays*.

In the next section, we will set forth some of the methods used by organic gardeners to control insect damage. We do not include all methods for the simple reason that new ones are being devised daily, as often as one careful observer of insects gets an idea. You will learn the methods used by people who have successfully made the transition from the separate gardening worlds of artificial and organic. While the way at times may have been confusing, their path has led them to a method compatible with their goals.

You'll learn about some strange ideas that work; the skeptics will scoff—but that's the role of skeptics, and we expect it. Organic gardeners and farmers have learned to be quite skeptical themselves about the majority view on insect control methods, so we're not sensitive when the roles are reversed.

The only thing we do hope is that the variety of control methods described in the following pages will show without doubt that poison sprays are not the answer to preventing plant damage by insects. Consider the warning of Nobel Prize Winner Joshua Lederberg of Stanford University: "Every mouthful of food any American eats in the next century," he explains, "will contain at least one molecule of DDT—even if DDT were never used again!" Put another way, the gardener or farmer who blithely sprayed this highly promoted poison back in 1942 (when it was first applied to food crops and entered water, soil, air, and all living things) had half of the DDT remaining in his own polluted environment in 1956, and one-quarter of it is still there today. What's more, in 1984, one-eighth of that poison will be right there causing trouble.

Since the mid 1940s when large-scale use of "hard" pesticides began, "something on the order of *a million metric tons* of DDT have been distributed over the earth," estimates Dr. Goran Lofroth of the Institute of Biochemistry, Stockholm, Sweden. Because of its persistence, much of this poison remains in the environment and in the tissues of living things. The concentration increases on the way up the natural food chain— amphipods (tiny sand fleas) contain approximately .014 ppm, the small fish that feed on them contain 3.6 ppm, and coho salmon as much as 20 ppm.

When accumulated poison reaches high proportions, damage to the organism results. Persistent pesticide residues present serious hazards to consumers. They simply do not deteriorate or disappear from our food, and neither washing nor cooking destroys them. Taken into our bodies, they are stored in fatty tissue—and evidence of their danger to both man and beast continues to mount. There is a close link between pesticides and cancer; reproduction is disrupted in birds and wildlife; mother's milk is now found laced with about four times as much DDT as is permitted in milk sold to the public; and residues discovered in stillborn and unborn babies are capable of doubling the mutation rate in man, according to famed British geneticist Dr. Osny G. Fahmy.

Turning to stronger and stronger insecticides certainly isn't the answer. Pests quickly develop resistance, then immunity to the chemical compounds used to clobber them indiscriminately. Look at it the way Dr. Robert van den Bosch, head of the University of California's Division of Biological Control at Albany, puts it: "Modern agricultural chemicals," he says, "are ecologically crude in their effect on insect components in the environment." These chemicals are designed to kill off 100 to 1,000 species, including the beneficial insects. (Remember, there are nearly 700,000 known species of insects—and one of people.) "Chemical sprays as they are used today create an insect vacuum for a time. Then, all the old pests come roaring back at a level increased 15 times. It's a disruption of the natural balance—and it's happening all over the world."

One final thought: Some people have trouble adjusting themselves mentally to the idea of working with nature instead of trying to dominate her. Insect control, as described here, requires that the gardener must put more trust in nature and disabuse himself of the notion that science has the answer for every problem. We must realize that man has yet to make nature knuckle under to his will. We must adjust ourselves to working with nature. Once that is done, the decisions, methods, and problems no longer seem so difficult to solve.

Recognition and Quarantine

A big step in any control program is knowing who the culprit is. With a little practice, you can learn to recognize at a glance the signs and symptoms of common pests.

The various chewing insects make their own patterns. Flea beetles make tiny round perforations; weevils produce rather typical angular openings; beetle larvae (grubs) "skeletonize" leaves, chewing everything but the epidermis and veins.

Sucking insects cause leaves to be yellowish, stippled white or gray. These insects, as well as their brownish eggs or excrement, can often be seen on the underside of foliage. Red spider can be spotted by yellowed leaves that are cobwebby or mealy underneath; whitish streaks mean thrips. When leaves are curled up or cupped down, look out for aphids. Deformed leaves may be caused by cyclamen mite; blotches or tunnels by leaf miners; round or conical protrusions by aphids, midges, or gall wasps.

The partial collapse and dying of a plant, termed *wilt,* may result from a number of causes—very often nematodes or grubs.

Quarantine for Plants

No one would think of going out of his way to visit someone who has a contagious disease. Yet this phenomenon occurs daily in gardens everywhere. The amusing hobby of keeping a "pet" diseased plant for anyone to handle should not be tolerated; it is very dangerous. Everyone who enters the garden is shown it and asked if he or she knows what the trouble is. While giving an opinion, the visitor does the natural thing—turns up the leaves to see the disease underneath and later examines plant after plant in similar manner, thereby infecting the entire garden.

There is a strong case for isolation and destruction of diseased and insect-ridden plants. Recent experiences show that it is not a good practice to use such plants as a mulch or, in fact, in sheet composting. It's risky trying to use infected plants, except in the compost heap, and even then you must be careful. When in doubt, it's better to destroy such material and to make certain of not spreading the trouble.

All gardeners should become health-minded and not worry too much about disease. If it comes, act promptly and destroy the first specimen. Feed the soil so that plants are in sturdy health, because all the remedies in the world are useless if the underlying cause is repeatedly neglected,

writes the English authority, E. R. Janes, in his book, *The Vegetable Garden*.

Safe Insecticides

When insect damage has been severe, organic gardeners have made use of certain nontoxic sprays ranging from dormant oil to pepper juice. Generally, even commercial insecticides which are advertised to be nontoxic should be used only in emergencies (and then with caution) because of the possibility of upsetting the natural balance.

Below we list some of the spray materials used from time to time by organic gardeners and which solved the insect problem for them.

1. Dormant Oil Sprays

Used properly, a 3 percent miscible dormant oil spray is effective against a host of chewing and sucking insects. Aphids, red spider, thrips, mealybugs, whiteflies, pear psylla, all kinds of scale insects, and mites fall before it. The eggs of the codling moth, oriental fruit fly, various leaf rollers, and cankerworms are destroyed.

A dormant spray is applied to fruit trees before any of the buds open. Some gardeners make it a practice to use it on all dormant trees, shrubs, and evergreens every spring, but this is rarely necessary if the plants have been organically grown for a number of years. Fruit trees, however, have many enemies, and dormant spraying should be a regular practice for them, along with a strict program of sanitation.

In early spring, insects that hatch from eggs laid on plants the previous fall can be readily killed because the shells of the eggs and the protective covering of hibernating scales become softer and more porous at this time. The dormant spray penetrates and makes a tight, continuous film over these, literally suffocating the organism to death.

It will, of course, form a similar film over leaves and injure them, which is why it is applied only while the trees are in a leafless state. Citrus trees, which do not shed their leaves, are given a very dilute spray, usually made with "white oils," highly refined oils that present the least chance of foliage injury.

Dormant oil sprays have a residual effect, too. An oil film covering the plant interferes with the successful establishment of any young insects that may hatch for several days after spraying.

Stock preparations of miscible oil sprays are sold by all garden supply stores, with instructions for dilution and use. You can also make your own, using a gallon of light-grade oil and a pound of fish-oil soap (an emulsifier) to a half gallon. These ingredients are mixed together, brought to a boil, and poured back and forth from one container to another until emulsified (thoroughly blended). Since all oil emulsions tend to separate into oil and water again, the mixture should be used as soon as possible after it is prepared. Dilute it with 20 or more times its volume of water for use.

Sometimes miscible oils are combined with Bordeaux mixture, arsenate of lead, or other strong chemicals to increase their insecticidal power. These are definitely harmful to plants and dangerous to handle, and should never be used. Lime sulfur is also employed as a dormant spray, but it is intensely poisonous, will harm the soil and plants, and is generally less effective than an oil spray.

It is difficult to apply harmful amounts of a miscible oil spray. If too much of the emulsion is applied, the excess simply runs off. A tree should, for this reason, be sprayed all at once, not one-half first (as when a sprayer goes down an orchard row), the other half later, after the first has dried. Almost twice as much oil would. in this case, be deposited where the coverages overlap, and this could conceivably cause damage on citrus trees, especially in arid areas. The drier and warmer the air, it seems, the more likelihood of damage, though probably quite slight. Always cover a tree thoroughly in one spraying.

Sometimes oil sprays are recommended for summer use, when the trees are in leaf. This is not a good practice as it can cause leaf burn and heavy leaf and fruit drop, as well as changes in the flavor of the fruit. The insects are destroyed just as effectively, or in some cases, more effectively, in the spring.

In recent years, fruit growers in the northeast have been using superior, dormant oil sprays. These highly refined oils, safer to use later than the regular ones, are sprayed after some new growth has appeared in the buds.

This later application is said to give a higher kill of, for example, European red mites, whose eggs become increasingly more susceptible to oil as their hatching period approaches. More mite eggs are killed with a 2 percent superior oil spray applied in the delayed dormant stage than by a 4 percent spray when the trees are still dormant. The delayed dormant stage of apples is said to be when about a ½ inch of leaf tissue is exposed in the blossom buds. A 3 percent superior oil concentration will destroy many oil-resistant pests.

2. Ryania—Plant-derived Insecticide

Discovered in 1943, ryania is a powder made by grinding up the roots of the South American plant *Ryania speciosa*. Although it is useful in controlling corn borers, cranberry fruitworm, codling moth, oriental fruit fly, cotton bollworm, and other insects, ryania has little effect on warm-blooded organisms.

The use of ryania may not actually reduce the number of harmful insects present, but it will protect the plant by making the pests sick enough to lose their appetites. Some species are not killed outright by it. They are induced into a state of "flacid paralysis."

We do not give an unqualified recommendation for ryania, or other plant-derived insecticides. There are many organic gardeners who are proud of the balanced insect populations in their gardens, and who don't need any other insect controls. Also, many people want food that is untainted with *any* insecticides, no matter how mild.

But there are certain problem plants that may cause you to lose all your crops to insects year after year—apples, for example. If you lose your apple crop to the codling moth, you will probably go out and buy apples from trees that have been sprayed up to 16 times in a season with the most deadly of poisons. Treating a few of your own trees with ryania is better than eating store-bought apples. So we are recommending ryania for those limited situations when you feel that you must give nature a helping hand.

When using ryania against codling moth, purchase 100 percent ryania dust and mix it with water at the rate of about one ounce per 2 gallons of water. If you want a stronger solution, you can use 1¼ ounce per 2 gallons of water. In larger quantities, it is mixed at the rate of 3 to 4 pounds per 100 gallons of water. About 5 sprays are needed during the season. Start spraying 10 to 14 days after the petals fall and continue at 10- to 14-day intervals until you have sprayed 3 or 4 times. When the second brood of codling-moth larvae hatch, give 1 to 3 additional sprays at 10- to 14-day intervals. Your county agent should be able to tell you when the second brood is hatching. An ordinary hand sprayer holding 2 to 3 gallons of solution should be sufficient for the small orchard.

3. Rotenone

Rotenone, sometimes called derris, is an insecticide derived from certain tropical plants, derris, cube barbasco, timbo, and a few others. It is a contact and stomach poison, often mixed with pyrethrum, and is of very low toxicity to man and animals. Like pyrethrum, it can be obtained in the pure state only from pet shops and veterinarians. It is a dustlike powder that is applied just like its more noxious cousins. When purchased in commercial dusts and sprays, rotenone is often mixed with synthetic compounds that may be toxic in varying degrees. Devil's shoestring (*Tephrosia virginiana*) is the only native plant which contains rotenone. It is a common weed in the eastern and southern states, and its roots may contain as high as 5 percent rotenone. Rotenone can be safely used on all plants and ornamentals. It kills many types of insects, and also certain external parasites of animals. However, it has little residual effect, and the period of protection it offers is short.

4. Grow Your Own Insecticides

The buds, flowers, leaves, or roots of some plants can be used as a safe means of insect control. And you don't have to be a chemist to be an insecticide grower; in some cases, merely *raising* the plants in your garden is enough.

For example, marigolds, asters, chrysanthemums, and related plants of the aster family are known to drive away some insects. Cosmos, coreopsis, and many herbs will also keep insects away. So plant a row of these colorful flowers in your vegetable patch; you'll get pest protection plus some more flowers for cutting.

Many old-fashioned gardens had their herb plot near the kitchen door—not only for convenience, but since insecticides were unknown in those days, a sprig kept the house free of "unwelcome visitors." Tansy, growing closely to the kitchen wall, kept out ants.

Coriander contains an oil used in an emulsion spray to kill spider mites and cotton aphids. Anise, another popular herb, has practically the same properties as coriander.

The *Missouri Botanical Garden Bulletin* has reported that the hedge apple, the large, green, ball-like fruit of the Osage orange tree, *Maclura pomifera*, is gaining a reputation as an insect repellant. "One green fruit, hedge ball, Osage orange, Osage apple, or whatever you want to call it, placed in a room infested with roaches and waterbugs, will drive the creatures out in a few hours." Such use was discovered by chemists at the University of Alabama.

Members of the cucurbit family, as pumpkins and squash, make effective fly repellents. Here's what to do. Nip leaves carefully from strong, growing vines. Crush them and rub on the backs and heads of cattle. For another fly (and flea) repellent, gather sprigs of mint leaves, hang them about doorways, place them in the dog kennel and where flies gather.

In India, the Peruvian ground cherry *(Nicandra physalodes)* is effective as a fly repellent merely by placing some bruised leaves around a room. If planted in quantity near a barn, the animals are said not to be troubled with flies; used in a greenhouse, the whitefly disappears.

Two researchers at the University of California, Peter Ark and James Thompson, have found that garlic is an effective destroyer of many bacteria that damage fruits, vegetables, and nuts. In their tests, they used diluted garlic-clove juice or powdered garlic extracts. They also discovered that garlic keeps its antibiotic properties for at least 3 years when stored in a dry place.

Here is an abstract of the research work of Professor Ark and Thompson entitled the "Control of Certain Diseases of Plants with Antibiotics from Garlic."

The juice of garlic cloves *(Allium sativum L.)* and aqueous as well as certain organic solvent extracts of commercial garlic powder possess strongly bactericidal and fungicidal properties. Both Gram-positive and Gram-negative plant pathogens are sensitive to garlic extracts in varying degrees. The volatile component of garlic preparations is equally toxic to plant pathogenic microorganisms. Downy mildew of cucumber, downy mildew of radish, cucumber scab, bean rust, bean anthracnose, early blight of tomato, brown rot of stone fruits, angular leaf spot of cucumber, and bacterial blight of beans were effectively controlled by sprays of 1 to 20 percent aqueous extracts of garlic powder preparations. Downy mildew of cucumber and bean rust were controlled by a dust formulation of garlic powder in pyrophyllite carrier. The objectionable odor of garlic in sprays was completely neutralized by water-soluble neutroleum. Garlic powder preserved its antibiotic property for three years, when stored at room temperature in a closed cardboard container.

5. Grinding Plants

Charles Coleman has come up with a unique way of making safe insecticides at home. Here's what he does: "I find some plant in the neighborhood which is not bothered by the pest (the one that is troubling my garden plants). Usually quite a few weeds are resistant. I run these through a meat grinder, or food chopper, saving liquid and residues, and add an equal amount of water. I use the ground-material soakings to spray or sprinkle the plants I want to protect. The soakings apparently contain the organic substances that keep the plant from being bothered. As simple as this sounds, it works very well."

Other gardeners, who have noted that the elderberry seems

to be always free of diseases and insect damage of all kinds, spray their plants with a concoction of elderberry leaves. This method appears to be successful in protecting plants from insects and disease.

6. Milk Stops Mosaic

S. B. Fenne, plant pathologist at Virginia Polytechnic Institute, says tobacco farmers who have had trouble with mosaic would do well to try the new milk method of control. He explains that tobacco mosaic is one of the older known diseases. It is caused by a highly contagious virus that is spread by contact. Little progress was made in its control during the past 25 years, but, in 1958 and 1959, scientists found that the use of milk in any form on tobacco at transplanting time will greatly reduce losses.

Two types of treatment have been used. The plant bed can be sprayed 24 hours before pulling the plants with 5 gallons of whole or skim milk or 5 pounds of dried skim milk mixed with 5 gallons of water per 100 square yards. Or the grower can use whole or skim milk or a mixture of 1 pound of dried skim milk to 1 gallon of water in which to dip his hands about every 20 minutes while pulling and transplanting plants.

Diluted milk will put a stop to the inroads made by tomato mosaic virus, reports J. Newell, John Innes Horticultural Institution. Results of tests, Newell says, show that if milk diluted with 9 parts of water is sprayed on tomatoes at 10-day intervals after transplanting, the plants will be practically free from virus. The tests were run on potentate tomatoes which normally are infected to an extent of about 95 percent with virus. Application of the diluted milk reduced infection to 5 percent.

A milk spray has also been found effective against one of the most destructive viruses of crops, sugarcane mosaic.

Whole cow's milk, sprayed directly on sugarcane and sorghum plants, prevents the destructive virus from taking a footing, Dr. Louis Anzalone Jr. of the department of plant pathology, Louisiana State University, Baton Rouge, explained in the *Science News Letter*.

The virus is now controlled by the use of resistant varieties of plants, he said. But new strains of the virus are causing damage to some plants, and other varieties of the plants could become important if protected.

The most effective inhibitor of infection tested by the scientist was common table milk before treatment. When mixed with parts of an infective juice extracted from an infected plant or used alone, it prevented infestation for some time after application.

7. Pepper Juice Fights Virus

Evidence that the juice of sweet peppers will put up a winning battle against the effects of virus are presented by C. D. McKeen in *Science*. Tests which have been run, McKeen says, show that the juice of sweet peppers infected with cucumber mosaic virus will cause an average of only 0.4 lesions when rubbed onto the leaves of indicator hosts. This is compared to 150.6 lesions on the indicator host plants when treated directly with the juice from infected plants.

In another test, the juice from healthy peppers was added to the juice of cucumber mosaic virus obtained from infected tobacco plants. When this was applied to cowpeas, 7.9 lesions were produced. In contrast, 220.7 lesions were produced in cowpeas when the untreated cucumber mosaic virus was applied.

Similar results were obtained with ring spot virus from tobacco and cucumber, and with tobacco etch virus. In all cases, the juice from sweet peppers seemed to have the power of almost completely inhibiting the growth of whatever virus it was tried on.

In a California study, natural juices squeezed from succulent plants have been found to protect other plants from viruses. They work against disease that is transmitted by insects or wind.

Plants suffer from a variety of ailments similar to man. Viruses are one of the most common problems, seldom killing the plants but stunting growth and reducing fruit yields.

The juices of several varieties of plants have been extracted and concentrated by Drs. John N. Simons and Ronald Swidler of the Stanford Research Institute's Agricultural Research Center in Menlo Park, California, and tested for virus-inhibiting effectiveness. The sprays were found effective against tobacco mosaic virus, potato virus *Y*, and several other viruses carried by pesky aphids by their mouth parts. The compounds do not kill the viruses, the scientists said, but change the plant so it is not susceptible.

Chemicals such as these are believed possible for use in preventing transmission of virus in the field. The material is not harmful to plants, as opposed to other types of chemicals, and is probably nontoxic to animals and man.

8. Sugar and Nematodes

The nematode is reported to be the most numerous of all plant pests, but it's a rare gardener who has ever seen one. They are tiny little worms—sometimes called wireworms— that burrow in the soil and often suck their nutrients from plant roots. Although nematodes rarely kill a plant, the Department of Agriculture states that they probably damage every crop each year.

Not long ago USDA plant pathologist W. A. Feder was looking for ways to stimulate the growth of fungi that capture and destroy nematodes. In one experiment, he added cane sugar to the soil, thinking it would stimulate the fungi. Next day when he went to check, he found that many of the nematodes had been killed. Following up on this chance discovery, he made some more tests and found that it took 5 pounds of sugar per 100 pounds of soil to kill all nematodes within 24 hours. And as little as 1,000 parts per million of sugar in the soil would kill some nematodes within 10 minutes.

Strange as it may seem, sugar kills nematodes by drying them out. Here is the Department of Agriculture's description of what happens. Enough sugar is added to the soil to produce a greater amount of dissolved solids in the soil solution than in the cell fluid of the nematodes. Because liquid tends to move from a less concentrated solution to one more highly concentrated (osmosis), the body fluid moves out of the nematodes, and they die as a result of dehydration (exmosis).

Field tests confirmed the effectiveness of sugar in controlling nematodes, but the trouble is that the cost of the treatment is more than the benefits produced, except in the case of certain garden and greenhouse crops that are particularly susceptible to nematode damage. Also, it was found that some plants don't like sugar in the soil, and it has to be flushed out 24 hours after treatment. The interesting thing about this discovery is that it points up the fact that common, ordinary substances can have a great effect on the soil and the creatures living in it. If a simple substance like sugar can wipe out nematodes, what can some of those fancy chemicals do to other creatures?

The most practical answer to the nematode problem for the average gardener is to build up the humus content of this soil. Fungi are the enemy of nematodes, as was mentioned previously, and if you want to have a lot of fungi in your soil, you've got to have a lot of humus. Chances are that if your garden soil is already rich in humus, you're playing host to only a few weak-kneed, second rate, and sickly specimens of the nematode tribe.

9. Personal Experience with Onion and Pepper Sprays

Recently Mrs. E. C. Shaver, an organic gardener from Houston, Texas wrote us about the following experience:

Since reading in *Organic Gardening and Farming* about making safe insect sprays out of plants growing at your own home, I have been experimenting and I think I have discovered two very good things.

First: I ground up green shallot onions in my food chopper, added an equal amount of water, and strained it through a cloth. Then I sprayed it on my roses, and in just a few minutes the aphids began falling off on the ground. I sprayed every day for 3 days and every aphid was gone. Since then I have never found another aphid on my roses.

Second: My vegetable garden is in the second year of organic gardening so I still have lots of insects. My worst trouble is with cabbage worms. I have tried all the simple remedies and nothing gets rid of them. I was determined not to use poison sprays so I looked around for something organic to use. I had several plants of a hot pepper that is so hot we can't eat it. I ground up several pods of the hot pepper, added an equal amount of water, and a half spoon of soap powder to make it cling to cabbage and collards. I sprayed with the hot pepper water and my cabbage worms are all gone.

I also tried the pepper spray on several insects of different kinds with very good results. It was very effective on ant beds, spiders, caterpillars and tomato worms. I was so pleased with the results of my pepper spray that I canned several jars of ground pepper to save for next spring when I won't have fresh pepper in my garden.

I have also planted garlic, mint and parsley to use for spray. I intend to try each plant alone, then try grinding them all together with pepper. I read in a book, "We learn wisdom from failure much more than from success. We often discover what will do by finding out what will not do; and probably he who never made a mistake never made a discovery."

10. Hot Water vs. Brown Rot

Just a bath of plain hot water was discovered to be an effective means of preventing brown rot in peaches. Placing freshly picked peaches in hot water kills the fungi causing brown and Rhizopus rots—and doesn't harm the peach, claims Wilson L. Smith of the USDA's Agricultural Marketing Service.

Smith gives the peaches a hot-water bath just before sending them through the hydrocooler. He explains that it's the heat, not necessarily the water, that eliminates the fungi which cause thousands of dollars in losses of fresh fruit annually.

California fruit growers have used hot water to kill fungi on lemons before shipment. But this is the first time this treatment has been used successfully on a soft fruit.

As is the case with lemons, you can use a number of combinations of temperature and timing without damage to the peaches.

Smith and his group have reduced post-harvest decay by dipping peaches in 120° F. water for 7 minutes; in 130° F. water for 3 minutes, and in 140° F. water for 2 minutes.

They made sure that they were killing the right organisms, too. They inoculated fresh peaches with both brown and Rhizopus rots. Then they dunked a sample of the inoculated peaches in 120° F. water for 7 minutes.

After 6 days in a room maintained at 70° F., only a fourth

of the hot-water-treated peaches showed traces of Rhizopus rot and less than a tenth showed brown rot. None of the untreated peaches were marketable due to both brown and Rhizopus decay.

Hot-water treatment is effective even when you can't give the peaches their bath until 24 hours or more after harvesting, Smith finds.

One big advantage for growers in the new treatment is that *there's no residue problem.*

Smith plans to try his hot-bath treatment on strawberries, raspberries, and sweet potatoes.

Fruit scientists in other countries also are experimenting with heat treatment of soft fruits and vegetables, Smith reports. Australian scientists, in particular, are making headway against decay fungi by treating fruit with hot air.

Companion Planting

Companion plantings—mixing one plant with another in the vegetable row or flower bed—have already been suggested as a good way to cut down on insect damage. Following are a few more examples of this practice.

Chives Chase Aphids from Roses

An old-timer once said to me, "If you want to keep aphids off your rose bushes, just plant clumps of chives between the plants."

"How ridiculous," I thought at the time. But the more I thought of it, the more I figured, "These old-timers are often so right; why not try it?"

So 3 years ago, I purchased a few clumps of chives which I planted in the rose bed. As they developed, I separated them and spread more clumps through the bed and also beside my rose climbers. I found that what he had told me is absolutely true—I never have aphids on the rose bushes. Furthermore, the neighbors on both sides of me are also using chives between their roses. When the plants grow too big and begin to blossom, you can cut them down, and they will come up again from the roots. However the purple blossoms are quite attractive in the garden.

The chives serve a double purpose. Besides keeping the aphids away, the tops are really delicious cut up in salads and soups. However, to have them tender and young, you must keep the old growths and blossoms cut off.—HELEN W. KORTZ.

Garlic against Peach Borers

To keep peach borers from killing our trees, C. C. Grant of Davenport, Iowa, plants garlic cloves around the tree as close to the trunk as possible. He lost 2 or 3 trees before he learned this, but not one since using the idea.

"We now have a new orchard started and have planted garlic around each tree," writes Mr. Grant.

Marigolds in the Bean Patch

Reports Mrs. Albert Kohler of Palmerton, Pennsylvania: "I planted marigolds in my bean rows and did not have any beetles to speak of, while my neighbors' plants were eaten up by the Mexican bean beetles."

Other gardeners have reported on different experiences with a wide variety of plants. In her book on *Gardening without Poisons,* Beatrice Trum Hunter lists the following:

Plant nasturtiums between fruit trees as well as vegetables to repel aphids; plant tomatoes near asparagus to fight off the asparagus beetles; green beans near potatoes against the Colorado potato beetle (in turn, the potatoes help keep the Mexican beetle from attacking the beans). If you have trouble with potato bugs, plant horseradish between the potato rows. . . . If you have ants in your kitchen, there is an old remedy. Plant spearmint, julip mint or tansy near the kitchen wall.

There are repellent flowers, especially in the aster family. Marigolds, asters and chrysanthemums repel some insects. Cosmos and coreopsis are also repellents. Plant them in the vegetable garden.

Herbs are also capable of providing other plants with added protection. Basil, anise, and coriander are a few found especially effective.

Of course, basic to any insect control program is a sound rotation schedule as well as good cultural practices.

Choose Resistant Varieties

By planting a variety with high resistance, you can prevent a great deal of trouble right at the start. Much progress has already been made in this work, so when you're checking plant catalogs, be sure to look for such terms as *immune* or *slightly susceptible* in descriptions of plant resistance.

Dr. Byron T. Shaw, Agriculture Research Service Administrator, rates the importance of resistant varieties as follows: "The ultimate answer (to the chemical residue problem) is the breeding of plants that have natural resistance to insect attack. . . . Once you get to that stage, you just plant one kind of seed instead of another."

An example of breeding work underway is the attempt to develop cotton varieties that would starve some costly insects out of fields by removing most of the nectar they relish as food. A comparison of one popular variety with a new selection showed that there were 7 to 10 times as many leafworms and loopers on the old variety as on the new one.

Sometimes a plant is more likely to escape infection when it matures before the season of disease infection occurs, the way early maturing, potato varieties may escape late blight disease. Other times, the fact that a plant is drought resistant can help increase its defenses against attack.

The list of vegetable varieties, resistant to one or another disease or pest, is growing all the time. To prove this, compare the latest edition of a vegetable seed catalog with one printed 5 years ago. In many cases, ⅓ to ½ of the varieties available today are resistant to a specific trouble. For information on insect-resistant vegetable plants, check the seed catalog, visit the local seed store, or write your agricultural college.

Healthy growth is one of the best natural deterrents against both disease and bugs. It may be possible for a strain of corn to be developed which has low earworm damage because the ear is so tight that the earworms can't penetrate. Or vines (such as squash) may be so tough that borers can't get a start.

In 1963 tomato varieties and breeding lines were reported that could resist leaf miners. In recent years, tomatoes have been reported that resist spider mites, potato aphids, tobacco flea beetles, and whiteflies. The resistance reported to spider mites and potato aphids is in horticulturally desirable lines that possess multiple disease resistance. *This means two-for-one benefits for the gardeners who work with tomatoes that can handle both insects and disease.*

Resistance to 8 insect species has been reported among the crucifers—cabbage, broccoli, cauliflower, etc. Insects studied include the cabbage looper, aphid, maggot, and worm. Resistance to the most destructive insect of beans, the Mexican bean beetle, has also been reported. *In some cases, "near immunity exists," regarding the potato leafhopper and snap and lima beans.*

The inescapable fact is that the organic grower has valuable allies, thanks to the ever-developing resistant varieties. And, in addition to working with disease-free seeds and plants, there's something else he can do—run his garden on soundly organic principles of annual crop rotation plus strict sanitary practices in the field. Here are 7 recommended garden practices which should keep disease either completely out of the garden or hold it to an absolute minimum.

Work with resistant varieties and seeds

Study the catalogs carefully, and when you order a new species or variety, make sure it is disease resistant for your area. If you pay close attention to your plant and seed catalogs, you'll notice that this information is included in plant descriptions and general information.

Fertilize and compost vigorously and thoroughly

Build up your compost and mulching program until it is a real factor in your gardening program. While we admittedly don't know all about the many and sometimes obscure diseases we are fighting, we do know that soils with a high humus content encourage the soil microorganisms which keep disease bacteria from flourishing and establishing colonies.

Observe recommended planting dates for your area

Strict adherence to planting by variety for your general area often permits plants to make a crop before disease appears or becomes serious.

Use care in watering

If you must water, try not to get the foliage wet, or water early in the day so the foliage dries out completely by nightfall. Sprinkling in the late afternoon tends to spread foliage disease more readily.

Touch wet plants as little as possible

Stay out of the garden when plants are wet. Bacteria or fungus spores can be present in the moisture on the leaves. You can be the prime infective agent by merely going down the row—spreading the disease by touching the plants as you go.

Good garden sanitation and residue disposal

Clean up the garden at the end of the season and get the vegetable waste into the compost pile where the heating-up process will destroy the unwanted spores and bacteria. Turn under the remaining residues to prevent disease and build fertility for next year's crops.

Rotate your crops to avoid monoculture

If possible, don't grow the same crop twice in the same plot or row. Many important diseases, notably the nematode induced, can be checked by rotation.

—MAURICE FRANZ

Biological Control for the
Home Gardener

As public worry over the danger from poisonous sprays builds up, pressure has also increased upon the Department of Agriculture to explore the area of biological control. C. A. Fleschner of California's Citrus Experiment Station defines biological insect control as:

the practice of reducing the numbers of a pest by the use of natural agencies such as parasites, predators and diseases. The aim of biological control is to achieve the most practical means of pest control. The fundamental basis of such control is the fact that life in nature exists in a state of balance which is maintained by the competitive inter-action of various forces. However, man through his diverse activities frequently disturbs this natural balance, often with disastrous results to his own well-being.

There are already over 100 insects resistant to one insecticide or another, contends F. R. Lawson, director of the USDA's Biological Control laboratory at Columbia, Missouri, "and a few which are resistant to all insecticides currently available. If you knock off all natural enemies also, you're in serious trouble."

To pit insect against insect is to identify and encourage the natural enemy of a pest in order to help keep it under control. Another promising development is the synthesizing of "juvenile hormones," substances similar to an insect's own natural hormones which regulate its growth. Applied in microscopic quantities at the right time, the hormones can prevent insect larvae from growing into adults and reproducing.

Still another exciting area of research is the use of microbes to fight insects. So far, some 280 insect viruses have been isolated. Unlike chemicals, but like natural enemies and hormones, viruses are highly specific. A strain of virus will kill just 1 type insect and will harm no other form of life.

Recent legislation calling for reduction of chlorinated hydrocarbons and other "hard" pesticides has prodded scientists to concentrate on these new methods of control. The Columbia laboratory, for instance, is investigating 3 types of natural enemies of pests. One is the predatory insect such as the ladybug, which can make quick work of aphids; another are the tiny wasps *(trichogramma)*, which lay eggs either in the egg or larva of cabbage worms. The wasp larva feeds on the eggs of the cabbage worm until only a husk remains. A third control is viral or bacteriological.

Bacterial control isn't more widely used yet, partly because of a lack of publicity and because of the way it acts. A worm quits eating an hour after being sprayed with bacteria. But may remain on the plant for 2 or 3 days before it dies. This can lead the farmer to think it doesn't work since he's used to seeing a strong pesticide curl up a worm instantly. "A worm killed by bacteria doesn't die as dramatic a death," Lawson says, "but he's just as dead."

The bug-eat-bug method of insect control is entirely reasonable. It encourages a healthy natural balance in the garden, orchard, or park. It avoids more contamination of our air and food with toxic sprays, and prevents further harm to wildlife and pollution of the environment. And it actually costs far less.

So that communities and home gardeners can understand how economical the method is, and contrast it with the expense of spray equipment and poisons, we emphasize costs: ladybugs, $6.50 a gallon, from 100,000 to 125,000 per gallon. Average gardens need only a pint or two for protection from aphids, mites, scale insects, etc. An adult ladybug eats 40 to 50 of them a day! Praying mantis cases, which hatch up to 400 insect-and pest-egg-eating young each, currently sell 8 for $3. Trichogramma wasps, 500 or more at a price of about $3. They come on a card because they are practically microscopic and are especially valuable in fruit orchards as well as among ornamental trees and shrubbery.

Take the case of Allen Casper of Concordia, Kansas, as an example of effective biological control. Allen manages a number of land areas for a nonresident owner. He said 258 gallons of ladybugs were distributed at the rate of one gallon per 15 acres at a cost of about 75 cents per acre. Almost complete control was obtained within 48 hours after the release, and the 30 tenants who farm the land he manages were all pleased with the results. "Why pay $2.50 per acre to have milo sprayed when you can accomplish the job with 75 cents worth of ladybugs?" Casper asked. Why indeed?

The ladybug has also accomplished the task of reducing an exceptionally high population of pine bark aphids at the H. W. Toumey Nursery at Watersmeet, Michigan. By no means will it eliminate all insect problems in the garden. However, the aphids *are* its favorite food. Each ladybug consumes 40 to 50 aphids a day and will also feed on other insects, eggs, and larva. The heavy-eating ladybug has several built-in protection factors. Water will not wash the beetle off the plant. When other insects attack the ladybug, she extrudes an odorous fluid detering the attacking insect.

Many people are now using ladybugs as a control in flower gardens, yards, greenhouses, parks, alfalfa fields, cotton and corn growing areas. Nursery Superintendent Stuart Slayton states he is not only enthused with the contribution the ladybugs provide for a better balanced environment, but also the reduction in cost by using this method.

Praying mantises do their work too. And they are "a lot friendlier than a can of DDT," says Edward S. Fisher, who raises the insects to control populations of other insects in his Billings, Montana yard. The mantises, which grow to 2 or 3 inches long, will eat any insect they can catch, including wasps. He started raising them about 5 years ago, purchasing eggs from a California firm every year. Fisher comments that fifty cents worth of mantises is enough to last all summer.

Among insect-disease weapons already showing dramatic results are the spore-type *Bacillus thuringiensis* (Thuricide), which halts caterpillars and worms unpopular as major pests of several vegetable crops; milky spore disease (Doom), which controls Japanese beetles surprisingly well and is the reason that they are no problem in Japan; and the nuclear polyhedral virus, a potent stopper for the costly cabbage looper and corn earworm. New discoveries include a mold compound that kills or dwarfs the pesky housefly. Isolated by Drs. Raimon L. Beard and Gerald S. Walton of the Connecticut Agricultural Experiment Station, the peptide made from a common mold *(Aspergillus flavus)* produced complete control of housefly larvae within 24 hours after exposure.

Use of juvenile hormones—a technique that turns the insect populations' own hormones against them—zeroes in on them and prevents pests from maturing into plant-eating adults. Active in extremely small amounts (Swiss researchers cleared mealworm infestations from 5 tons of stored wheat with 20 milligrams—1/140 of an ounce—of JH), the hormone is being produced by the Zoecon Corp, of Palo Alto, California.

Where to Order Natural Controls

LADYBUGS
Bio-Control Company
Route 2, Box 2397
Auburn, California 95603
L. E. Schnoor
Rough & Ready, California 95975

PRAYING MANTISES
Eastern Biological Con. Co.
Route 5, Box 379
Jackson, New Jersey 08527
Gothard, Inc.
P. O. Box 332
Canutillo, Texas 79835
Robert Robbins
424 N. Courtland
East Stroudsburg, Pennsylvania 18301

LACEWINGS (APHID LIONS) AND TRICHOGRAMMA WASPS
Vitova Insectary, Inc.
P. O. Box 475
Rialto, California 92376
Trik-O (Trade name for Trichogramma)
Gothard, Inc.
P. O. Box 370
Canutillo, Texas 78935

MILKY SPORE DISEASE
Doom

Fairfax Biological Laboratory
Clinton Corners, New York 12514

BACILLUS THURINGIENSIS DISEASE
Thuricide
International Minerals & Chemical Corp.
Crop Aid Products Dept.
5401 Old Orchard Rd.
Skokie, Illinois 60076
Biotrol
Kobes Dist. Co.
Orange City, Iowa 51041

Leave It to the Birds

One of the most successful and cheapest ways to control insects about gardens and farms is to get myriads of birds to do much of the work. Sixty or more helpful species of birds can be attracted to help with the eradication work in any agricultural area of the United States. These birds come with different appetites. Here's a list of the insects consumed by various birds:

Ants are relished by kinglets, tanagers, wood thrushes, brown creepers, nuthatches, titmice, barn swallows, and others.

Ant eggs are a special delicacy for chickadees, kinglets, gnatcatchers, titmice, nuthatches, and brown creepers.

Spiders are said to be the delight of downy woodpeckers.

Weevils, capable of doing five-hundred-million dollars worth of damage annually, are devoured by the beautiful bluebirds and yellow-throated warblers whenever they are near.

Scale, minute sucking insects, make highly prized food for the little ruby-crowned kinglets, juncos, and native American sparrows (not so-called English sparrows).

Moths would be the food most welcomed by many birds if the birds were nearby. The scarlet tanagers, phoebes, red-eyed vireos, flycatchers, gnatcatchers, and barn swallows find moths of all kinds very palatable.

Millipedes ("thousand-legged worms") bring great joy to the large fox sparrows.

Leaf hoppers are an attraction for gnatcatchers, several warblers, and others.

Grasshoppers are eagerly sought by flycatchers, bluebirds, mockingbirds, catbirds, brown thrashers, and meadowlarks, and some larger birds.

Crickets are relished by scarlet tanagers, blackbirds, and grackles.

Mosquitoes are most tempting to the "least" flycatchers and chimney swifts.

Other day-flying insects are regular "bill o' fare" for the flycatchers, gnatcatchers, phoebes, kinglets, barn swallows, and others.

Snails bring great satisfaction to the appetites of downy woodpeckers.

Ground insects are "gourmet specials" for towhees and juncos.

1. Identify Type of Birds

For purposes of practical identification, we can classify our bird friends as *vegetarians* and as *heavy meat eaters*. The vegetarians are the all-seed (or other plant life) eaters. Their *bills* are short, and fairly fine. English sparrows, pigeons, quail, bobwhites, mourning doves, and a few others are our all-vegetarian birds.

Of more importance from the standpoint of insect control are the meat eaters—birds which prefer to eat millions of insect life. A few birds prefer an *all-insect* diet. They include barn swallows, swifts, house wrens, gnatcatchers, flycatchers, brown creepers, and some of the several species of warblers. Their *bills* are long and straight, or long and curved; or they may be short and whiskered. Whippoorwills and the nighthawk family belong to this group.

Many of our most useful birds enjoy a mixed diet, eating both many kinds of insects as well as seeds and other plant life. Mixed-diet birds have *fine, sharp bills*. The finer and smaller the beak, the smaller the insect, the insect egg, or plant lice (aphids) such birds are able to reach and eat. In this way, many of the enemies of plant life are destroyed before they hatch; many are destroyed while they are still young and have not had time to grow and devour much of the cultivated crops. There are also those birds with *long, strong, sharp, boring bills*. Flickers, redheaded woodpeckers, and downy woodpeckers can make a thorough search in deep places for harmful insects and insect eggs. Boring insects make the favorite "banquets" for these birds.

It is important for us to know that the choice of the yellow-throated warblers is cankerworms. If troubled with these worms, then invite these warblers to live nearby. Plant lice are day-long treats for the little kinglets, for warblers, and for some of the finch family. Hairy caterpillars are consumed by yellow-billed cuckoos.

Dimensions for Various Houses

	DIAMETER OF INTERIOR (*inches*)	DEPTH FROM ENTRANCE (*inches*)	DIAMETER OF ENTRANCE (*inches*)	DISTANCE FROM GROUND TO ENTRANCE (*feet*)
house wren	4¼–5½	7– 9	1	8–18
black-capped chickadee	3¼–4	7– 9	1⅛	8–15
white-breasted nuthatch, tufted titmouse	3¾–4½	8–10	1½	12–25
tree swallow	4 –5½	6– 8	1⅜	8–30
eastern bluebird	4 –5	8–10	1⅝	8–20
crested flycatcher	5½–6½	9–12	2⅛	15–40
flicker	6½–7½	12–16	2½	10–35
purple martin	6 –7½	6– 8	2⅛–2½	12–14
wood duck, hooded merganser	7½	12–15	4	10–20
sparrow hawk	6½–7	14–16	3	20–50
saw-whet owl	6 –7½	14–16	2⅛	15–45
screech owl	7 –8	14–16	3¼	15–30

Nesting Box

common house finch	4½–6		open	10–30

Nesting Shelves

	WIDTH (*inches*)	LENGTH (*inches*)	HEIGHT FROM GROUND (*feet*)
robin	5–6	8 or more	8–30
phoebe	3½–4½	7 or more	3–20

Perhaps *beetles* and *caterpillars* head the long list of favorite insect foods for our birds; it is also possible that there are more of these foods available. Most gardeners and farmers feel that there is a great abundance of these chewers and crawlers on all their crops during all of the growing season.

2. Provide Materials and Protection

In spring and summer, provide suitable nesting areas and provide some suitable materials for making nests, so the birds will not have to carry materials far. While birds are very resourceful, a few strings, rags, hair, and feathers always help. Here are a few suggestions.

HAIR is used by house wrens, nuthatches, brown creepers, bluebirds, juncos, Baltimore orioles, indigo buntings, some warblers, some finch, and others.

RAGS, TWINE, STRING are used by robins, mockingbirds, and Baltimore orioles.

FEATHERS help house wrens, bluebirds, phoebes, titmice, chickadees, and others.

UPRIGHT WALLS are preferred by chimney swifts and barn swallows.

OLD TREES are the choices of woodpeckers, flickers, and chickadees.

MUD is needed by robins, phoebes, wood thrush, barn swallows, chimney swifts, and grackles for nestmaking.

BIRD HOUSES help invite some birds. Bluebirds and wrens are attracted to man-made nesting boxes or houses. Certain types of bird houses attract chickadees, woodpeckers, purple martins, and the little screech owls. Robins prefer open sheds or shelflike places as building places.

Most of the other wonderful insect-eating birds prefer to build close to nature, but *more* of them will build near places where you want them to be if it is a *safe place* and has plenty of building material nearby.

3. Provide Water

Another rule that is a very important one is *provide water* for the birds, especially near nesting times, so the parents will not need to leave the eggs or the baby birds later in search of water.

Also, you should provide water in places that are high enough for the safety of young birds when they are learning to fly, and for the older birds when they are weary from long flying.

Hungry birds, such as robins, catbirds, and others, prefer wild fruits, so cherry trees and strawberry beds are given protection when shadbush, other berries, or Russian mulberry trees grow nearby. The latter has a pretty bloom and makes good shade. Raspberry and blackberry fruits will have better protection when mulberry, chokeberry, or elders grow close to them.

Grapes are bothered less when wild black cherries, elders, or Virginia creeper grows nearby.

The *secret* is that birds *prefer* the strong-tasting wild fruits, berries, and other native foods first! They eat the bland-tasting cultivated varieties when the wild foods are not available or not plentiful.

4. Feeding Supplements

After a house, materials, and water, the fourth secret or rule for success in attracting birds is to provide feeding supplements, especially during the cold, hard winter. When you wish to provide a *year-'round* menu as an added incentive for birds to come early and stay long, here are some tips to remember.

BREAD CRUMBS AND KITCHEN BITS ARE RELISHED BY:

cardinals	brown thrashers
chickadees	robins
catbirds	house finches
scarlet tanagers	juncos, and others.
mockingbirds	

BEEF SUETS ATTRACT:

chickadees	flickers
titmice	kinglets
nuthatches	warblers
robins	woodpeckers, and others.

ORANGE AND APPLE SLICES, DRIED CURRANTS, AND RAISINS
APPEAL TO:

robins

mockingbirds

cedar waxwings

brown thrashers

some finches

catbirds, and others.

CRACKED CORN, AND SUNFLOWER SEEDS ARE SPECIALTIES FOR:

cardinals

nuthatches

cedar waxwings

chickadees

titmice

juncos

grosbeaks

goldfinches

purple finches

towhees

redwing blackbirds, and others.

A MIXTURE OF MILLET AND HEMP SEED IS PRIZED BY:

cardinals

nuthatches

chickadees

Good use can be made of dried seeds of melons and pumpkins which have been used earlier in the year. Dried baked goods are always good; rolled oats are good; crushed egg shells are sometimes greatly relished.

5. Attracting Birds with Plants

Here's some advice on making your garden more inviting to birds by using certain plants. Be sure to include sunflowers, cosmos, marigolds, asters, or California poppies. These will encourage many weed-seed consumers to remain around your land.

A hedge of multiflora or Rosa Rugosa roses, Japanese barberry hedge, bush cherry, bitter sweet, Michigan holly or winterberry, highbush cranberry, bush honeysuckle, snowberry, and many other kinds of shrubs carry equally good food for birds. A few mulberry trees will also prove more popular than your finest berry crops.

Keep the birds in mind when you're planting trees or specimen plantings in the yard. Many attractive landscaping trees will supply nesting sites for birds and often food as well. Sugar maple, often called "the aristocrat of all trees," flowering crab, the nut trees such as Chinese chestnut, Russian olive, sand cherry, wild plum, and other fruit trees serve a double purpose. Junipers, mountain ash, and the hollies are a few other recommended plants for attracting birds.

On a larger scale, plantings of native shrubs are useful along field borders and fence rows. Some farmers in the colder areas of the United States have discovered that planting asparagus and white clover between the last few rows of trees in a shelterbelt can keep pheasants from starving in periods of heavy snow.

6. Other Methods

Many insect-eating birds, such as house wrens, bluebirds, flickers, and purple martins, will use bird boxes. Place boxes at moderate elevations—4 feet for bluebirds, 6 feet for house wrens, 6 to 20 feet for flickers, and 15–20 feet for purple martins—on trees, poles, or sides of buildings near the garden.

Other birds, such as the ruby-throated hummingbird, are attracted to feeders of various types—red sugar water for hummingbirds, suet and sunflower seeds for cardinals, sparrows, grosbeaks, woodpeckers, and nuthatches. Feeds are especially valuable in winter when the natural supply of food is scarce.

Most birds love to splash in small pools of water. Small, natural-looking pools about 2 feet in diameter and 1″ deep are excellent. If possible, the water should be clear, cold, and slowly moving. Water which is slowly dropping from a slight elevation often works equally well. Almost every species which is found in the garden will, at times, make use of bird baths.

7. Keeping the Birds out of Your Fruit Trees

Although birds are helpful in controlling insects in the garden, they may also be troublesome to certain types of plants, particularly berry bushes and fruit trees. The following experiences of Kathleen Randall may offer some suggestions to fruit fanciers whose trees are going to the birds.

Everyone loves the songbirds in his garden, and I am no exception. Willingly do I share my earthworms with the determined robins, and my sunflowers with the bunting. When food is scarce in the winter, my bird feeder provides abundant feasts for all who come hungry.

But when it comes to the garden fruits, my attitude is less charitable. Fruit trees were nurtured to provide food for *my* kitchen table, and the harvest from my berry bushes is for *my* freezer—not for those confounded birds! I have tried everything—short of getting a hungry cat—to detour casual and friendly birds from my share of the harvest, but to no avail. Baby rattles, hung on the apple trees to scare them away, only provided a rhythmic background as the birds pecked into the ripening fruit.

Every bird passing through the area paused to scar our peaches. The only way we could salvage enough for the family was to pick the fruit when green, which did not compare in flavor with tree-ripened peaches, but which at least were whole. Our cherry trees were covered with cheesecloth before the fruit matured. This the birds considered a challenge. Some ripped holes in the cloth and merrily pecked my fruit, while others ignored the handicap to strip our trees bare. I was so angry with the few birds taking more than their share that I could not enjoy their melodious trilling in my fruit trees.

8. If You Can't Beat 'Em, It's Best to Join 'Em

The year the birds won our race in the strawberry bed, I decided to apply the old axiom. I'd obviously been unable to beat them. so there was nothing else left but to join them. It was the best gardening idea I have ever put to work.

Throughout that year, I contacted ornithologists in our area. Books in our public library also provided valuable information. I found the county agent more than willing to help me "join" the birds, as well as nearby nurserymen. With all the insecticides being used indiscriminately today, we have precious few birds left. All the specialists contacted were eager to help me arrive at a solution which would protect my fruit crop without harming the songbirds.

The following spring, armed with my knowledge, I

planted. The outcome was even better than I had hoped. For the past 3 years, the birds have been as happy as I with the results—and we *all* eat better.

To my surprise, I learned birds do *not* prefer the sweet, juicy fruits we humans enjoy. Instead, they like the bitter, sour, arid, or aromatic fruits we find distasteful. Only when these fruits are unavailable do the birds steal from us.

Hungry birds can be lured away from orchards by selective plantings of ornamental trees and shrubs which not only beautify our acreage, but also provide more delectable fare for our feathered songsters. Among those trees are varieties which grow almost anywhere in the United States, and in particular where fruit trees are raised.

The wild cherry or chokecherry, serviceberry, dogwood, thorn apple, holly, mountain ash, hackberry, and mulberry are trees which not only produce colorful fruit but also beautiful blossoms in the spring. Among our cherry trees, I planted a mountain ash so the birds could enjoy its berries in preference to our sour cherries. Since cherries—particularly our pie cherry variety—were the most enticing to the birds, I added 3 chokecherry trees in the orchard for good measure.

Among our 8 apple trees, we planted a dogwood as well as two Hopa crabs. The contrast of the Hopa's deep pink blossoms to the pale blossoms of the Delicious and Macintosh is breathtaking in the spring. An inexpensive thorn apple was also planted here.

In the shrub category, a nursery-compiled list was almost endless since practically all berry-producing bushes provide food. I chose the wild rose whose fragrance I have always loved, also some June berries, bayberries and elders which are successful in combating fruit-stealing birds. The blossoms of these bushes have encouraged pollen-laden bees—so necessary for an excellent fruit crop.

9. Berries Are Ornamental, Also Food for Birds

Berries from climbing plants are ornamental as well as appetizing to the birds. Wild grapes surrounding an arbor assure a peck-free domestic crop, and bittersweet not only brightens any yard with its clusters of brilliant orange in the fall, but also provides delicacies for birds. My bittersweet climbs protectively on the fence near my everbearing strawberries. The Virginia creeper — seen throughout the United States—is another colorful ornamental vine whose small clusters of berries are savored by the birds, while the vine provides housing for their numerous species.

Certain flowers are particularly sought by most native birds. Though I did not mind sharing my flowers, I threw a few extra seeds in my border plantings as an added enticement from the fruit trees. The bachelor's button, California poppy and sunflower are just a few of the colorful, "insurance," annuals which reseed themselves.

Three years have passed since I have planted and, as the ornamental trees and shrubs grow larger, fruit losses to the birds diminish in proportion. Last fall our loss was almost negligible.

Though my original purpose in planting trees and shrubs was to lure the birds from fruit destined for our table, we received an unexpected bonus. Not only were the songbirds made happy and welcome, but we added colorful plantings which will continue to beautify our yard for years to come.

10. Toads in the Garden

Aside from birds, there is another, more prosaic but effective insect eater—the toad.

True friend of the gardener, nearly 90 percent of the toad's food consists of insects and other small creatures, most of which are harmful. In 3 months a toad will eat up to 10,000 insects, 16 percent of which are cutworms. Mr. Toad delights on slugs and mole crickets. And golf course operators are aware of this fact. One southern club pays for a children's Saturday movie matinee every spring. Price of admission? A toad.

The toad relishes other pests too. Yellow jackets, wasps, rose beetles, spiders, ants, moths, caterpillars, flies, and squash bugs are all on its menu. In parts of Europe, toads are collected and brought to market, where they are bought by horticulturists. And before the advent of insecticides, tidy housewives kept a few toads in the house to eat cockroaches and other insect pests.

Toads, like people, feel there is no place like home, and possess a certain amount of homing instinct. So if you import yours from a distance, keep them penned up for a while so they can adjust to their new environment. After a spring rain, small toads can be found and collected in swampy, marshy lands, and around shallow ponds.

To encourage toads to stay in your garden, set out several toad houses. These are easily made with clay flower pots turned upside down. Break a small hole in the side for a door and bury them several inches in the ground, preferably under evergreen shubbery. The toad must have access to water, so keep a shallow pan filled in the garden. Toads must sit in the water, as they drink through their skins, not through their mouths.

Toads are night workers and do their good deeds when the sun goes down. In summer, you can watch your toads at work by turning on a yard light. In capturing various forms of insects, Mr. Toad is seldom interested in motionless food. Apparently only animate objects make an impression on its sensory apparatus. A toad's tongue is attached at the far end of its mouth, and is free behind. So it is an organ especially developed for flicking forward and capturing moving insects.

If weather is moderate, toads remain active from March to the middle of November. During the winter months, they hibernate in the ground. And statements claiming they are found under leaves, boards, or stones probably mean that Mr. Toad was a bit hasty in emerging in the spring.

Surprisingly, toads actually respond to friendly treatment. When kept as pets, they can distinguish between two people. And like other pets, they can be trained to a call for food. As an added bonus, the male toad has a song ringing with peace and tranquility. Could you ever find these ingredients in a can of poison spray?

—BEULAH WOODS ALLEN

What to Do If the Bugs
Are Already There

1. Ant

Keep ants away by banding plants with tanglefoot. That prevents insects from climbing up the plant. In home gardens, steamed bone meal has been found to discourage ants. If ants persist, a pepper spray may make them think twice. (Shellac the exterior of ruined bark or wood in nearby trees to take away their favorite habitats.) Tansy has been found to discourage ants. Plant it at the back door near the house foundation to keep both ants and flies from the house. The dried leaves of tansy sprinkled about, in cellar or attic, are a harmless indoor "insecticide."

2. Aphid

Enrich your soil organically, as aphids detest plants grown in organically rich soil. Some gardeners have had success by growing nasturtiums, which repel most aphids, between the vegetable rows and around fruit trees. However, often the nasturtiums themselves are plagued by the small, black bean aphid. One of the best controls for aphids of any kind is to encourage (or buy) ladybugs which eat many times their weight in aphids. Also, try making a trap with a small pan painted bright yellow and filled with detergent water. The aphids will become attracted to the bright yellow color, alight on the water surface, and trap themselves. Or you can trick aphids by placing some shiny aluminum foil around your plants so that it reflects the heat and brilliance of the sun. Aphids normally shy away from foil mulched plants.

3. Bagworm

Bagworms are caterpillarlike insects that get their name from carrying their baglike houses around with them. The bagworm moves freely with its bag, but fastens it to a twig with a silken thread whenever it stops to eat. These insects are easily removed by hand. Black-light traps are effective for catching the worms in their moth stage. Trichogramma, small parasitic wasps, are a natural and effective enemy. They are available commercially. (See more information and a list of sources in the section "Biological Control for the Home Gardener.")

4. Bean Beetle

Encourage the beneficial praying mantises, which have been most effective in bean beetle control, to live in your garden. Also, plant your heaviest crop of beans for canning and freezing early, because those plants are freer of the pest than late-season ones. Don't forget to use interplanting techniques with potatoes, nasturtiums, cloves, and garlic. Some gardeners have used a mixture of crushed turnips and corn oil to foil the beetle.

5. Cabbage Maggot

Create a strong alkaline area around the plants to deter the maggot by placing a heaping tablespoon of wood ashes around each plant stem, mixing some soil around with the ashes, and setting the plants in firmly. Protective canopies of polyethylene netting also prevent infestation by keeping the insects from laying their eggs in the young plants. In addition, practice general insect control measures such as the use of sanitation, rotation, and improvement of the soil condition. Interplanting might be able to beat the cabbage worm.

Surround your cabbage by cole plants such as tomatoes and sage which are shunned by the cabbage butterfly, the parent of the green worm. Further interplanting techniques include the use of tansy, rosemary, sage, nasturtium, catnip, and hyssop. Friendly insects like trichogramma are available from commercial sources. Avoid using poison sprays which will kill these and other most helpful insects. In addition, homemade, nontoxic sprays such as pepper sprays, sour milk sprays, and salt mixtures have been found effective.

6. Caterpillar, Tent

Perhaps the best control for caterpillar is the use of *Bacillus thuringiensis*. This nonharmful bacterial is eaten by the insects who become paralyzed and die in about 24 hours. Other control measures include the use of sticky bands so that the female worms, who are unable to fly, will not be able to crawl up trees and lay eggs there. You may wish to place burlap or shaggy bands around the trees to attract the caterpillars and trap them. Those caught can be destroyed daily. Light traps are also effective. Encourage praying mantises, and birds to live nearby. Trichogramma is effective against the tent caterpillar as well as the gypsy moth and cankerworm. Remove and destroy the brown egg masses from the branches of any wild cherry trees in vacant lots and other areas around your home. Every time a single egg mass is destroyed, the potential threat of 200 to 300 more tent caterpillars next spring is gone.

7. Chinch Bug

This little black sucking insect can cause large brown patches in your lawn, and all but destroy your sweet corn. Chinch bugs thrive on nitrogen-deficient plants, so heavy applications of compost will make your plants resistant and avoid much of the trouble. If present in your lawn, remove the soil from the spot, and replace it with 1/3 crushed rock, 1/3 sharp builder's sand, and 1/3 compost. If they show up in the corn patch, plant soybeans as a companion crop to shade the bases of the corn plants, making them less desirable to the highly destructive chinch bug.

8. Codling Moth

Place a band of corrugated paper around the main branches and trunk of affected trees. When larva spin their cocoons inside the corrugations, they can be removed and turned. Eliminate loose bark from trunks and limbs where moths like to hibernate. Trichogramma, tiny female insects, are helpful in biological control of moths. Also effective is a black-light trap which attracts and kills the moths during their summer sessions. One gardener suspended a container of molasses and water mixture in his trees to trap the moth. Ryania will discourage the codling moth, and birds are effective natural controls. Woodpeckers consume more than 50 percent of the codling moth larvae during the winter. Don't discourage them by saturating everything with viperous spray-can solutions.

9. Corn Borer

Destroy overwintering borers by disposing of infested corn stalks. Plow or turn under the refuse or relegate it to the compost heap. Plant resistant or tolerant strains of corn—consult your county agent for the best hybrids available locally. Because moths lay their eggs on the earliest planted corn, it is generally advisable to plant as late as possible, staying within the normal growing period for your locality. Encourage parasites like the spotted lady beetle which eats the eggs of the borer on an average of almost 60 per day. Trichogramma is also a natural enemy of the corn borer.

10. Corn Earworm

Fill a medicine dropper with clear mineral oil and apply it into the silk of the tip of each ear. Apply only after the silks have wilted and have begun to turn brown. Another easier control, but not as sure, is to cut the silk off close to the ear every 4 days.

11. Cucumber Beetle

Heavy mulching is a time-tested control. For bad infestations, spray by mixing a handful of wood ashes and a handful of lime in 2 gallons of water. Apply to both sides of leaves. Radishes, marigolds, and nasturtiums offer interplanting protection.

12. Cutworm

Cutworms chew plants off at the ground level. They work at night and hide beneath soil or other shelter during the day. A simple device for preventing damage is to place a paper collar around the stem extending for some distance below and above the ground level. Some gardeners get the same effect from using tin cans, with "electroculture" benefits as an added plus. Toads and bantam hens are natural feeders of cutworms. Cultivate lightly around the base of the plant to dig up the culprit first. Keep down weeds and grasses on which the cutworm moth lays its eggs. Interplanting with onions has been found to be effective in many cases.

13. Earwig

Traps have been an effective control for earwigs. Bantam hens feast on the earwigs and do a good job of eliminating them from the home grounds. Set out shallow tins of water which will attract earwigs so they can be destroyed.

14. Flea Beetle

Clean culture, weed control, and removal of crop remnants will help to prevent damage from flea beetles. Control weeds both in the garden and along the margins. Since flea beetles are sometimes driven away by shade, interplant susceptible crops near shade-giving ones. Tillage right after harvest makes the soil unattractive to egg-laying females and will assist in destroying eggs already laid.

15. Grasshopper

Virtually every kind of bird has a craving for grasshoppers. Some eat the eggs after scratching them from the ground. Construct birdhouses and otherwise attract birds to your garden if you experience difficulty from grasshoppers. Grasshoppers can be baited by using buckets or tubs of water with a light placed nearby. Because grasshoppers lay their eggs in soil not covered with plants, keep a good ground cover to prevent egg laying in the soil. Turn the soil in the spring to a depth of 8 inches so the eggs will not hatch. Eliminate any weeds around garden margins.

16. Japanese Beetle

Perhaps the most important control organism is the "milky spore disease," a bacterial organism that creates a fatal disease in the grub. The disease is caused by a germ not harmful to man and is available commercially. Since the beetles are attracted to poorly nourished trees and plants, be certain your soil is enriched by the addition of plenty of organic matter. Remove prematurely ripening or diseased fruit—an attractive dish for the beetles. Eliminate weeds and other sources of infestation like poison ivy and wild fox grape. Some gardeners get effective results by interplanting larkspur. Directions for use come with the product. See sources under "Biological Control for the Home Gardener."

17. Leafhopper

Leafhoppers seem to prefer open areas, so plant your crops near houses or in protected areas to avoid damage.

It's also a good idea to enclose your garden plants in a cheesecloth or muslin supported on wooden frames. Pyrethrum is an effective nonpoisonous control that can be dusted on top of the plants. Keep the neighborhood clean and raked so that insects will be exposed to the weather, particularly during the autumn. Avoid planting susceptible varieties.

18. Maggot

Use tarpaper collars around the stems to prevent the flies from laying eggs on the plants. Place plants in irregular rows so that the maggot is not able to find them easily. In the case of onions, this random technique often offers increased protection to neighboring plants because the onion smell is repulsive to many garden pests. Hot pepper spray is an easy and certain control.

19. Mealybug

Wash off plants with a strong stream of water or use fir tree oil. Denatured alcohol can be used on house plants and may be successful in light infestations. Cultivate or turn the soil for several weeks before planting to kill any grass or weeds which may be hosts. Also scatter bone meal to ward off fire ants which often carry individual mealybugs from plant to plant.

20. Mites and Red Spiders

These pests thrive in stagnate, very humid air, so try to give your plants good air circulation. Remove mites from plants by spraying forcibly with plain water, being sure to hit the undersides of the leaves. (Generally, spiders washed from plants do not return.) A 3 percent oil spray has also been found effective. Ladybugs are the mites biggest nemesis, so encourage their visit to your garden. An onion spray has been found effective but do not use poison sprays as they usually kill the enemies of mites and spiders but do not kill mites themselves. Pyrethrum is a safe dust-type control and can be used both indoors and out.

21. Mosquito

Mosquitoes may be controlled by draining stagnant bodies of water or by floating on them a thin film of oil. While this may be somewhat injurious to vegetation, it is not as dangerous as DDT or other poisons. Often rain barrels and other containers with water become mosquito breeding places. Eliminate those from the home ground. Perhaps the best control in your immediate area is to encourage birds like the purple martin, just one of which will eat 2,000 mosquitoes a day. The praying mantis is also a natural enemy. Agricultural experiment stations have had some success with using a garlic spray.

22. Nematode

The consistent use of compost will virtually eliminate nematodes. Avoid chemicals to exterminate them, as that will interfere with the proper functioning of beneficial soil organisms which tend to keep out all dangerous microbes and nematodes. Organic fertilization of infected plants induces the formation of roots and improves plant vigor, thus negating the harmful effects of nematodes feeding on the roots. The most practical answer to the nematode problem for the average gardener is to build up the humus content of the soil and to interplant with marigolds, especially the French or African varieties.

23. Peach Borer

Protect peach trees by keeping the ground beneath them perfectly clean of grass, weeds, and mulch for at least a foot in all directions to discourage rodents and other animal pests. This also enables birds to get to the young borers. Swab each one of your peach trees with tanglefoot (a commercially available sticky substance) before planting. The substance will catch the moths or the worms so that they cannot penetrate the material or get into the bark. Planting garlic cloves close to the tree trunk has been found effective against the borer as has the trichogramma.

24. Root Maggot

Repel root maggots by applications of large quantities of unleeched wood ashes or a mulch of oak leaves if available. Be sure to locate your growing area away from members of the cabbage family for at least 3 years. Maggots are particularly attracted to radishes, and some gardeners plant them as a trap crop to be discarded later. If infestation is heavy, test the soil and feed it. Then grow a cover crop to be turned under.

25. Scale

Best control is to spray infected trees early in the spring with a dormant oil emulsion spray. Ladybugs, available commercially, feast on scale insects and usually keep these pests under control.

26. Slug and Snail

Snails and slugs tend to be nocturnal. Take advantage of their nighttime habits by placing shingles, planks, boards, or other similar material in the garden to serve as traps. Each morning destroy those which have hidden away there for the day. The bodies of snails and slugs are soft and highly sensitive to sharp objects such as sand and soil, and dry, slightly corrosive substances as slaked lime and wood ashes. A narrow strip of sharp sand or cinders around a bed or border will serve as an effective barrier against them as will a sprinkling of slaked lime or wood ashes. Many gardeners have found that setting out saucers of beer, sunk to ground level, attracts slugs by the droves so that they can easily be destroyed.

27. Sow Bug

The best control for sow bugs is prevention. Look for and eliminate hiding places in and around the home garden area. Make certain that logs, boards, and other damp places are eliminated. Frogs, and poultry like to feast on sow bugs, so if you're lucky enough to have some around, turn them loose on this garden villain. If not, discourage him with a light sprinkling of lime.

28. Squash Bug

Squash bugs can be repelled from squash and other susceptible plants by growing radishes, nasturtiums, and marigolds nearby. Hand picking at either the egg, nymph, or adult stage is effective in a small garden. Because the squash bug likes damp moist protected areas, he often hibernates under piles of boards or in buildings. By placing boards on the soil around your plants, you might be able to trap him and easily destroy the bugs every morning.

29. Tomato Hornworm

Tomato hornworms may be hand picked and killed by depositing them in a small can of kerosene. On a larger commercial scale, the tomato grower may obtain effective control from light traps, since the hornworm must pass through the moth stage in its life cycle. If the back of the hornworm is covered with a cluster of small white bodies, do not hand pick. Those are parasites which will kill the worm and live to prey on others. Trichogramma, praying mantis, and a ground hot pepper dusting all prove good controls.

30. Whitefly

In the greenhouse or for indoor gardens generally, a planting of Peruvian ground cherry *(Nicandra physalodes)* is an effective white fly repellent. So is hanging fly ribbons on a stick. Outdoors, test for phosphorus deficiency in the soil. Ladybugs are fond of white flies, too. Many gardeners remove whiteflies from their garden area along with dandelion heads by using a vacuum cleaner to suck them up. In small greenhouses, improved air circulation by exhaust fans is also helpful.

31. Wireworm

Good drainage tends to reduce wireworm damage. Newly broken sod land should not be used for the garden if other soil is available. If sod must be used, it should be thoroughly plowed or stirred once a week for several weeks in early spring. Stirring the soil exposes many of the insects and crushes others. Enriching soil with humus will also improve aeration and reduce wireworm attacks. Plant radishes and turnips as a trap crop.

PART V

WHEN TO HARVEST

Vegetables must be picked at the psychological moment, at that stage in their development when they *taste best to you*. This is usually just before they go through chemical changes that convert sugar to starch and fiber to cellulose (wood). *Many vegetables are picked too late.*

How can you know the right time? Taste them again and again until you recognize the size and appearance at which they reach their peak of flavor and aroma (which has a lot to do with the flavor of things). You will never know what thrills you have been missing until you systematically test your own garden products from the earliest stages of maturity to the latest. They vary in quality and flavor far more than you might believe possible.

Some Harvesting Hints

1. Asparagus

Why dig down to cut it when it has a great, thick, tough white butt that takes so long to cook that the tender green tips are a mush by the time they reach the table? Butts have a strong flavor, too, and if there is any vitamin C in the tops, it has cooked away before the butts are done. Don't wait until the stalks spread at the top, either. Cut the young shoots when they are 4″ to 6″ tall. Clean and cook tenderly, then relax and enjoy a most delicious treat.

2. Beans

Snap beans? Pick them when they are 4″ long. Sliver and nibble them raw and serve in salad. Slice them once lengthwise and cook gently in just enough water to keep them from burning. Serve in their own liquor for maximum flavor and eat them with a spoon. (Peas, too.)

Lima beans have superb flavor when picked while they are still green, before the pods fill out. Some people feel that they never get their money's worth out of them at that point. Admittedly, they are hard to shell, but you've never tasted limas until you've known them young and tender.

Pick your beans early and often, and you will be rewarded with a bonus—the bushes go on bearing crop after crop until frost.

3. Broccoli, Cauliflower, Brussel Sprouts

Nip them in the bud. Broccoli and purple cauliflower repay early cutting of the main head with numerous side shoots.

For the fall garden, after first light frosts, they have no rivals when it comes to bringing the season to a triumphant close.

4. Corn

Enough has been said about the advisability of getting corn to the table with all speed after picking, but too many gardeners still let it grow until it has passed the milk stage of sweetness and delight. Corn that has reached the dough stage is hard to digest, tasteless, and sours when canned.

5. Early Greens

The season starts with dandelions, and by the time you notice them they are already too large to please a gourmet. Cut them before they are 3″ long, wash carefully, and serve in a tossed green salad, and you have the tastiest of spring dishes. Or cook them gently with a few evergreen bunching onions that have survived the winter in the open. After the flowers appear, both are too tough and bitter for pleasant eating.

For sparkling salads, there are no better tonics than upland cress and watercress, mustard, and roquette (garden rocket). But be sure to gather them in their "salad days." In their old age, they will fairly set your mouth on fire!

6. Eggplant

This is another near exception to the pick-when-young requirement. It changes very little from youth to maturity. Sauté the young fruit, and stuff or scallop the older with a chopped onion and a few tomatoes.

7. Later Greens

Lettuce comes in three types, iceberg for crispness, looseleaf for vitamin content, and butterhead for delicious flavor.

It "shoots" to seed and turns bitter with age. Plant early and often for a constant supply.

Spinach in its youth is a lively addition to the salad bowl. Later it improves with gentle cooking in a little water. It is not for the table after it has bolted to seed. Celtuce and New Zealand spinach and Swiss chard are reliable cut-and-come-again plants through a long season. The nicest leaves are the middle-sized ones.

Cabbage, if left too long, will crack or split, and it is definitely past its prime when that happens. Savoy is worth growing for its delicate flavor and texture in the raw state. Red cabbage is a rare delicacy when served with a sweet-sour dressing of vinegar, honey, and oil. Young cabbage, carrots, onions, and turnips cooked together enhance each other's flavor in stew, soup, or hash.

Celery is all good at just about every age. The greenest leaves may be tough and bitter but may be used to flavor a multitude of dishes either fresh or dried. The green stalks have the highest vitamin content, but the whole plant is rich in iron and even the core of the root is good eating.

Chinese cabbage is prime before the flower stalk develops. Some of the outer leaves are best discarded. Endive and escarole, too. All are at their most delicious combined with grapefruit in the salad bowl.

8. Okra

It turns to wood if it isn't gathered early and often. Okra is a nice thickener for soups and stews along with other vegetables.

9. Peas

Peas follow hard upon the heels of the asparagus early in June. They are never so good as when eaten raw as you pick them, young and tender, in the garden path. Some of my plantings never get past that stage, though I can sometimes salvage a few handfuls to serve raw in salad. Such peas never find their way to market, and none are better than the tiny, smooth seeded, early varieties like Alaska and the

French petits pois. Some of the later, commercial varieties have tough skins, are hard to digest at any stage, and are comparatively tasteless. Other wrinkled-seeded sorts and the edible-podded are as sweet as the little ones if picked in time. They have more body, and are more filling. Quality is recognized at every fair where canned peas are entered in competition. If you look carefully, you will see the blue ribbons on the cans of the youngest, tenderest, greenest peas.

10. Peppers

Big and green, they are excellent stuffed or raw, but let them turn red for the utmost in flavor—pimento style. Here is an exception to the "pick-early" rule.

11. Potatoes

Have you ever bored into a potato hill, without disturbing the yet-green tops, and felt around for early tubers about the size of a golf ball? Wash and cook them in their jackets with the last peas of the season or some young beans. Serve with chopped parsley and a little chopped mint, and admit you never had it so good.

12. Root Crops

All root crops—radishes, turnips, carrots, beets—are best before they ever attain their largest size. Young and tender, they are all delicious raw and a treat when cooked gently and just long enough to make them melt in the mouth. Young onions are more delicate in flavor than old ones and far more easily digested.

Salsify and parsnips haven't a chance in the summer garden, but when you go out in earliest spring and pry them out of the half-frozen ground, they can taste like manna from heaven to the winter-weary tongue. After the tops start to grow, however, the roots turn dry and corky, and nutrient values go into the seed heads. Young salsify leaves are a pleasant addition to any salad.

13. Squash, Pumpkins, Cucumbers

Bring them to the table in their tender adolescence. Squash, at its most delicious is cocozelle, caserta, no more than 6″ long. Slice and cook it gently in oil until it is golden brown, add a little water and simmer until done, for a revelation of what is stored in it to tickle your taste buds. Or scoop out the insides and stuff with meat and rice and simmer in tomato sauce until cooked through. If any stuffing is left over, roll it in young grape leaves that have been wilted in boiling water. These have a delicate acid that is an excellent foil for the bland flavor of the squash.

Grate young Alagold pumpkin raw into a salad or into a lime, lemon or orange jelly. Young carrots are grand served in the same way.

Cucumbers (the long-greens) are best before the seeds get tough, while they are all green and not too long.

14. Tomatoes

These, thoroughly ripened on the vine until plump and red all over, are altogether different from the same fruit picked with green still showing in the skins. People who buy them in stores never know what they offer to the gardener who grows his own to perfection.

—VIRGINIA CONKLIN

In harvesting produce from some vegetable plants like peas, beans, and cucumbers, take care not to damage plants. Injured plants may dry up partially and stop producing fruit. According to B. D. Ezell, plant physiologist of the USDA:

Maturity is the primary factor affected by the time of harvest and this perhaps is more closely related to quality and production problems such as taste, tenderness, yield, etc., than to nutritional factors. Nutrient content is affected in relation to the amounts of sugar, starch, fiber and to certain vitamins. Young, rapidly growing vegetables are usually richer in vitamin C than the older more mature ones. Other crops such as sweet potatoes may increase in vitamin A values as the season advances.

High humidity after harvest is important in preserving the appearance as well as vitamin C and probably other vitamins in leafy green vegetables. It is of less importance than temperature. Low temperatures are desirable but should not be low enough to cause injury to the product. Low temperatures are also of major importance in retaining quality factors such as taste and appearance.

How Harvesting Can Affect Vitamin Quality

When the housewife goes to market to buy greens for her family, she assumes that spinach is spinach regardless of variety, age, conditions of growth, and time of harvesting. She takes for granted that a pound of spinach or chard obtainable on one day is equal in quality to a pound on any other day, regardless of time and weather conditions. In the feeding of animals, the farmer even assumes that 2 hours pasturing of his stock in the early morning is the equivalent to 2 hours in the late afternoon.

Actually these assumptions do not agree with the facts. Definite differences in the amount of starches, sugars, proteins, fats, minerals, and of vitamins as well, may be found in plants subjected to different weather conditions especially

at and near the time of harvesting, or even in plants picked at different times of day. Differences, which are particularly noticeable in the leaves, may be found also in plants of different ages.

To increase our knowledge of one of the vitamins, namely vitamin C, studies were made by the United States Public Health Service to determine the effect of age, conditions for growth, and time of harvesting upon the quantity of this substance in edible plants. It was assumed that the amount of food in a pound of spinach or peas might depend upon how old the plants were when the vegetables were picked, on the age of the vegetables themselves, on the time of day when they were picked, and on whether the weather had been prevailingly cloudy or sunny during their growth, particularly around the time of harvesting. It was found that light has a remarkable effect upon the accumulation of vitamin C. Seedlings sprouted in light contained, after 7 days, more than 4 times as much vitamin C as seedlings of the same age grown in darkness. Plants grown in the greenhouse during May and June in the neighborhood of Washington, D.C., contained twice as much vitamin C as plants grown during December and January. In more northerly latitudes, it might be expected that the differences at the 2 seasons would be even greater. However, recent tests with tomatoes conducted at the USDA's Regional Laboratory at Ithaca, New York, yielded differences in vitamin C values in the summer and winter months similar to those which had been found with other types of plants at Washington, D. C.

Fruit from the shaded side of a tree has been shown by other workers to have a lower vitamin C content than that from the sunny side, and even in individual fruits, the sunny side has been found to have more than the shaded side. The changes in the amount of vitamin C in a plant under varying conditions of sunlight as compared to shade are noticed first in the leaves, though later differences may be observed in other parts, even in the roots.

Losses of vitamin C at night amounting to as much as 20 percent of the total quantity, and possibly even more, may occur in some types of plants. Appreciable losses at night occur only when the temperature is high enough to allow growth to take place. Similar losses of the vitamin may occur also during the day, but the quantity thus lost is not readily measurable because the vitamin is manufactured more rapidly than it is used. So the net result is an increase in vitamin C. Manufacture at a slow rate occurs at night, but its magnitude is difficult to determine because the vitamin is lost much more quickly than it is made. These facts suggest that the vitamin C is used by the plant in the process of growth. Just what it does with the vitamin is, so far, a secret with the plant. The evidence suggests, however, that it is used for some purpose in the growing regions such as in the tips of the roots and stems and in the development of the young leaves.

As a consequence of its own life processes, therefore, a plant starts the day with a lowered amount of vitamin C. If there then follows a succession of very cloudy days, and if the plant is growing rapidly, there tends to be a slow but progressive lowering of the amount of vitamin C. Comparable losses in the sugars and starches of plants under similar conditions have been recognized for a long time. Then comes a bright, sunshiny day. Marked gains in the vitamin are to be observed during the course of the day. Some types of plants may, under these conditions, have more than 25 percent more vitamin C by late afternoon than at break of day.

An interesting example of this variation in nutritional value of plants as related to time-of-day turned up in an experience in silkworm feeding. In sections of Italy where silkworm production has been an important industry from ancient times, it has been the practice to gather the mulberry leaves, used in feeding the worms, at dusk. These sericulturists have found by experience that leaves gathered at the end of the day tend to yield better results than leaves collected in the morning. Chemical studies of mulberry leaves have revealed why this is true. During the day, under the influence of sunlight, the leaves become enriched in nutritive substances, not only with carbohydrates such as starches and sugars but also with proteins, fats, minerals and, presumably, vitamins, too, since vitamin C, for example, is known to be present in relatively high concentrations in mulberry leaves. Moreover, the protein of young mulberry leaves nearing full size has been found to be superior in quality, quantity, and digestibility to that in well matured leaves.

It seems strange indeed that one should have to turn to the lowly worm for information on the subject of nutrition, but actually little is known of the influence of "time-of-day" for collection of food plants, or even of shading, upon their nutritive value to humans and to animals other than silkworms. It is true that variations in protein and nonprotein nitrogen have been observed in a number of types of plants harvested in late afternoon and evening in contrast to others collected in the morning. Just as in mulberry leaves, a greater amount of starches and sugars is found in plants kept in sunlight than in those kept in shade, and more also in plants collected in the evening than in those collected in the morning; but nothing was known until recently of the effect on variations in these different conditions on the amounts of any of the vitamins. It remains to be seen whether the amounts of the other vitamins in fruits and vegetables vary as does vitamin C with differences in light intensity, length-of-day, and time-of-day for harvesting. It seems probable that if differences occur, they won't be so great as those of vitamin

C, unless the vitamin in question, like vitamin C, is also used up in the life processes of the plant.

When the time comes to harvest fruits and vegetables, particularly vegetables of the leafy type, due consideration should be given to variations in the amount of light. Present results suggest that for good vitamin C values, the harvesting of vegetables should not be done before midforenoon, say 10 o'clock, after generally clear weather. It is preferable to harvest, if possible, after a spell of clear weather, or, if it must be done following cloudy days, collection should be made late in the day. Because of the tendency of vegetables, especially those of the leafy type, to lose vitamin C on standing, it would follow that when weather conditions permit, vegetables from the home garden should be freshly picked each day.

—MARY E. REID,
U.S. Public Health Service

Harvesting Vegetables

VEGETABLES	TIME OF HARVEST
asparagus	Not until third year after planting when spears are 6″ to 10″ above ground while head is still tight. Harvest only 6 to 8 weeks to allow for sufficient top growth.
beans, snap	Before pods are full size and while seeds are about ¼ developed, or 2 to 3 weeks after first bloom.
beans, lima	When the seeds are green and tender, just before they reach full size and plumpness.
beets	When 1¼″ to 2″ in diameter.
broccoli	Before dark green blossom clusters begin to open. Side heads will develop after central head is removed.
cabbage	When heads are solid and before they split. Splitting can be prevented by cutting or breaking off roots on one side with a spade after a rain.
carrots	When 1″ to 1½″ in diameter.
cauliflower	Before heads are ricey, discolored, or blemished. Tie outer leaves above the head when curds are 2″ to 3″ in diameter; heads will be ready in 4 to 12 days after tying.

corn, sweet	When kernels are fully filled out and in the milk stage as determined by the thumbnail test. Use before the kernels get doughy. Silks should be dry and brown, and tips of ears filled tight.
cucumbers	When fruits are slender and dark green before color becomes lighter. Harvest daily at season's peak. If large cucumbers are allowed to develop and ripen, production will be reduced. For pickles, harvest when fruits have reached the desired size. Pick with a short piece of stem on each fruit.
eggplant	When fruits are half grown, before color becomes dull.
kohlrabi	When balls are 2" to 3" in diameter.
muskmelons	When stem easily slips from the fruit, leaving a clean scar.
onions	For fresh table use, when they are ¼" to 1" in diameter. For boiling, select when bulbs are about 1½" in diameter. For storage, when tops fall over, shrivel at the neck of the bulb, and turn brown. Allow to mature fully but harvest before heavy frost.
parsnips	Delay harvest until after a sharp frost. Roots may be safely left in ground over winter and used the following spring before growth starts. *They are not poisonous if left in ground over winter.*
peas	When pods are firm and well filled, but before the seeds reach their fullest size.
peppers	When fruits are solid and have almost reached full size. *For red peppers,* allow fruits to become uniformly red.
potatoes	When tubers are large enough. Tubers continue to grow until vines die. Skin on unripe tubers is thin and easily rubs off. For storage, potatoes should be mature and vines dead.
pumpkins and squash	Summer squash is harvested in early immature stage when skin is soft and before seeds ripen. Winter squash and pumpkin should be well matured on the vine. Skin should be hard and not easily punctured by the thumbnail. Cut fruit off vine with a portion of stem attached. Harvest before heavy frost.

rutabagas	After exposure to frost but before heavy freeze.
tomatoes	When fruits are a uniform red, but before they become soft.
turnips	When 2" to 3" in diameter. Larger roots are coarse textured and bitter.
watermelon	When the underside of the fruit turns yellow or when snapping the melon with the finger produces a dull, muffled sound instead of a metallic ring.

—*Prepared by the University of Minnesota*
Agricultural Extension Service

Final Checklist at Garden Closing Time

In late autumn, most gardeners, having harvested their crops, have entirely forgotten about their gardens, which will be something for them to think about again when the seed catalogs roll in next February. Actually, the good gardener should be devoting a lot of time to his garden in autumn.

If you don't believe it, turn to nature. What is she doing in *her* garden? She is putting it to bed for the winter, blanketing it against the cold and the icy winds. If she has a garden in an open field, she lays down the grasses until they form a deep, matted mass, and she piles the dead stems of the higher plants on top to keep the grasses down. In the forest, she gently covers the floor with another layer of leaves and probably drops twigs and limbs on top; for forest trees are self-pruning. Look where you will, you will find that Nature is scrupulous in blanketing the earth against the rigors of the wintertime.

The best time to start making a protective winter covering for your garden is long before the garden year ends. Accumulate all the organic matter that you can find, from residue crop materials, manures, cut weeds, or outside products. Then lay down a thick mulch over the area to be planted to crops next year. All plant residues should be strewn over your garden for winter cover unless they are seriously diseased. Otherwise, gather up the infected plant residues, compost them, scatter the compost on the soil, and rake it in.

If you would like to grow a soil-conserving cover crop, cultivate the ground in the rows or rake it over and sow rye grass or some other quick growing, sturdy crop. You can do this between rows even earlier. You can do it at the last cultivation of your corn. Little by little, you can add to the protective carpet, for that is exactly what the rye grass will provide. At the same time, it will be making masses of roots that add humus to the ground.

Be sure to cut all weeds before they go to seed. The old adage says that, "One year's seeding makes 7 years' weeding." Use the cut weeds as mulch. Add any organic matter that will rot—the trimmings of your celery, the outer leaves of your cabbage, the clippings from your lawn, plant stems from your flower beds, the leaves from your trees, and so on —provided, of course, that the materials used are not diseased. Cornstalks cut into pieces are excellent to hold down the leaves. Or a little earth can be scattered over them.

Don't ever burn tree leaves. There is nothing you can use for mulch that may be as useful as tree leaves are. Suppose you use carrot tops or bean plants or beet leaves for mulch. How deeply do those plants forage? A few inches only. Whatever plant foods they secure must necessarily come from the top few inches of soil. And in those top few inches, much of the original supply of plant food may be exhausted, leached out, washed or blown away. But the tree leaves contain minerals that the roots brought up from deep down in the earth. Even though some of the minerals may be practically gone from the top 10″ of soil, there may be abundant supplies of these minerals 6″ below the surface of the ground. The tree roots will bring up some of them. The leaves will contain a part of what is brought up. Spread on your garden and eventually incorporated in your soil, these leaves will help replenish the dwindling supplies of minerals. So you see why tree leaves are especially valuable in your winter mulch or in compost.

Perhaps you cannot collect enough organic material to cover *all* of your garden thoroughly. In that case, you can mulch the areas which you want to be especially rich for your next summer's crops. This naturally suggests that you should plan your next year's garden *this fall*. Then you will know where you will plant this or that vegetable next spring. Beans may grow in very poor soil, but not all crops will. Muskmelons need a shovelful of good rotted manure under each hill. Perhaps you can't get manure. It becomes scarcer each year. But mulch or compost may do the trick for you.

The gardener cannot put back into his garden all that came out of it, because he has to eat the potatoes, tomatoes, beans, and corn, etc. But he can return the *equivalent*—and more. His grass clippings may make up for what is lost in the bean crop; his weeds may offset loss through carrot culture, and so on. If the gardener will put back into his soil, by composting, mulching, etc., all that it is possible for him to return to the ground, he may largely or wholly offset the annual loss of plant food. He can also add manure, tree leaves, and a host of other enriching products.

From time to time, he may need to sprinkle a little lime on his garden. Yet he should be careful where he puts it. Some plants do not thrive in soil that has been limed. He may need to apply ground phosphate rock, potash rock, and ground limestone instead of only lime.

Although your soil is the primary interest in caring for your garden in the autumn, there are many adjuncts to your gardening that also need to be considered now. Tools should be carefully cleaned, oiled, and put away. All broken or damaged implements, etc., should be mended or replaced. Wire trellises should be rolled up and stored in a dry place. Your complement of bean poles, tomato stakes, and other similar pieces of equipment should be made ready for spring. For when the spring rush comes, you will find it difficult to do repair jobs. Digging, planting, and cultivating will keep you more than busy. If there is anyone who needs to take time by the forelock, it is the gardener. And the best time to do it is in the autumn.

—Lewis E. Theiss

Clean Tools Before Storing

Gather all the rakes, hoes, spades, and other small tools which you won't be using until spring. Clean them well and paint with oil. Then hang them on the wall. If you have no regular hanging place for small tools, you can make one easily, using pegboard available at most hardware stores.

The care of power tools necessitates a little more work, but it will be rewarded with longer life and better operation. Follow these steps in winterizing power reel and rotary mowers, tillers, and shredders.

1. Check the manufacturers' booklets which came with the machines, as they will give very specific directions.
2. Disconnect the lead-in wire to the spark plug to prevent dangerous accidental starting.
3. Drain the gas tank completely.
4. Drain the dirty oil.
5. Clean off all matted clippings, mud, and other material from all parts of the machine. Use a wire brush, especially underneath rotary mowers. Paint the underside of the rotary mower with oil.
6. Using a kerosene soaked rag, wipe off excess grease and oil from drive chain, flywheel, axle, wheels, etc.
7. Remove air cleaner and wash upper part with kerosene.
8. Put a few drops of light machine oil on all drive chains.
9. Using a grease gun, grease all lubrication points on the power appliance with heavy lubricating grease.
10. Tighten all nuts, bolts, and screws.
11. Clean off rust spots with emery cloth and touch up with good quality paint.
12. Sharpen and clean cutting edges of attachments.
13. Check rubber tires on power units for cuts, nicks, and proper air pressure.
14. Refill crankcase with clean oil.
15. Remove spark plug. On your next visit to the gas station, have it tested, cleaned, and checked for gap size. Then replace it.

PART VI

THE ORGANIC WAY—
ANTIDOTE TO POLLUTION

Your Garden Is on the Front Line

There are still a few people around in favor of conservation who talk about banning DDT, but spray DDT and worse in their own gardens. Perhaps they don't read the label on the spray cans and therefore don't know what it is they are using. More likely, they are still prisoners of the insect-hysteria reflex that grips a large percentage of people. Compulsively, they go after any bug that strays into their range. Also compulsively, the people who broadcast persistent poisons around their homes haven't yet learned that it is possible to share both living space and some of our food with the insects, and still be happy, content, and affluent.

Your garden is now on the front line of the pesticide battle, for several reasons. First, your garden is where you live, and if you are spraying persistent poisons, you are creating an impure environment at the place where such pollution can hurt you most. Second, we have the chemical people on the run because for the first time the facts about the harm of chemicals are making an impact at the high levels of government. Politically, your garden is the grass roots of a chain of influence that leads right up to state capitals and to Washington. Just as each vote counts in an election, what you do in your garden has an impact on our national pesticide policy. As long as DDT sells in the stores to individuals who are willing to spray it where they live, the chemical industry can make the very strong point that people obviously want persistent poisons and want them right at home. A drying-up of the small-package sale of persistent pesticides would be the strongest possible vote in favor of a pure American environment.

Conservation organizations now recognize that a big battle in the pesticide war is being fought on the home front, and they are trying to encourage all Americans to take a closer look at their pesticide purchases than ever before. Home pesticide sales amount to about a quarter of a billion dollars of chemical industry volume each year, and that large segment of business is very profitable to the chemical companies. The DDT and other insecticides sold to farmers are often moved at cut prices because of stiff competition and large-package sales. But the dribs and drabs of poisons sold to home gardeners command premium prices. The USDA—long a close friend of the chemical companies—realizes the economic and political consequences of a home-garden revolt against DDT and its relatives, and is mounting a high-powered public relations campaign to get gardeners to "read the label" on insecticide containers. The phrase "read the label" is to some extent a nice way of saying "keep buying poisons." The USDA could and should be teaching gardeners how to get along *without* poisons. If you want to read the label, that's O.K. But for heaven's sake don't take that stuff home from the store and spray it all around where you live. Why poison yourself?

Further, do not be misled or lulled by halfway measures that the government may take. It does no good at all to ban the use of defoliants by homeowners while permitting state, county, and federal authorities to continue using deadly poisons along highways, in parks, and agriculturally. The battle against such poison is just that—a battle. We are all in it, whether we want to be or not. The choice of being a victim or a fighter is up to you.

One conservation organization that is very aware of the pollution battle being fought in gardens is California Tomorrow, a nonprofit group that publishes the attractive magazine *Cry California*. The Summer, 1969, issue was devoted entirely to "The Poison-Free Garden," and hopefully had an impact on growers in California, which is a highly chemicalized state.

"Every man can be a practicing ecologist; the hard pesticides can disappear from our backyards," says an editorial in *Cry California*. "And the word that they must be banished —and that they can be, without disturbing much of anything except the poison industry—will trickle upward to our legislatures."

Editor William Bronson explains the California Tomorrow program in more detail, and his words are worth quoting at length.

> We are not denying that we have pests that many people can't abide or that it takes a number of different poisons to control them all. But much of the presumed need for these compounds has been generated by skillful advertising which preys on fear and ignorance—fear of crawling things and ignorance of the essentially simple principles of successful gardening.
>
> There is something each of us can do. We can, right now, give up buying hard poisons for home garden use. In a world that seems sometimes beyond control, you can draw hope and inspiration from the simple personal act of forswearing the use of DDT and all its evil cousins in our gardens. You simply do *not* need them. And don't think your voice, by your action, will go unheard by the bodies politic or the industry itself. You will be pinching the latter where it hurts most.

It is a happy experience for us organic gardeners to see conservation organizations like California Tomorrow pushing the essential idea of poison-free gardens. Right around our homes is where the action is, and the sooner more people realize it the faster we are likely to get a total environment that isn't contaminated with persistent pesticides and other chemical hazards. When a lot of people start thinking and acting alike, things begin to happen.

Millions of people who never used to worry about the natural world very much are now forming the opinion that the land and the water and the air have a deep and significant value when they are pure. It's time for all of us to use our gardens as a means to tell everyone that a pure environment is something that we can all have, especially around our own homes. *Your* garden is on the front line.

—ROBERT RODALE

How An Activist Organic Gardener Can Help the Neighborhood

Because people are beginning to think organically, because they are beginning to see their true place in nature, we can now do many organic things we always have dreamed about but thought were impossible.

Here are a few examples:

Dr. Bargyla Rateaver of San Francisco long had a desire to teach organic gardening. Over a period of months she asked for the support of several colleges, junior colleges, and even county school districts, but was turned down. More recently, she took her plan for organic gardening classes to the University of California and was accepted. Now she has 150 students, and 50 of them are getting academic credit for their work. Dr. Rateaver is planning to expand her class schedule and even to set up an extension course for "urban gardeners," who will be shown how to grow things organically in cans and on apartment rooftops. I'm sure that interest in classroom studying of organic gardening will continue to grow because many people are thinking ecologically. And ecology leads right into organic gardening.

Another example: Have you ever thought that your organic plans were frustrated by neighbors who are spraying, and who are allowing their spray to drift on your garden? Now, chances are those neighbors are anxious to quit the hard-spray habit, and are looking for advice on how to garden organically or even on how to dispose of their unwanted poison packages. Organic gardener Mrs. Pamela Welton of Port Coquitlam, British Columbia, recognized the problem of safe disposal of unwanted pesticides and decided to do something about it. She and her husband organized a pick-up campaign, which was highly successful. Here is the story, in her own words.

We got coverage from two TV stations, and although our two major newspapers were on strike, we got excellent coverage from 4 smaller newspapers. We also got excellent cooperation from most of the managers of the shopping centers where we had our trucks parked. One hardware store gave us their entire stock of DDT, and one of our large department stores sent two cases of it from their warehouse. Of course, we still have a long way to go, for many gardening centers and hardware stores are still selling it, and are urging customers to use DDT and all other chlorinated hydrocarbons.

We got approximately 6 pickup trucks full of pesticides, and judging from the prices on these packages, they represented many hundreds of dollars. The reaction of the people bringing them in was one of relief at being able to get them out of their basements.

There was one amusing incident. An old man arrived with a cardboard box full of assorted pesticides, and handed them over to one of our volunteers. A few minutes later a younger man raced up, saying he was the son-in-law, and that the old man had cleared out his basement without his permission. He wanted the pesticides back! After some discussion, he left — empty-handed.

According to a newspaper report Mrs. Welton sent along, the chemicals were taken for storage at the Department of Agriculture office at Cloverdale, and hopefully will be burned "by a high-power incinerator at 2,000 degrees Fahrenheit." I hope that the burning will indeed get rid of them safely. Our County Agent, Glenn Ellenberger, recently testified to the Agriculture Committee of the Pennsylvania Legislature that he wasn't sure that there is a good way for homeowners to dispose of pesticides. Ellenberger is planning a pick-up in the Allentown area for gardeners who want to get the chemical monkey off their backs, yet he is puzzled about what to do after he gets the chemicals. But he is planning the pick-up anyway, and hopes that it will succeed and be copied by other counties in the state.

Chemical gardeners have gotten the message that pesticides can be dynamite in their hands. Ellenberg said at the Agriculture Committee hearing that "The hobbyist does more damage per acre than farmers. They use 5 to 6 times as much as farmers. They are in a hurry. They don't plan a program." How true! And how harmful much of the home-garden spraying has been to our environment!

Gardeners are now willing to change, though. If we organic gardeners will tell them how simple organic methods are, they will listen and will use those methods. The hearing I referred to above was for the purpose of seeking advice on a proposed state bill to license all people who apply pesticides, such as farmers and exterminators. I sat in the hearing room all day listening to testimony from chemical sellers, farmers, ecologists, and spray applicators. It was fascinating. How different now is the general attitude toward chemicals than it was 20 years ago! The chemical suppliers and users are now on the defensive—constantly trying to justify their affection for poisons. They are in a false position, but still have strength. However, I got the definite impression at that hearing that if we do a little better job of educating and demonstrating the effectiveness of organic methods, the "impossible" will be within our grasp.

The members of the Pennsylvania Agriculture Committee had all heard about organic farming, I am sure, but they didn't quite put two and two together and realize that the acknowledged impending bankruptcy of chemical-farming concepts is literally forcing everyone to at least move toward organic methods. They realized that many farmers were in trouble because sprays are less effective than they used to be (insects develop resistance) and because the harm that poisons do to the environment is becoming more clearly known each year. But I don't think these fine men quite gathered that the people who want a pure environment also want pure food, and that the end of an era of farm poison will lead to a new era of farm purity.

We have to explain these basic organic truths to the people who lead us, and who are faced with making decisions that will change the quality of our future environment. I testified to that committee in the afternoon, bringing in a bag of organic vegetables from our storage house. Plunking down a cabbage, turnips, beets, and carrots on the hearing table, I presented graphic proof that food *can* be grown without pesticides. Perhaps even more important, I read off the records of yields of feed grains from the Organic Gardening Experimental Farm, showing that for almost 30 years we have produced as much grain as the average production for our district—but without the use of any chemical fertilizers or pesticides. Another farmer also testified that he could grow alfalfa very well without spraying for spittlebugs. Hopefully, that kind of testimony will continue to mount in volume before our legislatures and congress.

Yes, we can do the impossible if we keep trying. A crucial but "impossible" task may be convincing the American housewife and consumer that small marks and insect bites on food can be signs of purity, meaning that the food hasn't been sprayed. The vegetables I brought to the hearing as evidence weren't marked, but many commercial growers are hesitant to try growing fruit and vegetables organically because they can visualize a whole crop lowered in value by superficial insect markings. Yet not all insects are dirty. Some are, in fact, much cleaner than the residues of insect killers which farmers use to try to keep the bugs off.

We must not let ourselves be limited in our horizons by false concerns about limits. In a world changing as fast as ours is now, the limits are changing too.

Did you realize, for example, that we organic gardeners and farmers have a much clearer understanding of the real problems of living today than almost any scientist or "expert" you can name? By wanting to live in tune with nature, by trying to produce pure food, by returning our wastes to the soil, we have involved ourselves intimately with the natural world. Scientists today tend to be so specialized in their studies and expertise that they seldom understand clearly what other scientists are doing, and are even further removed from the actual conditions and problems of life, in a broad sense.

We organic gardeners are more ecological than ecologists. I am indebted for that revelation to a little publication called *Earth People News,* published in Logan, Utah. "The current myth among a majority of scientists is that ecology is a science and that their practice of it as 'ecologists' is what ecology is all about," says Ron Warnick in an article titled "The Fallacy of Ecology as Science." He says that ecologists

have constructed valid ecological descriptions of the world as totally interrelated, but they don't feel themselves to exist this way. Their feeling of objective identity is alienation from the world rather than interdependence with it. They look at it and describe it objectively, but never become a part. Consequently, scientific ecology becomes just another way to manipulate a separate world, as if the world were not a living organism, but an inert stage upon which man plays out his actions.

Quite a challenging thought.

You and I, with our hands and feet in the earth, are really involved with the web of life. We are putting our wastes into compost heaps, and from there back into the soil as humus. We are eating natural food, not devitalized by processing, which is the only sane kind of food to eat. We are not poisoning ourselves by spraying our roses or cabbages with chlorinated hydrocarbons or organic phosphates. Most important of all, we comprehend that all these "organic" actions have a meaning to life, and we know what that meaning is. We understand that trying to manipulate the environment with technological tricks does not work, and we are proving in our own gardens and on our farms that organic, natural methods do work.

There was a time when I thought that convincing everyone of the soundness of organic ways was an impossible task. Now I am sure that it is possible, because I know that people are receptive and want to learn. The emptiness of the chemical-technological way of life has convinced them that there must be a better way.

We have that better way, and it is so simple. But we have to get some of the spirit that R. H. Conwell described in his famous talk, "Acres of Diamonds." We don't have to look any more for help or salvation from the chemical laboratories, or from tricks from science's magic black box. If we are willing to try, we can do the "impossible" ourselves. Under our feet are acres of diamonds. We can see them, and now we have to make sure that other people can see them too.

—ROBERT RODALE

The Organic Homestead—
Testing Ground for the
Preservation of Quality

The organic gardening homestead is likely to be the testing ground for the revolutionary antipollution and conservation methods that will be necessary to preserve the quality of life on earth as we know it today. Organic gardeners are already prepared philosophically for the job of research, innovation, and leadership that must be done to develop practical new ways of living. Perhaps even more important, organic gardeners and farmers are members of that dwindling group of Americans who still have close, direct attachment to the soil, and who have not forgotten what it is like to grow food and make the simple essentials of life.

Already, organic gardeners are recognized by many as holding a clue to the creation of a livable future world. "... We could be on the brink of the greatest period of human history," Wallace Stegner says in a conservation article in the December, 1969, issue of *American Heritage*. "And it could begin with the little individuals, the kind of people many would call cranks, who insist on organically-grown vegetables and unsprayed fruits, who do not pick the wild flowers, who fight against needless dams and roads." Many other thinking people and leaders of the conservation movement are also beginning to look with favor on the little American organic community, those people who for years have known how faulty is a synthetic world, operated by man as a manipulator instead of as an equal partner with the other interests of nature.

Right as we have been up to now, however, we can't rest

305

on our laurels. Conditions are changing. Within the past 10 years, we have learned that pollution is a worldwide thing. No matter how far from other people you live, pesticides in small amounts will trickle onto your land from the air and the rains. So we can no longer think of our organic gardens as islands of naturalness. We must accept the fact that our gardens and farms are linked in many ways with other land and the activities of other people.

If, 10 years from now, we are to feel as right about what we are doing as we feel today, we must lead further into new ideas and activities. To remain static in this fast-changing world is, in fact, to move backward. We must show others that advanced ecological and conservation methods are practical, so that they will be applied everywhere. Only by proving that people can live in harmony with the rest of the living things can we preserve indefinitely our ability to live the kind of natural life we cherish. Fail in that goal and we will be submerged in the pollution that will bury everyone.

The key to the really big fight is the concept of the "closed" system, in which all the resources we use to support life and to produce goods are recycled back into the land, water, and and air in their original form. In a closed system of life, population and industry would have to stop growing, or be severely limited. We could still produce power and manufacture goods, but would limit ourselves to ways and means that would allow us to end the process with the same natural resources with which we started. We could no longer burn coal or oil, for example, because there is no way to put fossil fuels back into their original form after use. Construction of homes, offices, and factories would be limited to replacement of existing buildings. We would build a simpler kind of life, using some of the techniques people used before advanced technology gave us the means to literally burn up our world.

Converting the whole world to a closed-system type of living is an enterprise that, as the saying goes, staggers the imagination. All that exists today is the bare idea that the open-end type of economy we now have is rapidly eating up resources, human health, open land, and natural beauty. To change everything to a closed system is going to require a drastic reorganization of science, possibly including the creation of whole new universities and disciplines of study. Even more important, the ingrained human urge to make things bigger will have to be curbed, or steered into areas more creative than just building bigness.

Stupendous problems and challenges have not stopped organic gardeners before, however, and they shouldn't stop us now. Our challenge for the 1970s is to take the first steps toward creating closed-system environments on our own homesteads. We are already living more of a closed-system life than other people because the organic method naturally led us to conserve resources and to put back useful things into the cycle of life. We have long known the efficiency of natural methods of insect control, for example, that are based on merging our interests with those of the world around us, rather than killing the offending bugs and not worrying what disruption was caused to the system those bugs were a part of. Almost all parts of the organic method we have used until now pointed toward a closed system without us realizing it. But now we have to go further in our experimenting and pioneering.

We can not be selfish. Some of the steps we will have to take to use a closed system will require us to think of the community as much—or perhaps even more—than we think of ourselves. We will have to prove that paying our taxes, voting, and serving in the military when called is not the limit of our civic duty. In the world of the future, for example, every person may also have to take responsibility for the growing of enough trees or other plant life to produce oxygen to offset what we consume. When we breathe, we convert oxygen into carbon dioxide. We do the same thing on a large scale when we burn fuel. Trees and plants are the main natural "factory" for converting that carbon dioxide back into oxygen, using the photosynthesis process. We are now burning so much fuel that the natural process of oxygen regeneration is threatened. Also, pollution by pesticides will soon hinder the oxygen-producing ability of oceanic organisms, which now account for a sizable percentage of total world oxygen production. So to be able to breathe freely and enjoy the other benefits of oxygen in the atmosphere, we are going to be sure that there are enough healthy trees and plants in the world. Admittedly, it seems ridiculous for each individual to grow a few extra plants now to make a tiny contribution to the world's oxygen stores, but we have gone past the point when it is merely symbolic to think green. *Each plant counts!*

Organic gardeners have made more than symbolic contributions in the past to the world's knowledge of safe methods of power generation. Harnessing the energy of the sun is thought to be one of the few safe methods of generating power that we will be able to rely on in the future. (Windmills are perhaps another.) Harold Lefever, a veteran organic experimenter from Spring Grove, Pennsylvania, built a solar-heated house over 10 years ago, using techniques he learned in his schooling at M.I.T. Described in the January, 1960, issue of Organic Gardening and Farming as being "as futuristic in design and conception as a 1970 automobile," the house caught the heat of the sun through large, second-story windows and transported it to special heat bins in the cellar through a piping system. From there, the heat was released into the living areas of the house as needed. The Lefever solar house was not completely successful, but it was the kind of pioneering experiment that is badly needed now—multiplied a thousand times—to help create the know-how we need to live healthily and happily without unbalancing the world's natural systems.

Another type of power system that merits renewed interest by organic homesteaders is the methane gas generator. If high-nitrogen organic wastes—like manure—are placed in an enclosed chamber and allowed to decompose without access to air, methane gas will be created. Isolated farms in underdeveloped countries have used such methane gas generators in the past, and possibly are still using them. They are interesting organically because the manure can be removed after it has decomposed and be used as fertilizer and soil conditioner. A lot of trouble, yes, but perhaps interesting when compared to life without any convenient form of energy, which is what some people may face in the future.

"We in America are especially vulnerable because only a very small percentage of us are self-sustaining," says W. E. Patterson, head of the Technocracy movement, in a recent letter. An immediate and very useful goal of our closed-system homesteading efforts could be to increase our ability to sustain ourselves without outside help, with the thought that future environmental crises could very easily deprive us of electric power and heating oil for example. (The manufacture and use of those energy sources creates pollution problems in addition to the occurrence of brownouts or blackouts.) The farm where I live was largely self-sustaining 30 years ago when we moved there. Water came from a pump operated by hand. Only a small portion of the house was heated, and a plentiful supply of meat and other foods was stored in various places around the homestead, not depending on electricity to keep them cool or frozen. Human wastes went into the privy, and garbage was fed to the chickens. Not a perfect setup by any means, but largely self-sufficient.

1. What Would Happen If Outside Help Were Cut Off?

Many times I have sat in our cozy house, watching a raging blizzard outside, and wondered what would really happen if our help from the outside were cut off. We would be very cold, for one thing. Our one fireplace would heat only the living room, and then only for about a day with the small supply of wood we have on hand. Water would be unavailable without electricity to operate the pump, which is buried 135 feet deep in the well. The toilets wouldn't work without water. The food in our freezer is plentiful, but it would spoil in a few days. We could survive without outside help, but would be not nearly as comfortable as the previous occupants of this farm. One of these days I am going to have another well dug and will equip it with an old fashioned hand pump. Either that, or we could build a cistern to catch rainwater. In past years, almost all the country houses around here had cisterns.

Even more important than self-sufficient homestead utilities is an efficient storage system of home-grown food. The Organic homestead of the future is going to have to be more productive of food, and to have available more efficient storage rooms. The quality of food available in stores has declined markedly in the last 10 years, and there is no immediate prospect of a return to the higher standards we accepted as routine in the past. (American food sold in stores never was as good as home grown as a matter of fact.) With improved composting and mulching methods, and efficient small power machines, we have the means to grow more food. But since central heating has become standard, most houses lack the cool damp storage places needed to keep vegetables, fruits, and root crops in good condition throughout the winter. We are up-to-date on that score at the Organic Gardening Experimental Farm, having built an above-ground, insulated house for vegetable storage. It has been a wonderful addition to our food-production facilities, and all gardeners with more than just a small plot under cultivation should give serious thought to providing better storage places, if they aren't now available. By doing that, you will be improving your family's chance to eat well and be healthy, and also will be helping in a small way to forge a link to a closed system of living.

Becoming more self-sufficient can help improve everyone's quality of living in an important subsidiary way—by lessening the need to transport yourself to the store and to other places. The constant back-and-fourth movement of people around where they live is one of the things that's spoiling our way of life. For every little thing that people need, they hop into their cars and drive somewhere. As a result, our land is being cut up with ever-expanding ribbons of concrete, and crusted over with cancerous parking lots. Auto exhaust, the prime cause of pollution in many places, is a direct result of the personal desire to move around.

2. Create More Fun at Home, Travel Less to Curb Pollution

We should create on our own homesteads more of the tangible things we need, and also places for recreation. Our gardens themselves are amusement parks, but give some thought to other fun places you can make on your homestead grounds. How about places to play games, like quoits or shuffleboard? Or a naturestudy area or wildlife area? Building walls and garden structures can be great fun, and will add to the value of your property. Put your imagination to work and you will see that there's practically no limit to the enjoyment you can have at home. By cutting down on travel to your places of enjoyment and to the store, you will expose yourself less to the frustrations of auto movement in urbanizing areas, and you'll help others by being one less care on the road. Voluntarily reducing the use and the size of our automobiles is a not so tiny step toward the better society that can be built in the future.

—ROBERT RODALE

A Young Man Tells Why He Lives
on the Land

Not everyone likes the thought, of youthful dropouts moving to the country, even for the purpose of farming and gardening organically. I got that message from some of the letters commenting on an editorial, "The New 'Back to the Land' Movement". But the majority of the people who wrote were receptive to the idea, and some were enthusiastic.

My favorite reader comment came in from a phone call one evening from a former city boy (now a student of art history) who is living in central Texas. The connection wasn't too good, but his message came through loud and clear. Rather than try to remember what Mr. Wray Rominger said, I invited him to write and tell his story in detail. Here in his own words is his story.

Dear Mr. Rodale:

It was really great to talk with you the other night and quite a feat for our old telephone. Often we can't make an audible connection with Austin, 30 miles away. Our recent rains not only ended the summer's drought and made us more optimistic about living in central Texas but also grounded our telephone better. We only have a single wire running from the exchange in Liberty Hill, and the last two miles it runs along the tops of the fence posts with beer bottles for insulators. I hope I didn't interrupt your dinner or anything with my call; my enthusiasm for your editorial was boundless. My wife and I had often talked of writing you on the very subject. Through an old friend who sought refuge with us after the disaster at Cold Mountain, we heard that story and also about different communities across the country, more or less done in by the mass media.

Ours is a different approach, described by my friend as "dropping out as far as possible and still staying in." Actually we came to our present (most of the time) happy situation through a search for alternatives for a wide range of dissatisfactions with contemporary American life. These alternatives which we have discovered or made form solutions in varying degrees to the sterility, ennui, decadence, low standards of health and life found in the American city.

Germany was the big turning point in my life. Returning from there in 1965 after a three-year tour of duty and with my German wife, I found the American city nauseating. An expatriot expatriate (albeit, an involuntary one) enjoys many freedoms from social responsibility, but I found that the freedom I missed most on returning was the freedom to enjoy tactile, life-charged urban spaces, to walk through the city delighting in the present moment. There are many others I missed in "the land of the free and the home of the brave": good fruit and vegetables at reasonable prices, good bread, the freedom to walk through forests, by streams and fields unhindered by barbed wire and "keep out" signs. To have a full, professional opera-theater-symphony season in a town of 60,000 would be impossible in America. The first reaction was against the low visual values manifest in the American city—that almost intangible, hard-to-define juxtaposition of positive and negative architectural spaces that makes day-to-day living in an urban setting enjoyable and full of surprises.

Dissatisfactions probably have a way of multiplying faster than joys; the next two and a half years spent in pursuit of a B.F.A. degree (sculpture) were sufficiently miserable. Forced to return to my hometown, Omaha, for financial reasons and because the University of Omaha would accept 30 credits made in the Air Force, we found ourselves in an apartment owned by my father on a major street and with a diminutive backyard, hard-packed by children and filled with cinders from the coal-burning era. We had to drive half an hour to see any country and were fenced out of what we could see. The

Missouri river is an open sewer, but you can only reach it at the public marina anyway. The banks are all private property and access is barred.

My wife Loni quickly developed an ulcer from the poor-quality food we were consuming. At any rate, the grievances were common enough and have been documented in critical articles in almost all of the national magazines, at one time or another. Yet I found that no matter how many people were decrying the environmental crises, the decay of the cities, etc., nobody seemed to be taking responsibility for the microcosm for which he could effectively care (except the organic gardeners). Our move to the country was not motivated entirely by negative reasons, however. We both love animals (in the quantity which is possible only on the farm). I do not think we had too many romantic notions about country life (and in this way we are probably different from some of the other young people moving into rural areas), although when I drive to school and watch the miles and miles of smoking live oak woods that are falling before the bulldozers and torches of Texas-style slash-and-burn developers, I find myself thinking that Liberty Hill is indeed the last frontier.

Like the American city, the American countryside is often sad. The land around us here is spectacularly beautiful (driving through at 60 m.p.h.), but a closer look reveals a pitifully overgrazed soil with all the symptoms of fertility decline brought about by that condition. There is little pride taken in most homeplaces, landowners frequently lease their pastures to large livestock holders or corporations. . . . Again I seem to be gravitating to the gloomy side. Actually the longer we live here the more positive we become. W have a very comfortable, 4-room house with about half an acre fenced for gardens and goats. The house was uninhabited for about six years and needed repairs and painting throughout (still in progress after a year) but the legacy we found of flowering shrubs and trees was worth the effort: paloverdes, oleanders, hybiscus, crepe myrtle, roses and many wildflowers. The large front porch is a haven of peace and quiet, the air is fresh, our animals (though demanding) are a constant joy (two milk goats, one angora goat, three dogs, seven cats, twelve bantam chickens, and a tame sparrow).

Unlike the wives of my fellow graduate students, Loni

does not have to work. We have no payments of any kind to make (except insurance and tuition—about $200 a year at the University of Texas). Our rent is $45 a month, and the absentee landlord has been generous with repairs and materials. Our telephone is $20 a year (a dubious bargain, it's both frustrating and fun), electricity runs about $5 a month, and gasoline for my 8-year-old VW, about $18. Feed for the animals isn't cheap, but we plan to lower those costs next year by growing more of it ourselves. From an older farm couple up the road we buy unsalted butter for 50c a pound, potatoes—10c, tomatoes—15c, figs—50c. I find the dogs will eat several vegetables that supplement their terrible package feed. They and the cats also consume about ½ of the goat milk. Out ten bantam hens take care of egg needs. Our garden is expanding—the compost pile, immense. From the place we have goat, cat, chicken and dog manure, as well as all the manure we can gather from the 40-head cattle herd owned by the landlord. With the passenger-seat removed (my wife is long used to riding in the back seat) the VW doubles as a pickup for hauling in granite dust from nearby quarries, bone meal from the feed store, and sawdust (for litter) from a millwork company in Georgetown, 11 miles away. We eat very little meat and most trips to the grocery finds us bringing home non-grocery paper and cleaning products.

My long hair and Yosemite Sam moustache bring relatively fewer "dirty looks" in Liberty Hill than they do in Austin where excesses of this nature are a common sight. Personally I believe that one can not make any life experience in America significant if one is in the middle of the endless flow of advertising propaganda from all media. In what was perhaps too grand a gesture, I flipped off the radio after Senator McCarthy's defeat, and with this also removed the last source of offensive advertising from the house except the mail. We do not own a TV or read any newspapers or national magazines besides yours, the *Dairy Goat Journal*, and several art magazines (they can give enough ulcers in their own way). Activist friends find this rather selfish and refuse to believe I didn't know about the moon shot. Other things just become more important. Sitting up with the goats all night during a thunderstorm isn't so remote. (If we know a storm is coming we take them in the bathroom where they behave very well, trotting out through bedroom and kitchen the next morning without having "made dirt".)

Reading this over, it seems rather lengthy, and I haven't touched on dozens of things I've thought about since I began reading your editorials exactly two years ago. Let me thank you again for talking to me the other night and for your letter, but most of all, for the invaluable information you've put at our fingertips. The oral tradition of gardening which was the repository for organic practices for centuries is lost to people like us, and without your books and magazines we would have been unable to cope with anything this year. I am sure you will receive many interesting responses to your editorial. The average, middle-class, organic gardener probably does not realize he has allies like us and our "further-out" friends.

> Best regards,
> WRAY ROMINGER
> Liberty Hill, Texas

Organic Gardeners in Action—
As Their Numbers Increase,
So Does the Quality of the World
Around Them

No matter where you live or where you go, an organic gardener is bound to appear. No matter what magazine you pick up or what program you turn on, the topic will sooner or later get to an "organic" subject.

You might be in a plane over Lake Erie, or in a bus passing alongside an apple orchard or in a supermarket produce department, just about anywhere—and someone says, "It's a shame the way we're messing everything up!" And, before you know it, two organic gardeners are linked in conversation.

A few years ago, you had to go to a meeting or somebody's garden in order to find a kindred spirit—someone who understood what you were talking about when you mentioned words like "natural balance," "ecology," "unsprayed foods," "additive dangers," "nitrate pollution." No more! Whether you're at the P.T.A., volunteer fire company, den mothers' meeting, or Little League banquet, take your "organic stand" and you'll find others at your side.

The change has been so steady—this shift to organic gardening—that we can only say: It's happened. Yet its gradual development can perhaps best be seen by what might be characterized as a 3-generation-takeover. Retired grandfathers and grandmothers remember how food tasted when they were growing up. Thirty-to-60-years-olds want to create their own atmosphere away from the frenzied pace of conventional urban-suburban living. College students seek to save an environment too long abused.

Organic gardeners see the mess around us and live a life

that makes no mess. And as their number increases, so will the quality of the world around them.

There organic gardeners have made a personal commitment to do something about the environmental crisis which exists today. While industry and government postpone making a meaningful commitment to improve the air we breathe, the water we drink, the soil we trod, and the food we eat, organic gardeners pioneer and persevere—living on an ecological frontier with obstacles every bit as harrowing as any in the past.

The struggle for survival (to those who recognize it) is both internal and external. Within, the battle is survival of the independent spirit, the fight against both mental and physical conformity. It is for conservation of the human drive that may show up in a woman's desire to bake her own bread—knowing she will never see it wrapped in plastic. Or it may show up in a man's yearning to put up a little outbuilding where someday he can house some goats, but in the meantime, it's a place to keep the tiller.

The organic frontiersman and frontierswoman have carved out his and her own battle plan against the environmental enemies. They have been the most avid and most understanding of Americans in trying to launch antipollution programs. They have rallied and continue to rally behind ecologists and public figures like Arthur Godfrey who stress that, "Incredible as it may seem, man now finds himself actually listed as one of the endangered species, not in the next thousand years or even the next hundred—*but within the next thirty years*—all that's left of the twentieth century."

Organic gardeners are not waiting for laws to ban cars in cities or for compulsory controls to be instituted. They do not wait for new standards that will ban certain additives in foods, or will limit the amount of crud that may be shunted into air, water, or land.

Organic gardeners are not waiting. They are living the best kind of life possible in today's unhealthy surroundings. They are the activists who put theory into practice. They are the Thoreaus of the 1970s, only they don't retreat to a Walden Pond (there's an industrial park next to the Pond anyway). They make a Walden Pond out of their home, their grounds, and their activities.

Inbred Ecology

A kind of inbred ecology that relates one organic gardener to another has sprung up. Just like the more intricate web of life that touches everything, this human network has an all-inclusive, far-reaching pattern of its own.

It's wrong, of course to say this organic gardening web has "sprung up." More correctly, it has been developing for decades on a firm foundation that only now—as we enter the 1970s—appears to be surfacing with tremendous vitality.

For example, 3 weeks ago, a midwestern farmer told me of a political science professor at the State University of New York—Robert Rienow who, with his wife, wrote *Moment in The Sun*, a book described as a "veritable ecological bible" which carefully documents the deterioration of our environment. I wrote to the Rienows, and Mrs. Rienow answered:

"You need not introduce us to *Organic Gardening;* we are fans from way, way back and my Dad before me . . . we are regular subscribers. We are also dyed-in-the-wool or dyed-in-the soil practitioners of organic gardening."

And so it goes. Person after person—all ages, all educational backgrounds, men and women, lower-middle-upper income—are tending their organic gardens. You can find your counterpart in any valley or plateau, along a river's edge, or a turnpike junction.

America is ready for organic gardening—and organic gardening is ready for America.

—Jerome Olds

GLOSSARY OF TERMS

ACIDITY-ALKALINITY: The soil condition is determined by the kind of rock from which it comes, and the partial or complete decomposition of vegetation. In the old times, a farmer tasted his soil. If it tasted sweet, he knew he could expect high yields. But if it tasted sour or bitter, he knew it wasn't good for crops. Today's gardener depends on pH reading based on soil testing. A pH of 7 is neutral; most plants do best around pH 6 or slightly acid.

ACTIVATORS: Compost activators are substances that some believe stimulate bacterial activity in a compost pile. This can work in two ways, (1) introduction of bacterial strains that break down organic matter, (2) increasing the nitrogen content of the pile to provide extra food for microorganisms. Good organic procedure calls for adding nitrogen-rich manures which also contain the bacteria necessary for complete decomposition.

ADOBE: Adobe soil is heavy clay, sometimes with silt mixed in. It is most likely rich in minerals, and almost entirely lacking in humus. Adobe, like sand, will benefit most conspicuously from organic gardening methods.

AERATION: The exchange of air in the soil with air in the atmosphere. Air is needed in the soil for the proper working of bacteria and fungi and aids in the breakdown of organic matter, especially roots of previous crops. The average soil contains about 25 percent air, and its fertility and optimum root functioning depend directly on the extent of air ventilation.

AEROBIC COMPOSTING: Decomposition of organic materials by airborne bacteria. The most common form of composting done by gardeners.

ALGAE: Microscopic green plants; that live as single cells or as large colonies of one-celled plants. They are present both in the land and in the sea, and also in fresh-water ponds.

ALKALI SOILS: Two types exist, white and black. White means an accumulation of soluble salts, usually the sulfates and chlorides of sodium, calcium, magnesium, and sometimes potassium. Black means large amounts of absorbed sodium that either are directly toxic to plants, or that harm them by making the soil impermeable to water. White is the commonest kind, found in almost all arid and semiarid regions. Both soils have a pH range of 8.5 to 11. (*See saline soil.*)

ANAEROBIC COMPOSTING: Composting without air. The heap is completely enclosed in an airtight container, and is worked upon by bacteria that exist in the absence of air. Escaping odors can become problem in anaerobic decomposition.

BLIGHT: Any of a number of plant diseases. Most blights are manifested by browning foliage caused by pathogenic organisms.

BUDDING: A form of grafting in which a single bud is fixed to a second plant in a selected location.

CARBON-NITROGEN RATIO: This means the proportion of the former to the latter in any organic matter. The C N ratio of young sweet clover is 12 to 1; rotted manure is 10 to 1; sugarcane trash is 50 to 1; straw is 80 to 1; and sawdust is 400 parts carbon to 1 part of nitrogen.

CATCH CROPS: Growing a quick-maturing crop along with the major crop to improve the organic content of the soil by plowing the former under for the benefit of the latter.

CHELATORS: By definition, a compound which literally clamps onto metals. Humus functions as a chelator, and most organic matter has some chelating ability which may, at times, attain considerable importance in the mineral economy of the soil. The chelating—fastening onto—action of manures is one explanation for the greater availability of phosphate fertilizers when applied with farm manures.

CLAY SOIL: The particles in a clay soil are so fine that it tends to compact, making cultivation difficult, and interfering with the oxygen supply of plant roots. A typical soil may be composed of about 60 percent clay, 20 percent silt, and 20 percent sand.

COLD FRAME: Usually a glass-covered (plastic can also be used) frame, higher in the back, and slanting down toward the front to admit more of the sun's low winter-time rays. No heat is used inside the cold frame. The cover is usually hinged in the back for ventilation.

COMPACTION OF SOIL: The hardening of soil into a dense mass caused by the continuous passage of heavy weights or vehicles. Plants growing in soil compacted by heavy tractors or combines cannot develop healthy roots.

COMPANION CROPS: Good plant neighbors have roots that occupy different levels in the soil, or find in each other's company the light requirements best suited them. Pole beans and sunflowers interfere with each other above and below the ground. But celery and leeks do fine together, also cabbage and beans, beets and onions, cucumbers and sweet corn, and carrots and peas. Do not plant your tomatoes next to kohlrabi.

COMPOST: Nature herself first made compost long before men began to garden. Leaves that fall to the forest floor and slowly decompose form compost. Last year's foliage, weeds, and grasses, combined with countless bodies of insects, birds, and animals are all part of the natural composting cycle. The compost pile in your garden is an intensified and somewhat speeded-up version of this seasonal transformation of protein into humus. Finished compost is the best-possible complete fertilizer for plants because it contains all the nutrients they require in readily assimilable form.

CONTOUR GARDENING: Plowing, planting, cultivating, and harvesting according to the terrain or prevailing slope of the ground. By fitting the furrows to the curves and swell of the land, water and soil are conserved. The curved furrows hold the rainfall, and reduce the amount of soil that is washed away. On the other hand, straight-up-and-down furrows mean washing away of soil, loss of water, and gullying.

COVER CROPS: Planting a crop before the main one in order to protect the soil and to add humus and nutrients to it by plowing it under before the second is sown. A good cover crop makes a great amount of growth in the shortest possible time. It should be adapted to the prevailing soil and climate, and easily incorporated into the soil. Summer cover crops include buckwheat, millet, oats, soybeans, and Sudan grass. Winter crops comprise rye, ryegrass, and wheat.

CROP RESIDUES: Most of the nutrients plants obtain from the soil remain in the unharvested portion—the foliage or root systems. Research has shown that these crop residues increase subsequent yields with the right management. Burning these materials results in an almost complete loss of their nitrogen and carbon. They can, instead, be used in the compost pile when combined with nitrogenous manures, tilled into the soil, or used as bedding for livestock.

CROSS POLLINATION: The transfer of pollen from one flower to the stigma of another. An easy way to do this is to pick a blossom when the pollen is ready, carry it to the other flower, and dust the pollen over it as soon as the blossom opens. Many gardeners are attracted to this aspect of plant propagation because of the infinity of possibilities it offers. In more sophisticated applications, an extremely fine paintbrush is used to brush on the pollen, and the pollinated plant is then isolated from any chance contacts.

CULTIVATION: Refers to the entire job of caring for the soil surface, and in some cases the subsoil. Cultivation also includes the operations that are completed prior to planting the crop. Soil cultivation, after the crop is planted, is done to keep the weeds down, and to save moisture in the soil. Cultivation should never be done when the soil is wet; it tends to break up texture.

DAMPING OFF: The wilting and early death of young seedlings soon after they emerge from the soil. The fungus attacks the seedlings at the soil line and causes them to break off at that point. Remedial measures include proper ventilation and drying off of the soil. It can be prevented by sowing the seeds in a mixture of equal parts of compost and sand, and keeping the young seedlings in a well ventilated and lighted cool place.

DORMANT OIL SPRAY: Should be applied to orchard trees before any of the buds open. Properly applied, a three percent miscible oil is effective against a wide array of chewing and sucking insects and destroys the eggs of the codling moth, oriental fruit fly, leaf rollers, and cankerworms. You can make your own, using a gallon of #10 oil, with a pound of fish-oil soap to each half gallon. They should be thoroughly blended by mixing, boiling, and pouring and used as soon as possible. Dilute the mixture with at least 20 times its volume of water.

DRAINAGE: Inadequate or defective, it can take either of two extreme forms, (1) the soil drains too rapidly and does not hold moisture for its plantlife, (2) it drains slowly or practically not at all and has degenerated into a swamp or bog. (*See aeration.*)

DROUGHT-RESISTANT PLANTS: Choose species and varieties best suited to your area. Don't be shy about asking the neighbors, the local nurserymen, and the county agent for recommendations. And then, when your mind's made up, be sure to go in for cover-cropping, mulching, and composting.

EARTHWORM: Learn to rejoice when you see them in the garden or in the compost pile—it means you're doing things right. Our topsoils have been made by earthworms. Aristotle called them the "intestines of the soil" because their castings are far richer minerally than the soil which they originally ingest. They also aerate the soil, going as far down as 6', and making holes for the rain. They also break up hardpan, and their dead bodies add as much as 1,000 pounds of valuable nitrogenous fertilizer to an area of highly organic soil.

ELECTROCULTURE: The system of growing plants that seeks to make use of terrestrial or atmospheric electric fields to stimulate growth and crop yield. Tests at various state experiment stations have indicated that plants benefit from the application of electricity. Gardeners frequently make use of metal—posts, fences, cans, etc.—to take advantage of local prevailing magnetic fields. At the present stage, electroculture is more of an art than a science. Much experimentation and vertification of results remains to be done.

ENZYME: Any of a group of complex organic substances that accelerate or catalyze specific chemical transformations such

as the digestion of foods in plants and animals. Without en-
zymes, plants would not grow, seeds would not germinate,
microbes would not function, and there would be no soil.

EROSION: Severe washing or wearing away of soil, generally
by rainfall but also by wind. Sheet erosion occurs when rains
puddle the soil and seal it so runoff occurs. Gully erosion is a
further (and catastrophic) development in which the results of
the steady loss in soil are made dramatically evident. Wind
erosion such as occurred in the mid-1930s lifted topsoil from
entire counties and deposited them hundreds of miles away.
Most of the U.S. soils are judged ruined when they lose 6
inches of topsoil, and are generally abandoned before they lose
the top 10 inches. (*See cover crops and mulch.*)

FERTILIZER, ORGANIC: Plant fertilizers have three vital
functions in addition to making the necessary nutrients available to plants, (1) improving soil tilth and structure, (2) improving the soil's water-holding capacity, (3) aiding
nitrogen-fixation. Organic fertilizers such as animal manures,
rock minerals, and complete compost serve all these functions
and serve to maintain a balanced soil economy by releasing
their nutrients gradually over a period of time, making them
available as needed. High nutrient chemical fertilizers do not
add humus to the soil, tend to harm rather than help its texture
and structure, and generally cause an imbalance by releasing
too much of a single kind of nutrient immediately.

FERTILIZERS, ARTIFICIAL: The organic school does not
accept the use of artificial chemical fertilizers for the following
reasons, (1) they are quick-acting, short-term plant "boosters"
that are known to pollute waterways, (2) they contribute to the
deterioration of soil texture, and actually create hardpans, (3)
they destroy much beneficial soil life, including earthworms,
(4) they alter the vitamin and protein content of some crops,
(5) they make some crops more vulnerable to disease, (6) they
prevent some plants from absorbing needed minerals, thus reducing flavor. The soil must be regarded as a living entity, and
an acid fertilizer can dissolve some of its constitutents which
hold it together and thus injure its structure. The recent wide-
spread dismay over pollution of the land, air, and water must
serve to establish the validity of the organic fertilizer position.

FUNGUS: Any of a group of plants—molds, mildews, rusts, smuts, mushrooms—that, destitute of chlorophyll, reproduce mainly by asexual spores. Most fungi are basically valuable, and essential to the processes of life. They help convert rock material into soil, and contribute to the manufacture of humus. They are also active in the decomposition of dead vegetation and animal bodies, restoring minerals to the soil. (*See microorganism and mycorrhizal association*.)

GARBAGE FOR COMPOST: Should be practiced whenever and wherever possible. Kitchen refuse, vegetable and animal, is particularly rich in nitrogen and other nutrients so essential to plant growth. Use of garbage on the average American homestead can help solve the overall pollution problem by eliminating one of the greatest offenders—dumping of raw garbage in landfills or in the ocean.

GARDEN CALENDAR: It is difficult, if not impossible, to make a planting timetable which will agree exactly with the vagaries of the weather prevailing in your area. But the wise and observant gardener will read the seasonal signs and follow the monitions of the local weatherman and old-timer alike. Sometimes he will guess wrong, and his plantings will suffer accordingly. But holding to some sort of schedule is necessary and, with an elastic and accommodating mulching program, the organic gardener should come through a "normal" growing year with a minimum of damage and frustration.

GERMINATION: Viability in seeds (the power to grow) varies greatly with the species and varieties. Some seeds will take root and grow after many years, some will not germinate after a single year. You know a seed has germinated when the young stem and leaves appear at the surface.

GLAUCONITE: An iron-potassium-silicate that imparts a green color to the minerals in which it occurs. It is a round, soft but stable aggregate of finely divided clay. The most common and best known glauconite mineral is greensand. Sand-sized glauconite acts like a sponge, absorbing and storing moisture. Its unique round shape also prevents the interlocking of soil particles and retards soil compaction. (*See Greensand*.)

GRAFTING: A graft is a shoot or a part of a tree or plant inserted into another tree or plant and fixed or protected so it becomes an attached and living part of the new identity. Probably the oldest purpose of grafting was to repair damage. But today its most important use is for propagating new or desired varieties of fruits or flowers for their perpetuation and multiplication. There is one other important reason for grafting—making dwarf trees. Grafting is also used to make trees more fruitful, or to improve the quality of the fruit, or adapt plants to adverse soils and varying climatic conditions.

GRANITE DUST: Granite stone meal is a highly recommended natural source of potash. Its potash content varies between 3 and 5 percent and sometimes more. The value of using potash rock over the chemical form is that it is cheaper and leaves no harmful chemical residue. It also contains valuable trace mineral elements.

GRASS CLIPPINGS: Can play an important role in improving soil. A good lawn doesn't need as much enrichment, added organic matter, or mulching as do the more heavily cropped plots. A rich source of nitrogen, these clippings can most often be better used elsewhere as a valuable fertilizer in the vegetable garden, a helpful addition in all mulches, and a major aid in converting leaves and other low-nitrogen wastes into best-quality compost.

GREEN MANURING: It fertilizes the soil deeply which composting alone cannot accomplish. The roots of the green manure plants decay deep in the soil year after year, leaving great stores of organic matter which is broken down into humus. It is worthwhile to devote part of your garden to a green manure crop, taking advantage of the new soil fertility as soon as decay is complete—about six weeks—and planting a "money" or yielding crop on the site.

GREENSAND: Glauconite greensand or greensand marl is an iron-potassium-silicate that imparts a green color to the minerals in which it occurs. Being an undersea deposit, greensand contains traces of many if not all the elements which occur in sea water. Greensand has been used successfully for soil building for more than a hundred years, and is a fine source of potash. (*See glauconite.*)

HARDENING OFF: Refers to the preparing of young plants to meet outside weather conditions. Young plants, especially non-hardy ones, are very vulnerable to sudden temperature changes. To put them outside, after their propagation in the protection of a greenhouse or other warm place, may easily be fatal. Therefore, young plants have to be introduced to the elements by degrees—the hardening-off process.

HARDINESS: That quality in plants that enables them to survive the climatic conditions of the particular area where they are to be placed. When gardeners speak of a "hardy" plant, they usually mean one that will survive the winter. But the term can also be applied to plants of a northern climate which will survive the winter. But the term can also be applied to the plants of a northern climate which will survive the heat of a more temperate climate. *All* plants are hardy in their natural climates, but when transported by man to foreign environments, many cannot survive.

HARDPAN: Hardpans are impervious horizontal layers in the soil that may exist anywhere from 6 inches to about 2 feet below the surface. A true hardpan is formed by the cementing together of the soil grains into a hard, stone-like mass which is impervious to water. A more common condition is an impervious layer in the subsoil caused by the pore spaces becoming filled with fine clay particles. Such tight clay subsoils, called *claypans*, are generally associated with an extremely acid condition, so that from both the physical and chemical standpoint they are objectionable.

HARROWING: The farm operation that usually follows plowing; its objective is to break up soil clods, similar to the job done by raking or rotary tilling in the home garden. Harrowing is done prior to seeding a crop.

HEAVING: A type of winter injury in which plants are loosened and frequently lifted from the soil as a result of successive freezing and thawing. It occurs in soils containing a considerable amount of clay or silt which alternately freeze and thaw in the spring. Protecting the plants and soil with mulch should eliminate the condition. A long-range remedy is to compost heavily, adding large amounts of humus to the soil and reducing its clay content.

HEAVY SOIL: Contains a high percentage of clay and/or silt. Heavy soils generally hold too much moisture and have poor drainage.

HOTBED: Similar to the cold frame, except that a source of heat is built into the unit. This can be electrical heating coils, electric lights, or a bed of fresh, raw manure.

HUMUS: Is organic matter in a more advanced stage of decomposition than compost in its early stages. In a compost heap, some of the organic matter has turned into humus, but the remainder will complete the decomposition process after it has been placed in the soil. Organic matter in the soil, in the early stages of decomposition, cannot be called humus. It must still be called organic matter. The process where organic matter turns to humus is called *humification*.

IRRIGATION: The objective of irrigation is to keep a readily available supply of moisture in contact with plant roots at all times. But all too often farmers and some gardeners depend on irrigation to the exclusion of soil building and management practices. Their soil is not in condition to receive and properly utilize the water falling upon it as rain or applied by irrigation. A soil rich in organic matter will catch and hold nearly all the rain falling on it. Thus much less irrigation water will be needed, and what is applied will be held better. Mulching, green manuring, strip cropping, contour plowing, and terracing are vital to cut irrigation costs and save the underground sources from going dry.

KITCHEN WASTES: Represent a tremendous potential of organic matter which can be returned to the soil. Reports show that the average person creates about 300 pounds of garbage a year. At present, most cities destroy garbage, burning it, burying it, or dumping it into the sea. In recent years, however, some cities have been adopting various methods of municipal composting, whereby all the city's garbage is composted and reduced to a fine material suitable for garden and agriculture use.

LATH HOUSE: Used to give plants more shade, a lath house has been described as a greenhouse without glass. The strips of wood are placed about one inch apart to allow sufficient circulation of air with less than half the usual amount of light.

LAYERING: This refers to a method of plant propagation in which the rooting of branches of woody plants takes place while they are still attached to the parent plant. Layering is used on certain woody plants, usually those which have become too "leggy," that is, too tall and gangling, with a few leaves growing at the end of a long stem. Its purpose is to produce shorter, stockier, more robust looking, and better foliage plants. The bark and cambium layer are cut or "wounded," and the injured area covered with sphagnum moss or selected soil. New, young roots generally form within 30 to 60 days.

LEACHING: Rainwater and irrigation are known to dissolve a certain amount of plant food elements from the soil, carrying them down to greater depths where they will be lost by the roots. This leaching is inevitable and should be remembered when fertilizing. Leaching also occurs in house plants, but this kind of leaching can be prevented by not over watering plants. Remember that every time water runs out of the drain hole and is thrown away in excess, it carries with it some soil nutrients.

LICHENS: Actually flowerless plants, active in the initial stages of soil fermentation. Long before men appeared on earth, lichens grew endlessly on flinty rock and sterile sand, in steaming tropics and icy tundra, perhaps the best example of the teamwork that is the very cornerstone of nature. Other organisms that work together to build soil from the inert substances of the earth's crust include aerobic and anaerobic bacteria, and earthworms that take over where fungi and molds leave off. All these tiny creatures form links in a chain, the end product of which is life-sustaining, fertile soil. But the lichen is the indispensable "starter" link in the chain.

LIQUID MANURE: Often recommended for fertilizing house plants as well as outside manure. The following method is easy, economical, and not a bit messy. As soon as the weather is warm enough to keep the water from freezing, get 3 large, 100 pound sugar sacks and fill each one with a mixture of fresh cow, horse, and chicken manure in equal parts. These are then suspended in 60-gallon drums, barrels, or containers, one to each drum, which then are filled with warm water. Be sure the sacks of manure are under water. Some city gardeners "bury" the drums in an inconspicuous place.

LOAM: Soil which is composed of a friable mixture of clay, silt, sand, and organic matter. The mixture of mineral and organic material in a good loam should provide 50 percent solid matter, and 50 percent space between the solids. Of the space, about half should be filled with water and half air for optimum plant growth. Clay, silt, and sand are particles of rock, usually of the rock which underlies the field on which they are found. Silt is composed of rock particles of less than 1/16 mm. in diameter which is or has been deposited on the bed of a body of water. Sand is coarser material, clay is finer rock material. If the mineral content of a loam is composed of more than half sand, it is said to be a sand loam. If clay predominates, it is a clay loam, or if it is mostly silt, it is a silt loam.

MANURE: The excreta of agricultural animals, along with stable litter, constitutes one of the oldest and most effective fertilizers known to man. The rise of chemical fertilizers in the 20th century has led to a decrease in the amount of manure utilized by world agriculturists. This wasteful misuse of natural fertilizer is often rationalized by farmers and agriculturists, who allege that the supply is not adequate for the need for fertilizers. This is faulty reasoning. In 1889, there were 13,663,000 horses in the United States and 50,331,000 head of cattle. Today there are fewer horses—about 3,000,000 total—but almost 100,000,000 cattle. There has also been a subsequent rise in the number of other livestock. The problem is not insufficient manure, but its misuse.

MICROORGANISM: There are many kinds and weights of microorganisms in the surface foot of soil in large numbers. Each kind of organism plays some significant role in the decomposition of plant and animal residues, liberation of plant nutrients, or in the development of soil structure. Many groups are dependent on each other; consequently one kind may tend to follow another.

MINERAL ROCKS: All solid rocks are classified by geologists into 3 major groups, (1) *igneous* or formerly molten rocks, (2) *sedimentary* or layered rocks, (3) metamorphic (changed) rocks. Besides having different origins, certain mineral and chemical compositions characterize each group. Because the different compositions influence soil types, erosion, and economic products, their differences are of practical importance.

MUCK SOILS: Muck lands are vast natural compost heaps. Over the ages, they were formed by the decomposition of aquatic plants growing in poorly drained areas.

MULCH: A layer of material, preferably organic material, that is placed on the soil surface to conserve moisture, hold down weeds, and ultimately improve soil structure and fertility. As with composting, mulching is a basic practice in the organic method. It is a practice which nature employs constantly, that of always covering a bare soil. In addition, mulching also protects plants in the winter by reducing the dangers of freezing and heaving. Practically any organic waste material can be used as mulch.

MUTATION: Any change in the character of a plant not brought about by crossing it with another plant is called a mutation. It may be a variation in color, size, flowering, yield, root, or top-growth habit, or any other characteristic. Sometimes only a part of the plant, such as a single branch, may show the new trait, as happens with roses and fruits. Cuttings of these branches will produce new plants having the alteration throughout. Generally, mutations appear most often in plants reproduced by seeds.

MYCORRHIZAL ASSOCIATION: Usually symbiotic (two plants necessary to each other which benefit from their proximity) of the mycelium (filamentary threadlike growths) of various fungi and the roots of seed plants. The fungi make various nutrients more available to plant assimilation.

NEUTRAL: Referring to soils that are balanced between acidity and alkalinity, having a pH of about 7.

NO-DIGGING METHOD: A school of gardening which adheres to the belief that no digging or soil spading is necessary to attain best garden results. Here are the basic principles: (1) to imitate nature closely by not inverting the soil; (2) to economize on compost and other organic materials by using them as a surface mulch, where nature keeps its fertility promoting materials; (3) to reduce weed growth by not bringing more and more seeds to the surface; (4) and, by all these methods, to maintain a balance of air, moisture, biological life, and plant foods.

NUTRITION: Proper nutrition is an integral part of the organic method of gardening and farming. Aside from the many other advantages of the organic method of gardening, the sound nutrition that is achieved from eating naturally grown foods is reason enough to follow the organic method. The relation between soil and health is as basic as the very process of nature; the axiom "you are what you eat" assumes greater and greater impact as experiments show the wonderful results of eating carefully selected, organically grown foods.

OIL SPRAY: (*See, dormant oil spray.*)

ORGANIC GARDENING AND FARMING: Calls for the maintenance of soil fertility and texture by replenishing soil with its own materials and readily decomposable matter which can be easily reassimilated. Natural animal manures, crop residues of every kind, plus compost are used as plant fertilizers and applied as mulch to conserve moisture and regulate soil temperature. The organic method also bans the use of artificial chemical fertilizers and toxic pesticides while advocating the use of naturally occurring minerals.

ORGANIC MATERIALS: Or organic matter is any part of any substance which once had life—animal, vegetable, or a by-product thereof. Most all organic matter can be composted to return its nutritive substances to the soil, thus continuing the cycle of nature. The wise gardener will avail himself of these various forms of organic matter and use them in the compost heap.

ORGANIC METHOD, HISTORY OF: The history of the organic movement had its inception in India in the researches and experiments of Sir Albert Howard over a period of 40 years. Sir Albert Howard was a British Government agronomist whose mind integrated itself with what his eyes saw. He noticed that results on government farms did not compare favorably with those of neighboring native husbandmen from the point of view of animal and plant disease, and also that the natives didn't make use of *artificial* fertilizers. In order to develop a system of farming that would keep disease down to a minimum, Sir Albert decided to use the method of the natives, but with scientific management. In this experiment, Sir Albert broke away from the accepted research procedures. He shunned the fragmentized approach of the agricultural stations. Instead of growing plants in handkerchief-sized plots, he farmed for 25 years on large acreage like any ordinary farmer. He attempted to prove conclusively that the use of chemical fertilizers degenerated plants, animals, and people through the poor nutritional quality of their food. His final findings had the strength of a heavily joisted and integrated structure.

PEAT MOSS: Is the partially decomposed remains of plants accumulated over centuries under relatively airless conditions. It is a highly valuable organic material for soil building. Peat moss loosens heavy soils, binds light soils, holds vast amounts of water, increases aeration, aids root development, stops nutrients from leaching away, and can be added to the soil or used as a mulch. When dry, it will absorb 15 times its weight in water. Its effect on water is to make a "crumb" structure that holds much more water due to the increased area of the soil particles.

PESTICIDES: Any one of a number of deadly chemical sprays which are used to kill insects and other harmful life in horticultural and agricultural areas. The use of pesticides is not condoned in the organic method because of the harm done to beneficial insects and soil life, and because of the potential threat to human health.

PHOTOSYNTHESIS: The process of forming starches and sugars that takes place in leaves in the presence of water and plant nutrients brought up from the roots, carbon dioxide from the air, chlorophyll in the leaf tissues, and light. Chloroplasts, microscopic bodies in the leaves, manufacture carbohydrates using radiant energy from the sun for their power source. Thus, leaves are the only known agents capable of transforming the sun's energy to food energy.

POLLINATION: Referring to the distribution of pollen; more specifically, the transfer of pollen to the stigma. It may be accomplished by insects, gravity, wind, birds, or by artificial methods.

Self-pollination: the transfer of pollen from the anthers of a flower of one variety to the stigma of a flower of the same variety.

Cross-pollination: the transfer of pollen from the anthers of a flower of one variety to the stigma of a flower of a different variety.

Pollenizer: the variety (plant, tree) used to furnish pollen; the male parent.

POTASH ROCK: naturally occurring rock containing a high percentage of potassium and therefore one of the most effective potassium fertilizers.

PROPAGATION: The great majority of plants can be propagated by seeds, cutting, division, and layering. For vegetables —annuals, biennials, and perennials—the most common reproducing method is by seeds.

PRUNING: Trimming out unwanted or unhealthy portions of a plant in order to help the portions which remain. The time of pruning varies with the type of plant that you want to prune, and with the results you wish to achieve through pruning. Some pruning is done at any time suitable to the gardener's convenience; some pruning must be done at a specific season. Pruning is not a mysterious process but a garden technique that requires an understanding of growth habits of plants plus an intelligent program of plant care and an appreciation of the beauty of plant forms.

QUARANTINES: The Plant Quarantine Act of 1912 is designed to prevent the spread of injurious insects and plant diseases. The secretary of agriculture is empowered to prohibit or regulate the importation and interstate movement of all plant materials that may harbor pests.

RABBIT MANURE: A fine source of nitrogen and other fertilizer values. The analyses differ according to the feeding practices, but an average sample is rich enough in nitrogen to produce good heating in a compost heap. The manure can be applied to the soil as it is taken from the hutches, dug in or used on lawns, and added between vegetable rows or around trees and shrubs all through the year. A large doe and her four litters of about 28 to 32 young a year will produce approximately six to seven cubic feet of manure annually.

ROCK FERTILIZERS: Rock dusts are potentially our most abundant source of plant nutrient minerals. Soil is formed primarily by the action of organic matter on crumbling rock dust. The rock basis for soil produces a continual supply of mineral-rich silt that keeps breaking down and in large part replaces the minerals that crops take from the soil. One of the most important points in favor of putting ground rocks on legumes is the fact that legumes are nitrogen producers. Rock fertilizers produce almost all the essential plant nutrients but nitrogen. Therefore, when they are used with legumes, there is achieved a balance of the plant's food needs.

ROOT CROPS: Any crop whose edible portion is taken from under the ground is commonly called a root crop. Popular ones are beets, carrots, onions, parsnips, potatoes, salsify, sweet potatoes, and turnips. Actually, onions are bulbs, and potatoes are tubers, rather than true roots.

ROOT PRUNING: When fruit trees fail consistently to set fruit and all other conditions are favorable, the grower may resort to root pruning. A trench about 2 feet deep is dug around the tree in the fall, at least 6 feet from the trunk, exposing the big anchor roots for cutting. If no big roots are found, there is very likely to be a wild taproot that must be located and cut. Any ornamental tree that has spread its roots out into areas where they are not wanted can be treated in the same way. A metal or cement barrier set in the trench will prevent subsequent spreading.

ROTARY TILLAGE: Simplifies and speeds up the process of preparing soil for planting. Ordinary tillage methods require the use of a plow, disk, and a harrow before seed can be planted. Rotary tillers do those three jobs in one operation. Rotary tilling has another advantage. It provides a better means of incorporating crop wastes and other organic matter into the soil than the plow-disk-harrow combination. Plowing tends to bury organic matter in a layer 4″ to 6″ deep, often too far below the surface to allow optimum decay and breakdown by microorganisms. Rotary tilling mixes such organic matter into the soil evenly through the full tillage depth.

ROTATION: Crop rotation means a regular scheme of planting whereby different demands are made on the soil each year. A 4-year rotation can be corn, oats, clover, and wheat in 4 fields of similar size. Each year the farmer has all 4 crops but in different places. The fifth year corn goes back where it started, and the repetition begins. Depending on need, you may have a 3, 5, or even longer rotation, sometimes leaving a perennial like alfalfa in each field for 2 or more years. This requires careful planning concerning time, and place, plus the right division of the farm into smaller units. It may take several years of trial and error to get just the right rotation for all the factors involved, each farm being an individual entity. But once rightly established, the rotation can go on indefinitely.

SALINE SOIL: Under hot, arid conditions, soluble salts often accumulate in the surface of soils whenever the ground water comes within a few feet of the surface. This can happen under natural conditions in the flood plains of rivers, the low-lying shores of lakes, in depressions in which drainage water accumulates, in any region where marsh, swamp, or other ill-drained soil would be found in humid regions. During dry periods, the surface of these soils is covered with a salt crust, which is dissolved in the soil water each time the soil is wetted. Saline soils are low in humus because natural vegetation cannot make much annual growth on them. The salts usually present in the soil are the sulphates and chlorides of sodium and calcium, though nitrates occur in a few places. (*See alkali soils.*)

SANDY SOIL: A typical "light sandy" soil may be composed of approximately 70 percent sand, 20 percent silt, and 10 percent clay. The particles in a sandy soil are comparatively large, permitting water to enter the soil and to pass through it so quickly that it dries out very rapidly, and often carries nutrients with it. Organic matter is especially important in improving the structure of sandy soils.

SANITATION: In gardening, this means the destruction of diseased, injured, or insect-infested plants or parts of plants, and certain other clean-up techniques that further aid in promoting the health and productivity of plants. Prompt removal of diseased or insect-damaged plants is the first rule of sanitation. It's a good idea to cultivate the habit of watching carefully for anything abnormal in the growth of your plants. Sometimes removing just a few sickly leaves or a single plant may prevent a bad infestation of bugs or the spread of a disease.

SEA MATERIALS: Approximately 8,000 kinds of plants and over 200,000 species of animals live in the sea. Every known element is found there, and acre for acre, the sea is probably as productive as the best soil on any farm. This is not surprising when we consider that, instead of a few inches of topsoil, the sea's productive area is limited only by the depth that sunlight can reach—about 200 feet. Seaweed, which makes up 25 percent of the Japanese diet, is made into flour, noodles, and other products. In Hawaii, over 70 species of sea plants are eaten. In Holland, Belgium, Scotland, and Norway, certain kinds of seaweed are consumed raw, cooked, or made into bread. In this country, industry has found that seaweed yields substances valuable in the making of everything from ice cream and salad dressing to burn ointments and dental impressions.

SEAWEED: Seaweed used as fertilizer belongs to 2 main groups according to habitat. Brown weeds grow between high and low water on rocky sites and also on rock bottoms below low-water, down to a depth of 60 feet. Rockweeds are relatively small plants, but their growth is usually dense, and they are easily collected by pulling or cutting from the rocks; 200 pounds per hour can be gathered easily from a good site. One of the basic tenets of seaside gardening is to never leave the ground bare to the drying action of the wind. Chopped seaweed makes a good mulch when used alone, or it can be mixed with shredded leaves, ground corncobs, compost, and other mulch materials. You can also dig finely chopped seaweed into the upper few inches of your soil at the rate of 50 to 200 pounds per 100 square feet in spring, well in advance of planting. Seaweed is low in phosophorous, so it's a good practice to mix in some rock phosphate or bone meal.

SEEDS AND SEEDLINGS: Seed may be saved from any annual or perennial garden plant, and from any shrub or tree, to be planted at a later time. Some seeds will keep well and will produce plants exactly like the parent plant, year after year. Other plants produce seed that quickly deteriorates, or seed that will revert in time to the species from which highly horticultural varieties were developed. Also, some plants take a long time to mature from seed, and are more efficiently propagated from cuttings or division. A knowledge of the life history of the plant will help the beginning gardener to know which seed is worth saving, and which should be purchased each year.

SEWAGE SLUDGE: The use of city-treated sewage sludge by gardeners and farmers throughout the United States has been climbing upward in recent years. In cities where municipal sludge has been sold, demand for sludge has been increasing. Most cities and towns don't sell their sludge, but make it available to local gardeners and farmers free at the plant site. In a few instances, there is a nominal charge, but in general, the sludge is available at no charge.

Activated Sludge is produced when the sewage is agitated by air rapidly bubbling through it. Generally, activated sludge is heat treated before being made available to gardeners and farmers; its nitrogen content is between 5 and 6 percent, phosphorous from 3 to 6 percent. Its plant food value is similar to cottonseed meal—a highly recommended organic fertilizer.

Digested Sludge is formed when the sewage is allowed to settle (and liquid to drain off) by gravity without being agitated by air. Digested sludge has about the same fertilizer value as barnyard manure. Nitrogen varies from 2 to 3 percent, phosphorous averaging about 2 percent. It often has an offensive odor that persists for some time after application to a soil surface during cool weather. This odor may be eliminated by storage in a heap during warm weather.

SHEET COMPOSTING: By this method, leaves, weeds, manure, and other waste organic materials are spread over the garden or field and worked into the soil to decompose. It's recommended to make several passes with a rotary mower over this material—cut-up material breaks down faster. Also add any lime, nitrogen fertilized bone meal, tankage, or dried blood, phosphate or potash rock at this time.

SHREDDERS: Compost shredders enable the home gardener to make compost in as little time as 10 days, and actually ease the task of making compost and mulches. It is now recognized that cut-up leaves, weeds, and other similar materials make better mulch than the rough raw product because they hold moisture better and form a thicker blanket which chokes off weeds. Breakdown of shredded materials is also faster, since the heap heats up more quickly. Shredders may also be used to grind and pulverize finished compost, which is ideal for lawns, potting soil, flowerbeds, and in greenhoues.

SILT: Particles are microscopic pieces of rock—much smaller than sand—that help make up soil. Silt of the nonquartz minerals is rich in plant food.

SOIL FAUNA: This is one of most important gardening assets. They include mites, worms, grubs, centipedes, etc. All feed either on each other, or the crop residues and leaves deposited on the soil. Through continual activity—biting, chewing, tunneling, crawling—they loosen and aerate the soil and thoroughly mix its various components. Where there is an abundance of organic matter, there is also a proportionate number of functioning soil fauna.

SOIL TEMPERATURE: Soil temperatures vary just as much as air temperatures. One part of a garden is probably hotter (or colder) than another depending upon its location, chemical and physical makeup. Here are some examples of how soil temperatures influence your garden results:
1. Germination of seeds depends upon warmth of soil below as well as upon air above.
2. Planting your first crop as soon as soil has warmed up enough in spring can mean that you'll have time for a late planting in the same spot.
3. A mulch or cover crop regulates the soil's temperature to your advantage.
4. You'll learn how to save plants from frost damage.
5. You can aid the work of helpful soil bacteria if you know at what soil temperature they work best.
Bacteria: Organic gardeners are well aware that their soil is

alive, and that it provides a home for many beneficial bacteria. These bacteria require special conditions of warmth, moisture, and free aeration of soil to do their best job. These conditions are found only in the upper cultivated layers of the soil, and are more easily obtained in sandy loams than in clays, where the moisture content is too high and the supply of oxygen is lacking.

SOIL TESTING: A good gardener wants to know as much about his soil as possible. He wants to know what general type of soil it is, what plants will grow best on it, and how to fertilize it. It is easy to see that many benefits can be gained by learning more about the composition and capabilities of your soil. There are two ways to find out what nutrients your soil is hungry for. You can send a sample of your soil to a laboratory or to your state college, or you can buy a testing kit and make many of the necessary tests yourself. It doesn't hurt to use both methods, because you will be able to double check your results. A home testing kit is valuable because it enables you to make frequent periodic tests of your soil. Most people don't realize that the nutrient content of the soil varies greatly from one season to another. A soil test will tell you what nutrients are "available" or soluble in your soil.

STONE MULCHING: A process which consists of placing rocks between and around growing plants. The stones are placed close together so that very little soil is exposed to the sun. This method greatly aids weed control without cultivation. The elimination of cultivation itself is of considerable value in that cultivating tools can sometimes cut into lateral-growing roots near the surface. Recent studies have shown that stone mulching:

1. Provides such beneficial conditions as the conservation of moisture.
2. Provides good soil aeration.
3. Reduces wind and water erosion on slopes.
4. Maintains ideal conditions for soil bacteria, earthworms, and burrowing insects.
5. Enriches the soil by gradual disintegration of the stone bottoms because of the erosive action of organic acids and moisture in the soil.
6. Protects the soil from the direct rays of the sun.

7. Prevents the growth of weeds and other plants in competition with food plants.
8. Provides a temperature regulator.

TANKAGE: Refuse from slaughter houses and butcher shops other than the blood freed from the fats by processing. Depending on the amount of bone present, the phosphorous content varies greatly. Nitrogen content varies usually between 5 and 12.5 percent; the phosphoric acid content is usually around 2 percent but may be much higher.

THINNING: Consists of pulling up certain seedlings in a row to give room to those that are left. Sometimes the pulled seedlings are kept and replanted, in which case the procedure is called pricking out.

Disbudding, the removal of some flower buds to make the remaining ones grow larger blooms, is also a form of thinning, which in fruit growing consists of pruning out some of the fruitlets as soon as they are set to prevent too much small fruit production.

TILTH: As ordinarily understood, tilth refers to the physical condition of the soil. Good soil tilth means a loosening to the depth necessary for root penetration and plant growth. A friable soil is one that has good tilth. In addition, soil tilth is also used to mean cultivation.

TOPDRESSING: The application of compost, lime, manure, and fertilizers to the surface of the soil. Usually the material is lightly raked into the ground around growing plants and along rows.

TRACE ELEMENTS: Trace elements are minor mineral nutrients needed by all plants, animals, and humans in extremely small or "trace" amounts. In order to be present, these micronutrients must be available in the soil in which the plants and foods are grown. Too little of one or more elements produces deficiencies which result in plant or animal disease. On the other hand, an excessive quantity of any trace element similarly brings about a host of toxic conditions in plants and sicknesses in animals and people. Just how important these elements are can be seen by the fact that although trace elements are can be seen by the fact that although trace elements may constitute less than 1 percent of the total dry matter of a plant, they are often the factor that determines the vigor of the plant. Even where good crops have been thought to be produced, trace elements additions to the soil have raised yields and improved crop quality often amazingly. Most soils originally contain a sufficient supply of these elements to sustain good plant growth. But intensive cropping, erosion, chemical fertilization, and the replacement of manure-producing animals with machines have caused wide-spread deficiencies to occur.

TRANSPLANTING: When seedlings are about a half-inch high or have their true leaves (those resembling the species, instead of the ones known as "seed leaves" which appear first), they have reached the proper stage for transplanting into other containers. These containers for transplanting purposes are practically the same as those used for sowing. Use a somewhat richer potting mixture, so that the seedlings will have plenty of available plant food. Dampen the soil and fill the containers loosely, smooth it off, and press it down with a flat board. With a small round stick, make holes in which to set the young seedlings. Be sure that these holes are wide and deep enough to accommodate the roots in their natural position without crowding.

TRENCHING: Might be called a soil exchange process whose aim is to replace enriched surface soil with soil from lower depths. This puts fertile soil down deep, and brings about better structure, drainage, and root development. Usually a trench is dug 12 to 18 inches deep, and the soil removed from it is hauled to the other end of the area to be trenched. Then a layer half as deep is taken off from the next strip. It is enriched with rotten manure, compost, rock fertilizers, and other organic materials and is dumped into the first trench. This is then filled to its original level with the remaining soil from the lower part of the second trench. This process is repeated until the last strip is reached, which is filled with the soil previously carried there from the first trench. Some gardeners bring up an inch or so of the subsoil of each trench and mix it thoroughly with the upper soil, thus making their soil fertile and friable to a greater depth each time they trench it.

INDEX

Index

Acidity, beets as indicator, 170
  See also Acid soil; Alkaline
    soil; Neutral soil
Acid soil, 25, 26, 27, 66
  organic preparation, 26
  rock phosphate and, 52
Adobe, explained, 23
Adobe soils, 23
Aerobes, 62
Aggregates, 15, 17
Air intake, 19
Alfalfa hay, as mulching mate-
    rial, 93
Alkali disease, 22
Alkaline soil, 25
  crop rotation and, 55
  legumes and, 55
  manure and, 55
Alluim sativum L. (*see* Garlic)
American Dust Bowl, 9
Angleworm (*see* Earthworm)
Animal manures, 34-35
Anise, 236
Antipollution methods, 305
Ants, birds and, 254
  control of, 265
Aphids, 230, 240
  birds and, 256
  chives and, 244
  control of, 256, 265-266
  ladybugs and, 250
  onion spray and, 241
  signs of, 230
Ark, Peter, 236-237
Arsenate of lead, 233
Artificial chemical fertilizers, 3-
    4
Artificial chemicals, mushrooms
    and, 196
Artificial gardeners, 3

Asparagus, 127
  harvesting, 279, 288
  planting information, 168-170
Aspergillus flavus, 252
Automobiles, effect on our land,
    310

Bacillus thuringiensis, 251, 253,
    267
"Back to the land" movement,
    311
  individual account of, 311-
    315
Bacteria, earthworms and, 58
  in humus formation, 58
  insect sprays and, 58
  soil fertility and, 58
Bacteriological control of pests,
    250-251
Bagworms, 266
Balance of nature, 249
Bamboo sticks, use in garden,
    129
Barnett, Frederick J., 38
Bark chips, as mulching mate-
    rial, 92
Bartlett, J. J., 68
  composting method in resi-
    dential area, 68-70
Basic slag, 29
Basset, F. W., 38
Bean beetles, control of, 265
Beans, bean rust and, 237
  marigolds and, 245
  seed culture of, 147
Bedrock, in soil formation, 14
Beetle larvae, signs of, 230
Beetles, 257
  on beans, 245
  marigolds and, 245

347